Sport and Development in Emerging Nations

For the first time, this book examines the strategies of leaders of emerging nations to use sport as a tool for reaching social, economic, cultural, political, technological or environmental goals and gaining international prestige. It assesses whether sport can really be an effective tool in international development.

The book explores the unique challenges, issues and opportunities offered by sport for development in emerging nations. Bringing together case studies of sport and development in countries including Brazil, China, Czech Republic, Hungary, India, Indonesia, Mexico, Poland, Qatar, South Africa, South Korea and Turkey, the book looks at policies designed to achieve development through, by and for sport, and whether they have achieved their socio-economic objectives. It considers the way that emerging nations have used major international sports events as political and developmental projects, as well as the importance of sporting infrastructure, professional leagues, participation programmes and the influence of nationalism and ideology.

With a truly global perspective, this book is important reading for any student, researcher or policy-maker with interest in sport management, sport development, development studies, international economics, globalisation or political science.

Cem Tinaz is Director of the School of Sports Sciences and Technology at Istanbul Bilgi University, Turkey. He is also an esteemed board member and Vice President of the Turkish Tennis Federation. Dr. Tinaz's research interests include sport policy and development, administration, legacies and impacts of sport mega-events – all integrated with his primary area of expertise in sport management. He was awarded a 2016/2017 Advanced Olympic Research Grant by the IOC Olympic Studies Centre for the project "Examining Positive Outcomes of Unsuccessful Olympic Bids".

Brendon Knott is Associate Professor in the Sport Management Department at the Cape Peninsula University of Technology, South Africa. His primary research interests include sport marketing, sport tourism and mega-event studies. He serves as Associate Editor for the *Journal of Leisure Research* and on the Editorial Board of the *Journal of Destination Marketing and Management*. He has a passion for sport and its impact on society, especially in emerging nations.

Routledge Research in Sport Politics and Policy

Series Editors:
Jonathan Grix, Manchester Metropolitan University, UK
Laurence Chalip, University of Illinois at Urbana-Champaign, USA
Barrie Houlihan, Loughborough University, UK

The *Routledge Research in Sport Politics and Policy* series aims to give shape to, and showcase, the burgeoning academic field of 'sport politics and policy'. Highlighting the political nature of sport, the series shows how sport can illuminate our understanding of wider political themes such as, issues around governance; sport, foreign policy and 'soft power'; gender politics, or the use of sport as a development tool. The series embraces all areas of sport politics and policy, including domestic, international and comparative studies, and includes work by world-leading and emerging scholars.

Available in this series:

Sport Policy in China
Jinming Zheng, Shushu Chen, Tien-Chin Tan and Barrie Houlihan

Sport, Statehood and Transition in Europe
Comparative perspectives from post-Soviet and
post-socialist societies
Edited by Ekain Rojo-Labaien, Álvaro Rodríguez-Díaz and Joel Rookwood

Sport and Development in Emerging Nations
Edited by Cem Tinaz and Brendon Knott

Sport and Development in Emerging Nations

Edited by
Cem Tinaz and Brendon Knott

Routledge
Taylor & Francis Group

LONDON AND NEW YORK

First published 2021
by Routledge
2 Park Square, Milton Park, Abingdon, Oxon OX14 4RN

and by Routledge
52 Vanderbilt Avenue, New York, NY 10017

Routledge is an imprint of the Taylor & Francis Group, an informa business

British Library Cataloguing-in-Publication Data
A catalogue record for this book is available from the British Library

Library of Congress Cataloging-in-Publication Data
Names: Tinaz, Cem, editor. | Knott, Brendon, editor.
Title: Sport and development in emerging nations / Edited by Cem Tinaz and Brendon Knott.
Description: First Edition. | New York : Routledge, 2021. | Series: Routledge research in sport politics and policy | Includes bibliographical references and index.
Identifiers: LCCN 2020048273 | ISBN 9780367903602 (Hardback) | ISBN 9781003024002 (eBook)
Subjects: LCSH: Sports—Developing countries. | Sports and state—Developing countries. | Nationalism and sports.
Classification: LCC GV689.2 .S74 2021 | DDC 796.09724—dc23
LC record available at https://lccn.loc.gov/2020048273

ISBN: 978-0-367-90360-2 (hbk)
ISBN: 978-1-003-02400-2 (ebk)

Typeset in Goudy
by codeMantra

To our families (Cem – to Pınar, Mehmet, Kerem, Tuvana and Ege; Brendon – to Kevin, Diane and brothers), thank you for your continuous support, love and inspiration.

Contents

Figures

Tables

Contributors

Selçuk Açıkgöz is a doctoral researcher in the Faculty of Sport Sciences, Trakya University, Turkey. He is also part of the (anti)racism pedagogy and critical sport study groups at the BoMoVu (Network of Sports and Body Movement for Vulnerable Groups) in Istanbul, Turkey. His research interests include different aspects of the sociology of sport with particular focus on social inclusion, youth studies, critical pedagogy and (anti)racism.

Bárbara Schausteck de Almeida is an independent scholar and entrepreneur. Prior to her current work, she was a lecturer at Centro Universitário Internacional (Uninter) and State University of Londrina (UEL) both in Brazil. She contributed as editor for the *Journal of Latin American Socio-cultural Studies of Sport*. Her main research interests include the Sociology of Sport, Mega-events and Funding in Sport.

Mahfoud Amara is Associate Professor in Sport Policy and Management and the Director of the Sport Science programme at the College of Arts and Sciences, Qatar University, Qatar. Previously he was Assistant Professor in Sport Policy and Management and Deputy Director of the Centre for Olympic Studies and Research in the School of Sport, Exercise and Health Sciences, Loughborough University, UK. He is most renowned for his work on sport in the Middle East and North African region and sport and multiculturalism debates in Europe.

Yeomi Choi is an academic intellectual in the field of socio-historical studies of sport and physical activity. Theoretically informed by post-colonial feminist scholarship, transnational studies and critical race studies, Dr. Choi's research interests are situated at the cultural and political intersections of race, gender, sexuality and nationalism in the mediated construction of sporting subjectivities. She is currently teaching at Korea National Sport University and also at Catholic Kwandong University in South Korea.

Gökben Demirbaş works in the Political Science and Public Administration Department at Trakya University (Turkey). Her thesis, entitled "Women's Leisure in Urban Turkey: A Comparative Neighbourhood Study", focuses on the relationship between gender, class, leisure and space, everyday lives in urban neighbourhoods and social in/exclusion practices, which also form her broader academic interests.

Vanessa García González is Professor at the Universidad Autónoma Chapingo, Mexico. Her research focuses on the social and cultural aspects of grassroots sports in Mexico, the intersection between physical activity, sport and health, and the relationship between sports, development and peace building. She is a member of the Editorial Board of the *International Review for the Sociology of Sport* and a member of the Executive Board of the *International Society of Qualitative Research in Sport and Exercise.*

Billy Graeff is Senior Lecturer in the sociology of sport at the Federal University of Rio Grande, Brazil. Billy has focused on topics such as sport mega-events, sport and development and Olympic studies. He recently launched the book *Capitalism, Sport Mega-events and the Global South*, by Routledge, and is currently developing the research project "South American Sport for Development voices and the Sustainable Development Goals", with funding from the Advanced Olympic Research Grant of the Center for Olympic Studies.

Reinhard Haudenhuyse is Postdoctoral Researcher in Sports Policy and Management at the Brussels Centre for Urban Studies, Belgium. His research focuses on youth, community sports, social in/exclusion, programme monitoring and evaluation, poverty and leisure.

Zsolt Havran is Senior Assistant Professor at the Department of Business Studies at Corvinus University of Budapest, Hungary. His research topics are human resource management in professional sport, the transfer market of professional football and leisure sport activities. He is a member of the Sport Business Research Centre at the Corvinus University of Budapest, the European Association for Sport Management and the Hungarian Society of Sport Science.

Wadih Ishac is Assistant Professor in Sport Management at Qatar University, Qatar. His research focuses on the social and political impacts of sport mega-events and foreign investment in the sport industry.

Michał Marcin Kobierecki is Assistant Professor in the Department of Political Theory and Thought, Faculty of International and Political Studies, University of Lodz, Poland. His research interests include sports diplomacy, politics and sport, and nation branding and public diplomacy with a specific focus on the use of sport. He is a principal investigator of the research project "Consensual and branding role of sport in diplomatic activities of states and non-state actors" funded by the National Science Center, Poland.

Vipul Lunawat is Founder and Director of the Institute of Sports Science and Technology, Pune, India. He is a Level 2 Short Track Speed Ice Skating Coach, certified by the Australian Ice Racing and the Olympic Solidarity programme. He is the Head Coach at India's biggest short track ice skating club, the Snovit

International Ice-Skating Club, Pune, India. His research interests include sport technology, business development and innovation in sport.

Yang Ma is Lecturer in the School of Physical Education at Shanghai University, People's Republic of China. His research interests reside in sport governance in China in general and Chinese football governance in particular.

Agus Mahendra is Associate Professor in the Department of Sport Education at Universitas Pendidikan Indonesia. His research topic is physical education pedagogy in elementary schools and motor learning practicality in gymnastics. He is the Head of PETE for Elementary Schools, member of International Physical Literacy Association (ISPA) and the Country Leader of Active Healthy Kids-Indonesia as part of Active Healthy Kids Global Alliance (AHKGA).

Amung Ma'mun is Professor in the Department of Sport Education, Faculty of Sport and Health Education at Universitas Pendidikan, Indonesia. His research topics are sport leadership and policy and sport history. He is the Head of Sport Education for Master's and Doctoral degrees at the School of Postgraduate Studies, UPI. He is a member of the Executive Board of APASS (Asia-Pacific Association of Sport Studies), Indonesian Sport Scholars Association and former Expert Staff to the Minister of Youth and Sport, the Republic of Indonesia.

Roberto Martín-González is a doctoral candidate and member of the Department of Geography in the Faculty of Tourism, University of Málaga, Spain. His research deals with sport tourism, surf tourism and smart tourism in urban destinations. He spent two years at the Department of Tourism and Events Management, Cape Peninsula University of Technology (Cape Town, South Africa) as a member of the research unit Centre for Tourism Research in Africa (CETRA) in the framework of the Erasmus Mundus EUROSA+ programme from 2014 to 2016.

Tünde Máté is Senior Assistant Professor at the Department of Business Studies at Corvinus University of Budapest, Hungary. Her research focuses on the impacts of international sport events and programmes on the residents of the host city. She is a member of the Sport Business Research Centre at Corvinus University of Budapest and the Hungarian Society of Sport Science.

Simona Šafaříková is Assistant Professor in the Department of Development and Environmental Studies (Faculty of Science) at Palacky University Olomouc in the Czech Republic. She teaches the use of sport in solving development problems at the Faculty of Physical Culture. She focuses her research on the topic of sport for development and has been involved in projects all around the world. She is a member of the Advisory Board of International Sociology of Sport Association.

Arnošt Svoboda is Assistant Professor at the Faculty of Physical Culture, Palacký University Olomouc, Czech Republic. He is a sociologist with a research interest in the cultural role of sport in society, sport for development and sporting subcultures. He teaches general sociology, sociology of sport and methodology of social research.

Kamilla Swart is Associate Professor in the Masters of Science in Sport and Entertainment (MSEM), Division of Engineering Management and Decision Sciences, College of Science and Engineering, Hamad Bin Khalifa University, Qatar. Kamilla was instrumental in developing the 2010 FIFA World Cup Research Agenda and served as the City of Cape Town's Research Coordinator for 2010. Her work has been focused on contributing to sport, tourism and event knowledge in the developing context and in the global South in particular. Kamilla also serves as a Senior Research Associate in the School of Tourism and Hospitality, University of Johannesburg, South Africa.

Ágnes Szabó is Senior Assistant Professor at the Department of Business Studies at Corvinus University of Budapest, Hungary. Her research interests cover workplace health, sport consumption, economic effects of leisure sports. She is a member of the Sport Business Research Centre at Corvinus University of Budapest and the Hungarian Society of Sport Science.

Nadyne Venturini Trindade is Associate Lecturer at the University of Northampton, UK where she teaches sport management and sociology of sport, leisure and tourism modules. She has an interdisciplinary background and her research reflects an interest in the relationship between sport and leisure participation, social justice and well-being. Currently, Nadyne is a PhD candidate at Loughborough University, UK and her research focuses on the emergence of equitable and inclusive policies and practices for gender diverse (intersex, trans, gender nonconforming and non-binary) participants in competitive sport and physical activity.

Huan Xiong is Professor in the School of Physical Education and Sports Science at South China Normal University, People's Republic of China. Prior to working at South China Normal University, she was a lecturer at the School of Asian Studies at University College Cork, Ireland. She is a member of the Editorial Board of *Asian Journal of Sport History & Culture*. Her main research interests include the Sociology of Sport, Urban Studies and Gender Issues in Sport.

Foreword

In the opening chapter of this collection, Cem Tinaz and Brendon Knott discuss the variety of interpretations of development in relation to sport. Their discussion captures the multiple interpretations of 'sport development' particularly the extent to which sport development is both an activity of those working in the sports sector and a resource for non-sport businesses, not-for-profit organisations and governments. The plasticity of the concept of sport development is demonstrated to powerful effect in the chapters of this collection. Almost 20 years ago I wrote a book with Anita White which had the sub-title *Development of Sport or Development through Sport* (Houlihan and White, 2002). Over the intervening years the implied tension between the two interpretations of sport development has remained and has arguably intensified. The range of developmental objectives to which sport has been attached has remained broad with sport being utilised by governments in a wide variety of ways including as a diplomatic resource, a tool of social control, a health strategy, a resource for community integration and a strategy for sanitising corrupt political regimes. Similar examples of the use of sport for non-sport objectives can be found in relation to business involvement in sport. In the last 40 years or so sport development as a business sector has become an important part of many national economies. While the growth of the business of sport development (whether the development of young elite athletes or the provision of community sport opportunities) has widened the opportunities for participation it has also been used by some businesses to project a more positive brand image – a strategy particularly notable among the manufacturers of unhealthy junk food.

One of the principal virtues of this collection is the way in which it demonstrates the variation in the motives of governments, the extent and methods of intervention and the impact of governmental intervention. Furthermore, two important tensions are amply illustrated: the first is between market freedom and government control (Chapters 3, China, and 5, Hungary, are particularly valuable in this regard) and the second is between investing in elite sport (often for nation-branding/promotion purposes) and investing in community sport/sport for all (Chapters 4, Czech Republic, and 7, Indonesia, being good illustrations of this tension). Perhaps the most interesting exploration of the motives of governments is in Chapter 3 which examines the professional football in the People's Republic of China (PRC). As the authors make clear achieving international success in football remains a political priority despite the PRC having clearly demonstrated its 'sports power' status at successive recent Olympic Games. Sporting success as an indicator of international status and as a measure of national self-confidence needs no clearer illustration.

The increased involvement of governments and large corporations in sport development requires the analysis of not only the motives for involvement but also the distribution and exercise of power in the sport development field. The theme of power was a thread that ran through a collection of studies that I edited in 2011 with Mick Green (Houlihan and Green, 2011). The particular focus was on the attraction of sport development to governments and the ways in which they sought to utilise sport not only for socially beneficial, but also for deeply cynical, ends. The collection demonstrated *inter alia* that major attractions of sport to government included its relatively low cost, its high visibility and its low risk. Whether the issue concerned youth unemployment, low educational standards, poor health indicators or urban unrest sport was often presented as a panacea. Politicians would regularly refer to the 'power of sport' as though it had magical properties. The mythologising of the potential of sport development to address complex social and personal problems has deep cultural roots in many countries making the objective analysis of the impact of sport development a challenge for researchers. As Fred Coalter persuasively argued, 'such myths contain elements of truth, but elements which have become reified and distorted and "represent" rather than reflect reality, standing for supposed, but largely unexamined, impacts and processes' (Coalter, 2007, p. 9). The collection of studies in this volume reinforces Coalter's emphasis on the need to challenge the mythologising that surrounds sport development and to examine evidence from a disinterested and sceptical standpoint.

Apart from the critical examination of the claims made on behalf of sport development the other strength of this collection is the focus on a range of countries that are often on the margin of Western academic research. As an academic community we know far too little about the policy and politics of sport and sport development in the majority of the 207 countries that attended the 2016 Olympic Games, the 61 national members of the International Council of Sports Science and Physical Education, the 53 member states of the Commonwealth who subscribe to the organisation's strategy for development and peace through sport (Dudfield, 2014) or many of the states who contributed to the UN report the role of sport in peace and development (United Nations, 2020). The focus of this volume on analysing the interpretation and implementation of sport development policies in countries from Asia, Africa, the Middle East, South America and Eastern Europe greatly enriches our understanding of sport development as a global phenomenon. Furthermore, the collection of studies in this volume will be of particular interest to scholars whose research focuses on the tension between attempts to maintain a set of national policy objectives and the priorities of global sports organisations, broadcast media and sports businesses. Understanding how, and the extent to which, emerging nations are able to develop strategies singly or collectively to protect their interests is an important direction for research that this volume indicates.

by Barrie Houlihan

References

Coalter, F. (2007) *A wider social role for sport: Who's keeping the score.* London: Routledge.

Dudfield, O. (ed.) (2014) *Strengthening sport for development and peace: National policies and strategies.* London: Commonwealth Secretariat.

Houlihan, B. and White, A. (2002) *The politics of sort development: Development of sport or development through sport.* London: Routledge.

Houlihan, B. and Green, M. (eds.) (2011) *Routledge handbook of sports development.* London: Routledge.

United Nations (2020) *Sport: A global accelerator of peace and sustainable development.* New York: United Nations.

Acknowledgements

The editors wish to thank the following individuals for their support and assistance in this project:

Katy Herrera: Thank you for your assistance with proofreading the chapters. Your gift for writing excellence helped us greatly.

Simon Whitmore and Rebecca Connor (Routledge Publishing): Thank you for encouraging us in this project, being flexible and helpful in all that we needed.

Thank you to the series editors: Barrie Houlihan – Thank you for your encouragement of our project proposal and for writing the foreword. We respect your contribution to the global sport development academia. Thank you also to Jonathan Grix and Laurence Chalip for your contributions and support.

Each of the contributing authors: We thank you colleagues for your participation in this project. We believe that you have made a significant contribution to the academic literature on sport and development in your country.

Istanbul Bilgi University and Cape Peninsula University of Technology: Thank you to our academic institutions for your support of this project and your ongoing support of our academic development.

Thank you to our mutual friends, Douglas Michele Turco and Risto Rasku for connecting us and supporting, mentoring and encouraging our professional development.

Chapter 1

Introduction

Defining sport and development in emerging nations

Cem Tinaz and Brendon Knott

The sport industry has been enjoying increased benefits and expanded opportunities through the process of globalisation. As Jarvie (2006) has stated, the global era of sport has presented fundamental challenges for sport organisations. Still, it has also created the opportunity for sport to be a social force for internationalism, reconciliation and international development.

Sport is currently linked to a wide variety of development initiatives as it is often posited as a tool to assist in economic and social development. With great optimism, many countries facing acute demographic shifts towards youth tend to see sport as a means to suppress delinquency, unemployment and drug use. Each month multiple new organisations using sport to achieve specific results have been established (Hayhurst and Frisby, 2010).

At the same time, sport can provide physical, mental and social benefits to improve the well-being of an ageing population. It can be used to promote social inclusion of otherwise marginalised people. As Kay and Bradbury (2009) have suggested, involvement in sport is understood to confer life skills, leadership qualities, social knowledge and values. However, it would be very naive to say that such positive outcomes happen naturally or organically through participation. In other words, solely playing sport does not lead to developmental outcomes; in order to have a productive effect on development, sport programmes should be organised and structured in purposive, systematic ways. According to Coalter (2009), although participation in sport can be a useful mechanism for development, it is not sufficient alone to engender social change. Hartmann (2003) emphasised that the non-sport components of any sport-based social interventionist programme are what define its strength.

Houlihan and White (2002) argued that the area of sport development is not static; the objectives, practises, primary agents and recourses change over time as does the definition of sport development. Hartmann and Kwauk (2011) stated that one of the most critical initial challenges for understanding and theorising the field of sport and development is the ambiguity and multiplicity around conceptions of development. Furthermore, the interpretation and definition of sport development has different meanings to different agencies, such as sports governing bodies, clubs, corporations and NGOs. In its most comprehensive meaning, sport development refers to participating in sport itself and promoting the opportunities and benefits of such participation, and as Kidd (2008) argues, it is a project of sport organisations. The potential outcomes of sport development may include betterments of the sport itself, plus individuals who are involved in sport for various benefits and experiences, and in a wider sense nations and communities. From a practitioner's perspective, Astle (2014, p. 15) defined sport development as:

> The sustainable provision of, and access to, integrated pathways of relevant, appealing and affordable sporting opportunities for individuals, irrespective of age, ability, interest or gender, to participate, enjoy and progress in a supportive environment that has the infrastructure and services, capable of offering high-quality experiences, that satisfy their diverse and changing needs, motivations and expectations, and ensure their continued involvement in sport.

Initial attempts to define sport development considered two aspects: the development of sport and development through sport (Houlihan and White, 2002). Intending to build sport capacity, development of sport refers to the development of the sport itself or, in other words, the creation of opportunities for participants and the enhancement of the sport. Mainly, these are the activities designed both to excel in performance and increase participation. On the other hand, development through sport focuses on the role sport can play in enhancing the well-being of individuals, communities and societies (Ha, Lee and Ok, 2015). According to this approach, sport constitutes a powerful tool for social integration, promotion of health and disease prevention, creating physical and psychological benefits for individuals, development of the community and social capital and empowerment of minorities, girls and women (Levermore, 2008a). As a result of this approach, recently sport has gained increased importance as a tool to promote health, education and peace. Nevertheless, as Levermore and Beacom (2009) have expressed, we should bear in mind that these socio-economic aspects and sport are not mutually exclusive. As they state, different social aspects such as leadership, inclusion and capacity building are linked to sport aspects such as coaching, performance and physical skills.

In his conceptual framework, Coalter (2009) defined two ends of sport and development: sport plus and plus sport. In this conceptualisation, sport plus programmes focus on the development of sport-oriented initiatives such as sustainable sport organisations, programmes and development pathways, while plus sport programmes focus on achieving non-sport goals, such as social or economic development. The main concern of plus sport programmes is how sport can aid social and economic development.

Astle (2014) reworked these definitions by providing the following six sub-categories of sport development:

- Development IN sport: the extent to which authorities adapt sport to make them more attractive to audiences.
- Development OF sport: breaking down barriers to participation.

- Development FOR sport: the production of elite talent.
- Development THROUGH sport: community initiatives in nations.
- Sport FOR development: promoting sport in developing nations.
- Sport AND development: the connection between sport and humanitarian issues.

However, we should consider that these sub-categories are not mutually exclusive and can often overlap as a result of the occasionally interchangeable nature of the terms sport and development. As Schulenkorf, Sherry and Rowe (2016) have stated regarding the focus and purpose of sport development initiatives, these interpretations are interconnected and share much in common. Each interpretation represents a different perspective of sport development, which is defined by key features that reflect the interests and expectations of the different agencies involved and the environment in which they operate (Astle, Leberman and Watson, 2018).

According to Astle, Leberman and Watson (2018), "development IN sport" considers how sport has evolved and adapted its content and appearance for the benefit of itself and its stakeholders. Development IN sport focuses on the emergence, codification, diffusion and adaptation to change of different sports (Astle, Leberman and Watson, 2018).

The development OF sports has been defined as a traditional approach representing the creation and development of sport initiatives aimed at building sport capacity (Green, 2005). This framework is focused on ensuring that community sport remains up to date by providing flexible opportunities and ways of experience that attract and retain participants in sport in order to ensure the future growth and sustainability of sport (Astle, Leberman and Watson, 2018).

According to Astle, Leberman and Watson (2018), development FOR sport has similar aspects to development OF sport, except essentially its primary focus, which is developing elite sport. Here, the particular concern is on developing children and youth into high-calibre performers.

As explained earlier, development THROUGH sport approaches sport as a driving force in conducting various development programmes, covering issues such as the resolution of intergroup conflict, the physical and psychological benefits of sport, the promotion of cultural understanding, the development of physical and social infrastructures, the empowerment of girls, women or disadvantaged groups and social inclusion (Ha, Lee, and Ok, 2015).

Levermore (2008b) grouped sport FOR development initiatives into six clusters, namely conflict resolution and intercultural understanding; building physical, social, sport and community infrastructure; raising awareness, particularly through education; empowerment; direct impact on physical and psychological health as well as general welfare; and finally, economic development/poverty alleviation. Astle, Leberman and Watson (2018) distinguish development THROUGH sport from sport FOR development mainly through the geographical setting, as development THROUGH sport deals with community sport in developed nations and sport FOR development deals with community sport in developing nations.

Finally, sport AND development is related to the capacity of sport to contribute to personal and social development. It is claimed that sport has inherent physical, social and moral qualities, and the experience of participating in sport provides individuals with opportunities to inspire confidence, learn to accept gain and losses and develop qualities such as work ethics and team spirit (Astle, Leberman and Watson, 2018).

Sport and development in emerging nations

As has already been stated, globally, sport has been used as a practical and discursive tool for development. Not only developing countries but also those that are more developed try to take advantage of certain sport attributes to assist with objectives linked to international development/relations (Levermore, 2008a). The role of sport in development initiatives has grown dramatically in recent times, now finding a place in the UN's sustainable development goals. The business of sport and its role in development is a growing academic field, with specialist sport management courses emerging to cater for the increased professionalisation and global reach of the sport industry. Sport development has gained a lot of interest during recent years not only from academic scholars but also practitioners. In many countries, large-scale or sport mega-events have become key factors in local and national development strategies. Hosting sport events is seen to be a key to boosting tourism, local investment and employment, although genuinely sustainable legacies are unfortunately an exception. As Grix, Brannagan and Lee (2019) have stated, sport mega-events such as the FIFA World Cup and the Olympic Games, which until recently were only hosted by developed countries, have become the perfect soft power project for emerging nations such as Brazil, South Africa and China, as well as Qatar. Additionally, sport has the potential to provide opportunities to challenge dominant social structures which have long existed in these nations. Globalisation offers new opportunities for sport leagues, teams, events and manufacturers in developed economies. These organisations aim to promote their products and service specifically in emerging nations (Zhang et al., 2018). The emerging nations are undergoing rapid urbanisation and development; this has been instrumental to growth across the sport industry. One of the essential factors which led to the fast growth of the global sports industry during recent years was the fast growth of emerging nations. Therefore, it is vital to continue to explore the impact of new changes and trends in globalisation in relation to the development of sport industries in growing economies.

Grix, Brannagan and Lee (2019) indicated that an outcome of the 20th century has been the decentring of wealth and power from the major developed states – the United States, Japan and Europe – to the fast-developing nations in Africa, Asia, the Middle East and South America. Similarly, we have seen a shift in the sport industry, especially in the hosting of sport mega-events from the developed West to the developing nations. Most of these nations have faced very different challenges compared to the established Western nations. Besides the prevalent issues relating to social and economic under-development, many of these nations have experienced recent political and ideological regime changes or global isolation as a result of their political standing. Yet, the common denominator among these nations is a recognition of the opportunities that sport provides for both social and economic development. Both the public and private sectors are seeking to harness sport opportunities in various forms as a means to develop and promote their society and stimulate their economy. Recently, the importance of sport has risen unwaveringly in emerging nations. Governments' spending on the development of the sport industry, specifically in hosting sport events, setting up sport infrastructure and building sport, has increased.

According to MSCI Market Classification Framework (2014), an emerging market is a market that has some characteristics of a developed market but does not fully meet its standards. They are moving away from their traditional economies that have relied on agriculture and the export of raw materials. As a result, they are rapidly industrialising and adopting a free market or mixed economy. It is evident that decision-makers or investors in emerging nations tend to use sport as one of the tools for reaching their social, economic, cultural, political, technological or environmental goals. By doing so, their countries can also gain international prestige.

The Morgan Stanley Capital International Emerging Market Index (MSCI, 2020) lists 26 countries. MSCI analyses indicators relating to sustainable economic growth, monetary policy, price stability, fiscal discipline, debt position, trade and current account balance. These are Argentina, Brazil, Chile, China, Colombia, Czech Republic, Egypt, Greece, Hungary, India, Indonesia, Korea, Malaysia, Mexico, Pakistan, Peru, Philippines, Poland, Qatar, Russia, Saudi Arabia, South Africa, Taiwan, Thailand, Turkey and the United Arab Emirates.

Aim of the book

This book only uses cases from emerging nations and thereby studies the relationship between sport and the development of a country. Yet each case has a unique focus on an aspect of sport, with a diversity of topics including sport policy, sport infrastructure, sport mega-events, professional sport leagues and sport development programmes. The chapters present a holistic perspective on sport development, including references to different perspectives such as economic development, sport participation, social and cultural transformation, nationalism and ideology, and sport for peace.

This book aims to deepen the knowledge of academics and practitioners who already have a background in sport business or development. The sport industry is rapidly professionalising around the globe and has a need for those in managerial roles to have an understanding of the global nuances and challenges of the sport industry, especially within the emerging economy context.

A national and international benchmarking exercise among academic institutions offering sport management-related programmes revealed that there has been a growing recognition and inclusion of globalisation topics and the role of sport in development. Globally, programmes have been adding features to their courses that examine the societal context of sport from a developmental perspective, linked to economic and social sustainability.

In this book, we have aimed to identify and examine local sport and development practices, local knowledge, sociocultural and political-economic contexts, and the needs and desires of local communities in emerging nations. The collection offers a systematic and balanced approach to the study of the theory and practice of sport and development. It aims to add to the body of knowledge on the globalisation of sport industries through highlighting the unique challenges, issues and opportunities provided by sport for socio-economic development in emerging nations. Specifically, it will provide answers to the following question: "How is sport contributing to development (in terms of social, economic, cultural, political, technological or environmental advancement) in emerging nations?" This book deepens the knowledge of academics and practitioners who already have a background in sport business or development.

Structure of this book

The book is comprised of 12 country-specific cases as well as a conclusion chapter that draws together the specific issues and challenges highlighted through these cases and offers potential solutions for sport and development in emerging nation contexts. The chapters outline vital topics, theories and applied research undertaken on sport and development-related issues, outlining the significant critical insights, enabling readers to have a broad grasp of the key areas, issues and research across a multi-disciplinary and global geographical perspective.

The editors, themselves based in emerging nations, made use of their professional academic network within sport management to identify reputable and esteemed academics from multiple emerging nations featured in the MSCI list. The editors particularly aimed to find a good spread of contributors to represent the different global regions of emerging nations. These academics were invited to submit an abstract for consideration in the book. After further review of the abstracts by the editors, the publishers and external reviewers, the list of contributors was refined to reflect the 12 nations represented in the following chapters. Figure 1.1 below gives a clear indication of the diversity and spread of emerging nations covered in this book.

The opening country-case chapter aims to present the relationship between sport and development in Brazil in the 21st century, pertaining to two main perspectives. The first of these discusses how hosting sport mega-events impacted public policies, funding and communities in host cities (mainly for the 2014 FIFA World Cup and the 2016 Olympic Games). The authors demonstrate how these mega-events had adverse outcomes for Brazil's more excluded communities, while temporary funding was mainly channelled towards elite sport

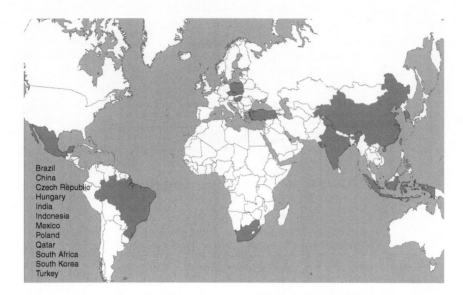

Brazil
China
Czech Republic
Hungary
India
Indonesia
Mexico
Poland
Qatar
South Africa
South Korea
Turkey

Figure 1.1 The diversity and spread of emerging nations covered in this book.

(development-for-sport). The second perspective focuses on how public programmes and not-for-profit organisations promote sport as part of development
programmes for disadvantaged youth. It discusses these programmes' and organisations' structures, management, challenges and strategies to promote sustainable
initiatives, based on their reports and academic publications.

Chapter 3 uses the development of professional football in China as a case to
demonstrate how sport has been interwoven with the country's social and economic development. By reviewing the historical background to the rise of professional sport, the commercialisation process of professional football and the status
quo of the professional football industry in China, the authors argue that for
China, football is not just an economic booster but also an indicator of social development. The contemporary party-state has reanimated football as a vehicle for
its nation-building projects. A flourishing domestic football industry, combined
with internationally competitive performances, has a role to play in the New Era
through the promotion of domestic consumption, civic participation, cultural engagement and national pride. However, the process of China's football reform still
lags far behind the transformation and development of Chinese society.

Chapter 4 provides an overview of the role of sports in the social, cultural and
political development of the Czech Republic. The goal of this study is twofold:
First, the historical part outlines the cultural and political position of sporting
activities and new organisations within the establishment of Czech civil society
under the surveillance of Austro-Hungarian authorities throughout the 19th and
the beginning of the 20th century. Then, mass sporting activities as a tool for

support of the Communist regime are presented. Following this, the last three decades of evolution of sport for development initiatives are introduced, together with a critical appraisal of several specific projects. Theoretically, the chapter builds on Coalter's sport plus and plus sport typology and Astle's continuum of (a) sport and development for the parallel coexistence of sports and society, (b) sport for development for sports as an accelerator of international territorial recognition and multicultural integration and (c) development through sport for the deliberate use of sport in legitimising political regimes.

The aim of Chapter 5 is to analyse the trends of leisure sports markets and people's physical activity in the Central and Eastern European (CEE) region, with a specific focus on Hungary. Comprehensive data collection was conducted between 2010 and 2019 on the regional and national level in eight post-soviet countries in the CEE region, all of which are members of the European Union. The results show that in the case of an emerging country, the development of the economy can result in a significant increase in the service sector, including the leisure sport industry. The study demonstrates that although spending on sports goods and services has risen, the degree of physical activity and the number of people involved in leisure sports are decreasing.

Chapter 6 examines the definition of 'sport development' in the Indian context, exploring 'on the ground' perspectives that centre fundamentally on recruiting new athletes as well as retaining and nurturing existing ones. The research lens is also extended to other challenges such as access to good infrastructure, organisation of big events, development of coaches and allied support staff, training officials, generating revenue streams and more. While India is a country with rich and diverse sporting history, it is known almost exclusively for its most popular sport, cricket. With the launch of the Indian Premier League (IPL) in 2008, an array of corporate, government and even private investors started pumping money into the sports industry. Many other sports like Kabaddi, wrestling, football, tennis, table tennis and volleyball followed the IPL format to start professional leagues in India, which opened doors to new areas in sport development, hence boosting what had been a stagnant sport market in India. This study focuses on mapping these developments and tries to predict the opportunities and challenges the industry may face.

Chapter 7 discusses sports development policy in Indonesia during the *Reformasi* era (1998–present). Sports development practices are discussed along with the more open and liberal political and social system in which they are situated. At the beginning of the Reformation era, sports development received less attention. However, in 2005, the Law of the National Sports System was successfully enacted through which the scope of sports was divided into educational sports, recreational sports and competitive sports. Sports development policy in Indonesia has always intersected and aimed at building a self-image related to the economy, politics, culture and wider society, reaching its peak when Indonesia was trusted to host the 2018 Asian Games. The development-of-sport framework has generally been the dominant paradigm throughout this period, although within certain limits, the development through sport approach has also been applied, especially when hosting large-scale international sporting events.

Chapter 8 identifies a gap in the literature regarding specific sport for development and peace (SDP) practices in Latin America, particularly in Mexico. The purpose of this chapter is to identify the scope and diversity of SDP initiatives operating in Mexico, providing an overview of the Sportland field in the country. The analysis was conducted following the methods proposed by Sevensson and Woods (2017), with the findings showing that there was a boom of NGOs and community-based organisations delivering SDP programming in Mexico between 2007 and 2017. SDP programming was delivered in partnership with business corporations, the Mexican government, international funding agencies and national universities, predominantly targeting children, youth or both. SDP organisations are concentrated mainly in urban settings, with soccer, boxing and martial arts being the particular sports of preference. Education was the primary focus of more than half of the SDP organisations. There was a lack of evidence provided by the organisations under analysis to support the results they reported, indicating that further research is needed to understand the link between sports practices and their reported or intended outcomes.

Chapter 9, which looks at the Polish context, discusses how development through sport can be observed from the perspective of elite and mass sport. The chapter is dedicated specifically to focusing on development for sport. As a post-communist country, Poland has been undergoing a complex transition, which has also been reflected in sport. The level of elite sport and mass participation in sport both decreased after the fall of communism in Poland, whereas today, several social roles are assigned to sport, such as increasing the level of health and fitness of society and developing social capital. The study includes a review of the strategic goals of sport development in Poland, which are then compared with their actual implementation. Key observations include relative stability and consistency of Polish sport policy in recent years despite alterations of governments and certain discrepancies between the strategic documents and the actual implementation of sport policy.

Chapter 10 turns to The Middle East, which is expected to be one of the fastest growing emerging markets for the sports industry in the next few years. In the last decade or so, Qatar in particular has been heavily investing in sport as a means of branding and of positioning the country as a modern monarchy-state, while also tackling health problems related to physical inactivity, particularly among the youth. Since winning the bid to host the 2022 FIFA World Cup, Qatar has been under the spotlight, having to respond to criticism regarding the working conditions of labourers involved in the construction of football stadia as well as other regulations related to the Kafala system – a system of sponsorship that binds workers to their employers. In response, a number of reforms have been implemented, including the raising of the minimum wage and the lifting of the requirement for workers to get permission from their employers to change jobs or exit the country. The other strategy in sport has been to invest more in sport for a development agenda, internally and externally. Internally, the strategy is to develop sports projects targeting workers, centred on health and well-being, and celebrating cultural diversity, while externally it is to position Qatar in the international network of sport for development through collaborations with different NGOs and international sport clubs/brands. The chapter focuses on football for development as led by Generation Amazing, a branch of the Supreme Committee for the Delivery and Legacy of the 2022 FIFA World Cup.

Chapter 11 focuses on South Africa, a country with a rich, albeit contested, sporting history. It is also known for being a "sport-mad" nation. The development of sport in South Africa is an illustrative case of how sport is a microcosm of the broader socio-economic and political factors that contribute to the shaping of society. It is therefore not surprising that apartheid, South Africa's segregation policy which sanctioned political, economic and social discrimination against non-whites, has played a central role in the development of sport in South Africa. This chapter provides a historical context for the development of sport in South Africa, with a particular focus on sport in an apartheid society and the transition to post-apartheid sport in a democratic era. The governance of sport in South Africa is also presented. Furthermore, it highlights unique challenges faced by the industry currently, such as women in sport and the use of sport in positioning South Africa as a globally competitive tourism and investment destination. The study further addresses other contemporary challenges and trends such as sustainability. Finally, precursory observations of how the global coronavirus pandemic affected major sport events in South Africa conclude the chapter.

In Chapter 12, the focus shifts to Korea, a divided nation since 1948, where sport is frequently used as a vehicle to influence the political linkages between North Korea and South. The 2018 Winter Olympics held in PyeongChang, South Korea, is a notable example. The South Korean government highlighted the significance of this sporting mega-event as a 'Peace Olympics' in order to ease tensions on the Korean Peninsula and improve inter-Korean relations. North and South Korea's joint women's national ice hockey team was part of such an initiative. This state-led ideology on peace and national unification, however, caused controversy in South Korean society, especially among those in their 20s and 30s. Given this context, this study examines the media's construction of the controversy surrounding the unified team. Through a critical reading of media texts, close attention is paid to the produced meanings of the Olympics and sport diplomacy in long-divided Korea, North and South Korean/ness and the reunification of the two Koreas. This case study provides new insights into the changing relationship between sport, politics and nationalism in today's complex global system.

The final case chapter looks at Turkey, where sport has received an increasing amount of attention in developmental initiatives since the turn of the 21st century. Since its re-establishment in 2011, the Ministry of Youth and Sports (MYS) has invested in infrastructural and institutional developments such as hosting international sport competitions and investing in athlete development. Along with 32 football stadiums and over 2,000 neighbourhood sports fields, the MYS has built over 300 youth centres since 2012. Although this has increased participation in sports competitions in Turkey, the low figures of youth participation in sports activities suggest that the legacy of sport-for-development investments in Turkey should be questioned. The youth centres can be defined as one of the major initiatives of the Turkish government in aiming to contribute to community sport participation. Through use of Lefebvre's theoretical framework (1991) on the production of space, this analysis of qualitative research conducted in three youth centres provides insights into the government's neoconservative and sport-related objectives and their actual outcomes. The findings suggest that the youth centres are at risk of being unsustainable, due to their physical distance from disadvantaged communities, lack of personnel and an inconclusive vision for implementing long-term community transformation programs for young people.

Ultimately, Chapter 14 concludes the book by highlighting similarities across the cases in order to draw together the specific opportunities that sport offers for development in these nations. It also identifies the unique challenges faced by emerging nations in a sport development context. Based on the findings from the cases, the chapter offers potential solutions for sport and development in emerging nation contexts and identifies areas for further research.

References

Astle, A.M. (2014). *Sport development – Plan, programme and practice: A case study of the planned intervention by New Zealand Cricket into cricket in New Zealand.* Unpublished PhD thesis, Massey University, Palmerston North, New Zealand.

Astle, A.M., Leberman, S. and Watson, G. (2018). *Sport development in action: Plan, programme and practice.* London and New York: Routledge.

Coalter, F. (2009). Sport-in-development: Accountability or development? In: R. Levermore and A. Beacom, eds., *Sport and international development.* Hampshire: Palgrave Macmillan, pp. 55–75.

Green, B.C. (2005). Building sport programs to optimize athlete recruitment, retention, and transition: Toward a normative theory of sport development. *Journal of Sport Management,* 19(3), pp. 233–253.

Grix, J., Brannagan, P.M. and Lee, D. (2019). *Entering the global arena: Emerging states, soft power strategies and sports mega-events.* Singapore: Palgrave Pivot.

Ha, J., Lee, K. and Ok, G. (2015). From development of sport to development through sport: A paradigm shift for sport development in South Korea. *The International Journal of the History of Sport,* 32(10), pp. 1262–1278.

Hartmann, D. (2003). Theorising sport as social intervention: A view from the grassroots. *Quest,* 55, pp. 118–140.

Hartmann, D. and Kwauk, C. (2011). Sport and development: An overview, critique, and reconstruction. *Journal of Sport and Social Issues,* 35(3), pp. 284–305.

Hayhurst, L.M.C. and Frisby, W. (2010). Inevitable tensions: Swiss and Canadian sport for development NGO perspectives on partnerships with high performance sport. *European Sport Management Quarterly,* 10(1), pp. 75–96.

Houlihan, B. and White, A. (2002). *The politics of sport development.* London: Routledge.

Jarvie, G. (2006). *Sport, culture and society.* London: Routledge, 2006.

Kay, T. and Bradbury, S. (2009). Youth sport volunteering: Developing social capital? *Sport, Education & Society*, 14, pp. 121–140.

Kidd, B. (2008). A new social movement: Sport for development and peace. *Sport in Society*, 11(4), pp. 370–380.

Lefebvre, H. (1991). *The production of space*. Oxford: Blackwell Publishing.

Levermore, R. (2008a). Sport in international development: Time to treat it seriously? *Brown Journal of World Affairs*, 14(2), pp. 55–66.

Levermore, R. (2008b). Sport: A new engine of development? *Progress in Development Studies*, 8(2), pp. 183–190.

Levermore, R. and Beacom A. (2009). Sport and development: Mapping the field, ed., *Sport and international development*, 1st ed. Hampshire: Palgrave Macmillan, pp. 1–25.

MSCI, (2014). *MSCI market classification framework*. [online] Available at: https://www.msci.com/documents/1296102/1330218/MSCI_Market_Classification_Framework.pdf/d93e536f-cee1-4e12-9b69-ec3886ab8cc8 [Accessed 12 Jan. 2020].

MSCI, (2020). *MSCI emerging markets index*. [online] Available at: https://www.msci.com/countries-heat-map [Accessed 12 Jan. 2020].

Schulenkorf, N., Sherry, E. and Rowe, K. (2016). Sport for development: An integrated literature review. *Journal of Sport Management*, 30(1), pp. 22–39.

Zhang, J.J., Kim E., Mastromartino, B., Qian, T.Y. and Nauright, J. (2018). The sport industry in growing economies: Critical issues and challenges. *International Journal of Sports Marketing and Sponsorship*, 19(2), pp. 110–126.

Chapter 2

Sport and development in Brazil

Lessons from multiple sport mega-event hosting and sporting programmes in disadvantaged communities

Bárbara Schausteck de Almeida, Billy Graeff and Nadyne Venturini Trindade

Introduction

Brazil, in South America, has the sixth largest area in the world, fifth largest population size and ninth largest gross domestic product (CIA, 2019; World Bank, 2019). Although Brazil is rich in resources, it has one of the highest inequality indexes globally, reaching 53.3 on the GINI index (World Bank, 2019). Consequently, the majority of its citizens suffer from inadequate public services and/ or cannot afford adequate health, education, security or urban transportation. Therefore, development in the context of Brazilian sport must be understood within its economic and social spheres.

During the 2000s, Brazilian policy strategies and economic growth, combined with the inclination to reach further territories by sport governing bodies, allowed Brazil to win the right to host two sport mega-events: the 2014 FIFA Men's World Cup and the 2016 Olympic and Paralympic Games (see Almeida et al., 2015; Gaffney, 2014). The country has also hosted other major or mega-events such as the 2007 Pan and Parapan-American Games, the 2011 Military World Games, 2013 FIFA Confederations Cup, among other regional and international sporting events. Having the Brazilian government as the major sponsor and funder, hosting these events intended to portray Brazil as a regional leader and world-player (Almeida, Marchi Júnior and Pike, 2014; Resende, 2010). After Rio de Janeiro's election to host the 2016 Olympic and Paralympic Games, the former Brazilian president, Luiz Inácio Lula da Silva, claimed that Brazil had won its "international citizenship" (Almeida, Marchi Júnior and Pike, 2014, p. 278). Yet, "mega-events are characterised by contradictory statements, sentiments, and tendencies that are not easily resolved" (Müller, 2017, p. 235). As it was seen during and after these events in Brazil, paradoxes of development within underdevelopment, world-class facilities causing exclusion and redirection of investment should be critically assessed as part of sport mega-events.

This chapter shows that sport became part of the scope of national policy and politics beyond those events but was significantly influenced by them in the last decade. Nevertheless, the use of sport as a developmental tool precedes the preparations for the sport mega-events. It is important to note the increase in local non-governmental organisations (NGOs) that used sport as a tool for development and peace beginning in the 1990s. The fast-growing offer of sporting programmes relates to a context of political and economic reforms, in which sport and leisure became rights afforded by the 1988 constitution. Since then, NGOs have been receiving public and private funding, sometimes as the only institutional presence to offer sport and leisure services for the population.

By reviewing the consequences of hosting sport mega-events and sport for development (SFD) programmes by NGOs, this chapter discusses the relationship between sport and development in Brazil in the last two decades. Initially, it presents how the political strategy of hosting mega-events was beneficial to a few sport sectors while influencing negatively disadvantaged populations. Then, it shows how public programmes and not-for-profit organisations target disadvantaged populations, adapting to external forces to keep their work sustainable over time.

Through a descriptive approach, this chapter dialogues with Brazilian and international literature, exposing theoretical debates and empirical data to discuss sport mega-events, public policies and non-governmental programmes related to sport and development. It is divided into two main sections: the economic sphere and the social sphere. In the economic sphere, we first present data on public funding of sport over the period from 2004 to 2018, pointing to the influence of sport mega-events on funding and sport public policy. Then, we examine how the projects associated with these events impacted communities living in host cities. Finally, we reflect on how hosting sport mega-events related to development. For this discussion, we gathered official government data on funding, reports from independent organisations and academic literature on the impact of sport mega-events.

In discussing the social sphere, we include a review of how sport activities are developed in Brazil and who they focus on. Importantly, we highlight the rationale of these interventions, which are aimed at children and teenagers living in disadvantaged communities. For a deeper understanding, we explain the development of public programmes on a national scale and other non-profit initiatives. The data presentation also includes Brazilian and international literature as well as official data available regarding these programmes.

The chapter addresses several interpretative strands of sport and development as proposed by Astle (2014). Initially, the section on the economic sphere presents the development *for* sport, when hosting sport mega-events attracted significant attention and resources with the expectation of generating international visibility. Additionally, it shows how funding was directed to elite sport, aiming to improve Brazil's position in the medal rankings. Although some of the mega-events' evangelical messages announced SFD goals, as communities would benefit from the related economic investments on urban infrastructure, our analysis shows that these aims did not materialise.

In the social sphere section, we discuss how public and private programmes aimed at sport *and* development on the basis that sport has inherent values. From this perspective, sport becomes a tool not only to target antisocial behaviour in disadvantaged communities in particular but also to promote education and health-related benefits (development *through* sport). As the strands are a continuum without sharp boundaries (Astle, 2014), this chapter demonstrates how sport has been used through public and non-profit programmes to promote development in Brazil.

Economic sphere: impact of sport mega-events on funding, public policies and communities

In this section, we analyse how hosting sport mega-events impacted funding and public policies of sport as well as communities living in host cities in Brazil. Given the relevance of the aforementioned sport events hosted by Brazil between 2007 and 2016, several studies have been published, including evaluating the consequences of PAN 2007 (Curi, Knijnik and Mascarenhas, 2011; de Oliveira, 2011), the impact of sport mega-events in Rio de Janeiro (Almeida and Graeff, 2016; de La Barre, 2013, 2014; Gaffney, 2010; Penglase, 2016; Sánchez and Broudehoux, 2013; Silvestre and Oliveira, 2012) and the process of community resistance in Rio de Janeiro (Donaghy, 2015; Gutterres, 2014). However, most of these studies address specific issues, often leaving aside the possibility of reflecting on more general aspects and the connections among different sectors. Thus, our perspective here is motivated by an initial consideration of the impacts of sport mega-events on these three sectors: funding, public policies and perspectives of communities living in host cities in Brazil.

The budget of the Ministry of Sport gives indications of how sport mega-events were important for more resources to be brought into the area of sport (Athayde, Mascarenhas and Salvador, 2015), as seen in Figure 2.1.

As Figure 2.1 shows, from 2007 onwards, when the Pan American Games took place and the other sport mega-events began to be granted to Brazil, there was a significant increase in the sport budget in the Ministry of Sport. In 2011, the funding reached its peak, as the projects related to the FIFA World Cup began. Much of the structural work would have to have been ready by 2013 for the Confederations Cup and some even earlier for FIFA inspection. In 2016, Figure 2.1 shows another peak, which included the costs associated with the Rio de Janeiro Olympic Games and several unfinished World Cup projects that needed supplementation.

The literature has shown that the phenomenon of sport mega-events cannot, on its own, explain the variations and the increase in the Ministry of Sport budget in Brazil during the period studied (Almeida et al., 2018). However, such events have been considered an essential part of the context of such changes in the financing of sport in the country. Moreover, the literature in the area also indicates that most of these resources were intended for areas including support

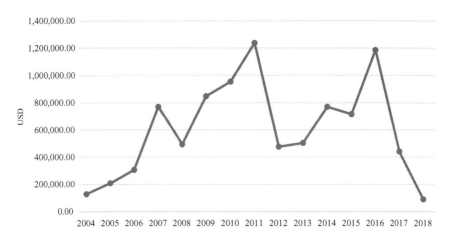

Figure 2.1 The budget of the Brazilian Ministry of Sports.

for athletes, bid and promotion of events, elite sport facilities, scientific and technological centres and events, initiation in elite sport and doping control (Castro et al., 2016). Such areas can be linked to what is referred to as "elite sport" in Brazil as well as sport mega-events. It is relevant to remember these results so that we can advance the debate at the end of this section.

A second explanatory variant for the increase in sport budgeting can be attributed to the beginning of the "popular front" governments of Lula and Dilma Rouseff. Social policies began to receive more government funding during the period and sport was not forgotten. Lula's and Dilma's political party (the Workers' Party) had kept a sector to discuss public policies of sport and leisure since 1998 (Castelan, 2011). With Lula's election in 2002 and the consequent formation of a Ministry of Sport in 2003, the area started to achieve a superior status in comparison to former governments, advancing diverse public policies. Policies created in the period included funding for sport and leisure facilities, financial support for athletes and sport programmes in schools (Carneiro, Athayde and Mascarenhas, 2019; Matias, 2014).

Additionally, the narrative of sport participation, from the popular front and the Workers Party, reached the sport sector. One indicator of this is the hosting of National Sport Conferences (Brasil, 2004) in 2004, 2006 and 2010 (Araujo, 2013; Souza, 2012). Such a narrative focused on sport participation gradually starts to compete for space and resources with sport mega-events. Accordingly, for many, sport mega-events were negative for public policies of sport in the country. Furthermore, evaluations indicate that in the context of sport mega-events, public sport policies had little or no consequence and only short-term outcomes (Broudehoux and Sánchez, 2015; Reis, Souza-Mast and Gurgel, 2014; Sánchez and Broudehoux, 2013).

Finally, one may argue that there is a similarity between public funding and public policies during the preparations and hosting of sport mega-events. Just as the budget was influenced by sport mega-events, so was the public policy. Thus, it can be said that, as in relation to financing, public policies of the sport sector were dominated by the narrative of sport mega-events and their initiatives to the detriment of public policies more distant from such events.

Sport mega-events and their impacts in host communities in Brazil are a vital facet of what happened in the sport sector in Brazilian Society during the period. Initially, it is necessary to understand that the announcement of the 'coming' of sport mega-events to Brazil caused a significant change in the executive and legislative spheres of the Brazilian public powers both in the federal level as well as in states and municipalities. Many have referred to this moment as the creation of a "state of exception" in Brazil and especially in Rio de Janeiro (Almeida and Graeff, 2016).

It is also necessary to emphasise that sport mega-events have been associated with several human rights issues, as pointed out by Graeff and Fernandes (2019), among them: the creation of exception laws and an impediment to participation in decision-making processes (last-minute legislation and exclusionary policies); denial of the right to information; discrimination of race, homeless and migrant people; forced evictions; illegal expulsion of specific populations without appropriate reward; and interruption or attack on the continuum of adequate housing.

Some of the most problematic issues involving communities affected by sport mega-events were linked to state violence and displacement of people (Almeida and Graeff, 2016; Butler and Aicher, 2015; Gaffney, 2010; Graeff, 2019; Sánchez and Broudehoux, 2013). We cover issues related to the latter subject here. As Rolnik (2009) points out, sport mega-events have contributed to the deterioration of living conditions for significant slices of already-disadvantaged and vulnerable populations. In Brazil, it was no different.

Displacement processes were confusing and violent in Brazil during the sport mega-events period and affected principally less fortunate communities (National Coalition of Local Committees for a People's World Cup and Olympics, 2012). Second, displacement processes displayed disregard to international standards of adequate housing (United Nations, 2011). These processes were hurried and brutal. As an example, on diverse occasions, "most individuals were given less than 30-minutes notice that their home was designated to be demolished" (Butler and Aicher, 2015, p. 307).

Also, according to Graeff (2019, p. 106), during the period of the World Cup, in Porto Alegre

> works were advancing amid partially unoccupied streets, mixing abandoned houses, destroyed houses and fully operational homes. Visually, the consequences of such a mismatch was a combination of untouched areas, with spaces occupied by houses and other buildings and regions that mixed

demolition debris and construction sites. This disparity also manifested itself in other areas. For example, garbage collection and other basic services were interrupted several times.

This created a sense of abandonment by the communities affected by sport mega-events in Brazil and transformed many of these communities for the worse, making them look like war zones.

In terms of housing, also in relation to Porto Alegre, the overall results of the sport mega-events period can be considered negative. "Threats, misinformation, lack of public debate and disconnected, disjointed and ineffective policies were the main factors leading to such conditions" (Graeff, 2019, p. 110). These perceptions have been found, more or less evenly, in other research in several Brazilian cities that hosted sport mega-events in the same period (Costa, 2013; Curi, Knijnik and Mascarenhas, 2011; Gaffney, 2010; Vico, Uvinha and Gustavo, 2019).

Social sphere: public and non-profit sectors

The military regime (1964–1985) was a period in which government-led sport programmes with a focus on social outcomes were popularised (Da Costa and Miragaya, 2002). When Brazil undertook a formal turn to democratisation, access to sport and leisure became a constitutional right. Timidly and unevenly, the right to access sport and leisure activities became part of the agenda by both civil and social rights movements in the 1990s (Linhales, 1996).

The neoliberal reforms in the next three decades influenced the sport sector and fostered the creation of a variety of programmes aiming to promote development through sport for a wide range of social groups (Melo, 2005). Led by public, private and non-profit organisations, these sport programmes have targeted a plethora of development objectives such as the improvement of health and education outcomes, the promotion of social skills, the prevention against drug abuse and the involvement in criminality.

While some scholars argued that sport and leisure have not been part of social welfare policies in Brazil (Linhales, 1996; Silva, Romera and Borges, 2014), others have interpreted the growing number of sporting social projects in urban centres in the country as resulting from an existing grey space in which the public, private and third sector interact in both cooperative and competitive ways (Martines, 2009; Trindade, 2017). Despite the overlap between objectives, areas of activity and target groups, for the purpose of contextualisation, the discussion on initiatives provided by the public sector, and the third sector will be presented separately in this part of the chapter.

A major characteristic of sporting social programmes in the country is the focus on specific demographics (e.g., schoolchildren and elderly people) and spaces (e.g., inner city), which is often justified as a compensation measure for the deleterious effect of poverty and extreme socioeconomic inequality in such contexts

(Luguetti, 2014). For instance, 84.5% of children in the country attend school in the morning or the afternoon for four to five hours (Todos Pela Educação, 2020). Due to the reduced school times and the limited offer of free programmes, there is a strong demand for after-school programmes, especially in underserved areas affected by poverty and inequality.

In the same vein, it is estimated that only 22.3% of the Brazilian population over 15 years of age meet the World Health Organisation's guidelines for physical activity (IBGE, 2015), which is further aggravated by the existence of significant social disparities across the population (Guimarães Lima et al., 2020). The narrative that emerges from the collection of this data is based on (1) concerns about the unavailability and inadequacy of existing spaces for the use of children and adolescents from poor communities and (2) the occupation of free time as a solution to prevent youth involvement with illicit, harmful activities.

Public initiatives

After 2003, the appeal for the use of sport and leisure activities as a tool for social development influenced the government strategy and the programmes promoted by the Ministry of Sport. Publicly funded initiatives such as the Second Half programme (*Programa Segundo Tempo*) and Sport and Leisure in the City (*Esporte e Lazer da Cidade*) were implemented across the country in partnership with local and state-level government, higher education institutions and Civil Society Organisations of Public Interest (Figuerôa et al., 2014).

The Second Half programme was conceptualised with a focus on the democratisation of access to sport and its intentional use as a tool to counteract social exclusion and social vulnerability (Ministry of Sport, 2019). The programme was created in 2003 as a combination of two pre-existing federal programmes that were aimed at public school students and the population residing in underserved areas. Thus, as its main characteristic, the Second Half programme seeks to promote educational sport activities to children and adolescents in the after-school hours. Due to the particularities of school hours in Brazil, the programme is implemented in alternative spaces such as public and private clubs, outdoor sport courts and public squares.

The use of sport as a tool for development is justified under the premise that it can be a valuable instrument in reducing social vulnerability and promoting social inclusion (Knijnik and Tavares, 2012). Furthermore, the fundamental problem that the programme seeks to address is the difficulty of children and adolescents exposed to situations of greater social risk (e.g., child labour, abuse, involvement with the production and trafficking of drugs and other criminal activities) in practising educational sport in idle time (Ferreira, Cassiolato and Gonzalez, 2009).

The Sport and Leisure in the City Program is the biggest community sport programme in the country and aims to expand and universalise the access of all age groups to sport and leisure activities. It is a decentralised programme that uses inter-organisational networks composed of universities, research institutes, municipalities and trained local leaders to offer activities around 400 recreational and leisure sport centres in the country. The programme has another two branches that target: (1) people over 45 years of age (*Programa Vida Saudavel*) and (2) indigenous, rural and traditional communities (*Povos e Comunidades Tradicionais*).

Both programmes were affected by the reductions in the budget for community and educational sport due to the contingencies that resulted from hosting sport mega-events. As the investments in sport infrastructure became the priority during this cycle, the expansion of sport-for-all programmes was compromised due to the reallocation of public investments.

Third-sector initiatives

The recent surge in *sport plus* social projects led by third-sector organisations in Brazil was preceded by numerous *plus sport* social projects that were offered by civil entities, primarily community-based NGOs and religious institutions such as Christian churches (Zaluar, 1994). These initiatives were scattered over time and lost most of their presence to larger NGOs that were able to establish inter-organisational connections among them. Due to this shift, the use of the label 'third-sector organisations' is problematic as it blurs the significant differences between a variety of organisational formats adopted by community programmes, philanthropic entities and corporate social responsibility institutions in the country.

The extent to which sporting and leisure social programmes can survive economic austerity is perhaps dependent on the increasing number of third-sector sport organisations responsible for holding up the field (Rossi and Deanes, 2018). These organisations are designed to fill the gaps left by reduced funding for community and educational sport (Kenyon, Mason and Rookwood, 2018). Austerity politics such as the continued reduction in public spending, advocacy of privatisation and reduction in taxes have led to a precarious environment for SFD initiatives where greater competition for resources (often funding) has resulted in NGOs having to adapt to survive (Trindade, 2017; Widdop et al., 2018).

One of the outcomes of this has been that sport social initiatives are being asked to address additional social outcomes within their aims and become more business-oriented in their approach to access the limited funding available, while also exploring additional revenue streams (Kenyon, Mason and Rookwood, 2018; Reid, 2017). This has led to the aims, values, missions and day-to-day practices of SFD organisations becoming increasingly blurred between the interests of the funders (either the state or private donors) and the so-called "public interest", which leads to a natural shift towards social entrepreneurial approaches (Cardoso and Costa, 2014; Rivera-Santos et al., 2015).

This appears to align with the contemporary conceptualisations of SFD, which primarily aim to use sport as a tool to address social objectives (Biscomb, Medcalf and Griggs, 2016). The growing global trend towards organisations identifying as a social enterprise in sport (Bjärsholm, 2017; Ratten, 2011) and SFD is further demonstrated through international SFD organisations employing social entrepreneur approaches as part of their policy and practice. It means that they are operating as cooperatives, trading charities or community interest compasses while also using third-sector models. Examples of such organisations operating in Brazil are *Love Futbol* and *Fight for Peace*.

Within the broader political-economic context, social entrepreneurship offers a different model for organisational survival and sustainability across multiple disciplines and fields (Rivera-Santos et al., 2015). Ultimately, organisations that adopt social entrepreneur approaches aim to achieve social change through the adoption of business-like practices, which include the reinvestment of some or all profits back into the organisation (Smith, Gonin and Besharov, 2013; Weerawardena and Mort, 2006). Furthermore, the ability of such organisations to extend the definition of entrepreneurship into the third sector is done through emphasising ethical integrity and maximising social value rather than private value or profit.

At the governmental level, endorsement for the flexible nature of social entrepreneurial approaches and their perceived compliance with good governance standards has emerged in key legislations. For instance, the Sport Incentive Law (Brazil, 2006) redefined the grey area in which third, private and public sectors interrelate by allowing companies and individuals to invest, respectively, up to 1% or 6% of their income tax in sport projects approved by the federal government. In the same vein, with the New Regulatory Framework for the Third sector (Brazil, 2015), organisations offering SFD projects can be certified as *Civil Society Organisation of Public Interest*, which confers benefits such as the simplification of the process of raising and managing public funds.

These legal reforms favour highly pragmatic organisations, particularly those that have initial capital to invest (e.g., social entrepreneurship or corporate social responsibility institutes) in public funding applications. This is a result of not only the nature of the qualification process itself but also the demands that arise from the execution and the accountability process. There are several requirements that not-for-profit organisations need to attend to in order to qualify for public funding as a civil society organisation of public interest, and qualifying often requires specialised personnel, which is a challenge for the limited human resources available in smaller NGOs. Even though the qualification processes are designed to facilitate public fund-raising, the use of the public investment and the accountability process are bureaucratic, and there are an increasing number of consultancies established in the country nowadays that offer these services. Thus, given the need to guarantee investments for projects via tax incentive laws and direct public financing, third-sector organisations increasingly outsource the fund-raising and accountability process.

In 2007, with the support of Nike and the United Nations Program Development, the Sport for Social Change Network (SSCN) was founded in Brazil by

27 SFD organisations that were developing sport projects that aimed to promote human rights, health, economic development, diversity, inclusion, disability sport and environmental education (Sport for Social Change Network, 2017). The network has significantly expanded and is now composed of 127 selected SFD organisations that are internally (e.g., through the promotion of inter-organisational knowledge exchanges between members) and externally (e.g., moderated debates and collaborations between the participant organisations and the public and private sector, international cooperation agencies and academic institutions) represented by SSCN, which is ultimately responsible for the strategy of coalition building. The majority of the affiliated SFD organisations are corporate social responsibility projects of large private companies, philanthropic institutes founded by ex-athletes, charitable foundations linked to higher education institutes and a small number of local sport providers (Sport for Social Change Network, 2019).

As an advocacy organisation, SSCN works on different areas of policy development, including campaigning and lobbying (e.g., increasing the visibility of participant members through print, television and digital media), engagement with policymakers (e.g., regular debate sessions with public managers and members of organised civil society) and defensive strategies (e.g,. mobilisation to maintain unaltered the legislation that secures funding for third-sector organisations in the states Rio de Janeiro and São Paulo).

The consolidation of SSCN is a response to the need of third-sector organisations in the country to incorporate social entrepreneurial approaches in order to remain competitive while facing the consequences of austerity. The development of strategic advocacy elements by SSCN is emblematic because it indicates an unprecedented articulation between public, private and the third sector in regard to the social agenda of sport in Brazil.

In fact, given the disputes for legitimacy and funding in the third sector and the secondary place of sport in the social agenda, engagement in collaborative networks denotes the necessity for a nuanced and hybrid approach of SFD organisations in the country. When compared to self-organised community organisations and local projects in the country that target specific groups (e.g., girls, people with disabilities, refugees), particular social issues (e.g., school dropout, involvement with drugs and crime, psychomotor development for people with disabilities) or small-scale projects using alternative pedagogies (emancipatory pedagogy) and sport modalities (radical and/or alternative sports), SSCN's organisation members are often criticised for abandoning the reformist and progressive character of smaller civil society organisations. The criticism comes from the interpretation that there are irreconcilable differences between social and economic objectives.

First, pragmatic organisations that adopt a social entrepreneur approach are adapting to austerity policies in order to survive in the third sector rather than challenging the aggravating effect of neoliberal forces in other sectors. As a result, the problems that these organisations aim to address in the first place are arguably perpetuated, providing a basis for the continued existence of these programmes.

Second, there are similar challenges when it comes to monitoring and evaluation. As most of the SSCN's organisation members have their own developmental
objectives for their programmes and do not necessarily support the offer of sport
and leisure as a right, there are inconsistencies in their extensive use of efficiency
measures, such as quantitative data on participation. The generic nature of the
objectives of SFD projects affects the adoption of an integrative set of indicators
(i.e., the use of both qualitative and quantitative data to evaluate the effectiveness
and the efficiency of the programmes), which makes it unsuitable for ascertaining
the ethical integrity and social value of such programmes beyond the self-reports
of accountability.

Within the broader political-economic context in the country, social entrepreneurship offers a different model for organisational survival and sustainability
across multiple disciplines and fields. Ultimately, third-sector sport organisations
that adopt social entrepreneur approaches aim to achieve social change through
the adoption of business-like practices that allow them to fill the gap between the
social demands and the existing public policies.

Conclusion

In the last two decades, economic and social factors have been influencing Brazilian sport. On the economic side, we analysed how hosting sport mega-events
impacted the funding and public policies of sport and in communities living in
host cities in Brazil. From the research, one may conclude that hosting sport
mega-events in Brazil was aimed at SFD (i.e., bringing benefits for the communities through mega-events). Yet, their main impact was a temporary increase in
funding for elite sport (development for sport), as shown by reviewing the Ministry of Sport budget. In terms of public sport policies, throughout the article, we
also show that sport mega-events strongly influenced them, draining resources. In
terms of the impact on host cities' communities, violence and lack of policies ad-
hering to international standards for removals and displacement set the negative
tone of our assessment.

On the social side, while public sport programmes funding was affected by sport
mega-events, non-profit organisations innovated in their management to become
sustainable. Difficulties in accessing public and private funding challenged the
existence of community-based programmes. Currently, the bigger organisations
that promote SFD activities are part of a network, supported by Nike and the
United Nations, showing a higher level of professionalism by management to sustain their activities.

Through the examination of both areas, we argue that sport has been used as
a tool for development in Brazil to promote economic and social benefits. Yet, the
outcomes of public and private programmes in these key areas should be critically
reviewed, particularly through the improvement of planning, transparency and
evaluation processes. Aiming for economic and political goals, sport mega-events
highlighted the social inequalities targeted by SFD programmes and organisations.

In this sense, the issues noted in the Brazilian case might be experienced by other emerging countries bidding or preparing to host sport mega-events as well as by those creating public and private programmes based on SFD purposes.

References

Almeida, B.S., Bolsmann, C., Marchi Júnior, W. and Souza, J. (2015). Rationales, rhetoric and realities: FIFA's World Cup in South Africa 2010 and Brazil 2014. *International Review for the Sociology of Sport*, 50(3), pp. 265–282.

Almeida, B.S., Castro, S.B.E., Mezzadri, F.M. and Souza, D.L. (2018). Do sports mega-events boost public funding in sports programs? The case of Brazil (2004–2015). *International Review for the Sociology of Sport*, 53(6), pp. 685–705.

Almeida, B.S. and Graeff, B. (2016). Displacement and gentrification in the "city of exception": Rio de Janeiro towards the 2016 Olympic games. *Bulletin Journal of Sport Science and Physical Education*, 70, pp. 54–61.

Almeida, B.S., Marchi Júnior, W. and Pike, E. (2014). The 2016 Olympic and Paralympic Games and Brazil's soft power, *Contemporary Social Science: Journal of the Academy of Social Sciences*, 9(2), pp. 271–283.

Araujo, S.M. (2013). Conferências nacionais de esporte: o debate sobre controle social. In: *VI Jornada Internacional de Políticas Públicas*. [online] São Luís-MA, Brazil: Universidade Federal do Maranhão. Available at: http://www.joinpp.ufma.br/jornadas/joinpp2013/JornadaEixo2013/anais-eixo8-direitosepoliticaspublicas/conferencias nacionaisdeesporteodebatesobrecontrolesocial.pdf [Accessed 03 Feb. 2020].

Astle, A.M. (2014). *Sport development – Plan, programme and practice: A case study of the planned intervention by New Zealand Cricket into cricket in New Zealand*. PhD thesis, Massey University. Available at: https://mro.massey.ac.nz/bitstream/handle/10179/6619/02_ whole.pdf?sequence=2&isAllowed=y [Accessed 06 Feb. 2020].

Athayde, P., Mascarenhas, F. and Salvador, E. (2015). Primeiras aproximações de uma análise do financiamento da política nacional de esporte e lazer no Governo Lula. *Revista brasileira de ciências do esporte*, 37(1), pp. 2–10.

Biscomb, K., Medcalf, R. and Griggs, G. (2016). *Current issues in contemporary sport development*. Newcastle: Cambridge Scholars Publishing.

Bjärsholm, D. (2017). Sport and social entrepreneurship: A review of a concept in progress. *Journal of Sport Management*, 31(2), 191–206. Available at: https://doi.org/10.1123/jsm.2017-0007 [Accessed 3 Jan. 2020].

Brasil, (2004). Decree of 21 January 2004. [online]. Available at: http://www.planalto.gov.br/ccivil_03/_Ato2004-2006/2004/Dnn/Dnn10107.htm [Accessed 12 Feb. 2020].

Broudehoux, A.M. and Sánchez, F. (2015). The politics of mega-event planning in Rio de Janeiro: Contesting the Olympic city of exception. In: V. Viehoff and G. Poynter, ed, *Mega event cities: Urban legacies of global sport events*, 1st ed. London: Taylor and Francis, pp. 109–123.

Butler, B.N. and Aicher, T.J. (2015). Demonstrations and displacement: Social impact and the 2014 FIFA World Cup. *Journal of Policy Research in Tourism, Leisure and Events*, 7(3), pp. 299–313.

Cardoso, M.L.M. and Costa, D.M. (2014). O que a perspectiva antropológica tem a dizer sobre a avaliação de projetos sociais apoiados pela cooperação internacional? *Horizontes Antropológicos*, 20(41), pp. 117–140.

Carneiro, F.H.S., Athayde, P.F.A. and Mascarenhas, F. (2019). Era uma vez um ministério do esporte… Seu financiamento e gasto nos governos Lula, Dilma e Temer. *Motrivivência*, 31(60), pp. 01–22.

Castelan, L.P. (2011). *As conferências nacionais do esporte na configuração da política esportiva e de lazer no Governo Lula (2003–2010)*. Master's Degree dissertation. Universidade Estadual de Campinas.

Castro, S.B.E., Starepravo, F.A., Coakley, J. and Souza, D.L. (2016). Mega sporting events and public funding of sport in Brazil (2004–2011). *Leisure Studies*, 35(3), pp. 369–386.

CIA, (2019). The World Factbook: South America – Brazil. [online] Available at: https://www.cia.gov/library/publications/the-world-factbook/geos/br.html [Accessed 03 Feb. 2020].

Costa, G. (2013). Social impacts, pros and cons of hosting mega sporting events, focusing on a global south city: Rio de Janeiro. *Territory*, 64, pp. 19–27.

Curi, M., Knijnik, J. and Mascarenhas, G. (2011). The Pan American Games in Rio de Janeiro 2007: Consequences of a sport mega event on a BRIC country. *International Review for the Sociology of Sport*, 46(2), pp. 140–156.

Da Costa, L.P. and Miragaya, A. (2002). *Worldwide experiences and trends in sport for all*. Aachen: Meyer & Meyer Sport.

de La Barre, J. (2013). Choque do Futuro: o Rio de Janeiro e os Mega-Eventos. *O Social em Questão*, 16(29), pp. 43–68.

de La Barre, J. (2014). Future shock: mega-events in Rio de Janeiro. *Leisure Studies*, 35(3), pp. 352–368.

de Oliveira, A. (2011). Mega-events, urban management, and macroeconomic policy: 2007 Pan American Games in Rio de Janeiro. *Journal of Urban Planning and Development*, 137(2), pp. 184–192.

Donaghy, M. (2015). Resisting removal: The impact of community mobilization in Rio de Janeiro. *Latin American Politics and Society*, 57(4), 74–96.

Ferreira, H., Cassiolato, M. and Gonzalez, R. (2009). *Uma experiência de desenvolvimento metodológico para avaliação de programas: o Modelo Lógico do Programa Segundo Tempo*. Brasília: INEP. Available at: http://agencia.ipea.gov.br/images/stories/PDFs/TDs/td_1369.pdf [Accessed 3 Jan. 2020].

Figuerôa, K.M., Sevegnani, P., Mezzadri, F.M. and Moraes e Silva, M. (2014). Planejamento, ações e financiamento para o esporte em tempos de megaeventos. *Motrivivência*, 26(42), pp. 55–71. Available at: https://doi.org/10.5007/2175-8042.2014v26n42p55 [Accessed 1 Dec. 2019].

Gaffney, C. (2010). Mega-events and socio-spatial dynamics in Rio de Janeiro, 1919–2016. *Journal of Latin American Geography*, 9(1), pp. 7–29.

Gaffney, C. (2014). The mega-event city as neo-liberal laboratory: The case of Rio de Janeiro. *Percurso Acadêmico*, 4(8), pp. 217–273.

Graeff, B. (2019). *Capitalism, sport mega events and the global south*. London: Routledge.

Graeff, B., & Fernandes, D. V. (2019). Human Rights and the Olympic Movement: estrangements and approximations. *Diagoras: International Academic Journal on Olympic Studies*, 3, 153–172.

Guimarães Lima, M., Malta, D.C., Monteiro, C.N., Sousa, N.F.S., Stopa, S.R., Medina, L.P.B. and Barros, M.B.A. (2020). Leisure-time physical activity and sports in the Brazilian population: A social disparity analysis. *PLoS One*, 14(12), e0225940. Available at: https://doi.org/10.1371/journal.pone.0228095 [Accessed 12 Jan. 2020].

Gutterres, A. (2014). "It's not easy, I ask for public mobility and the government sends skull against me": An intimate account of the political protests in Rio de Janeiro (June & July, 2013). *Anthropological Quarterly*, 87(3), pp. 901–918.

Housing and Land Rights Network; Youth for Unity and Voluntary Action, (2011). Handbook on United Nations basic principles and guidelines on development-based evictions and displacement [pdf]. Available at: www.hic-sarp.org/documents/Handbook%20on%20UN%20Guidelines_2011.pdf [Accessed 29 Oct. 2019].

IBGE, (2015). *Práticas de esporte e atividade física*. Rio de Janeiro: IBGE. Available at: https://biblioteca.ibge.gov.br/visualizacao/livros/liv100364.pdf [Accessed 14 Nov. 2019].

Kenyon, J.A., Mason, C. and Rookwood, J. (2018). Emerging third-sector sports organisations and navigating uncertainty in an 'era of austerity': A single ethnographic case study from Liverpool. *International Journal of Sport Policy*, 10(1), pp. 25–42. Available at: https://doi.org/10.1080/19406940.2018.1425732 [Accessed 7 Jan. 2020].

Knijnik, J. and Tavares, O. (2012). Educating Copacabana: A critical analysis of the "second half", an Olympic education program of Rio 2016. *Educational Review*, 64(3), pp. 353–368. Available at: https://doi.org/10.1080/00131911.2012.671805 [Accessed 8 May 2019].

Linhales, M.A. (1996). *A trajetória política do esporte no Brasil: interesses envolvidos, setores excluídos*. Ph.D. thesis, Universidade Federal de Minas Gerais. Available at: http://cev.org.br/arquivo/biblioteca/4019029.pdf [Accessed 14 Jan. 2019].

Luguetti, C.N. (2014). *Moving from what is to what might be: Developing a prototype pedagogical model of sport addressed to boys from socially vulnerable backgrounds in Brazil*. PhD thesis, Universidade de São Paulo. Available at: https://teses.usp.br/teses/disponiveis/39/39133/tde-20022015-093608/pt-br.php [Accessed 11 Jan. 2019].

Martines, I.C. (2009). *As relações entre as organizações não governamentais e o governo do estado do Paraná no campo esportivo*. Master's degree dissertation, Universidade Federal do Paraná. Available at: https://acervodigital.ufpr.br/handle/1884/18870 [Accessed 14 May 2019].

Matias, W. (2014). Política social de esporte e lazer no governo Lula. *SER Social*, 16(34), pp. 134.

Melo, M.P. (2005). A Vila Olímpica da Maré e as políticas públicas de esporte no Rio de Janeiro: um debate sobre a relação lazer, esporte e escola. *Movimento*, 11(3), pp. 89–106.

Ministério do Esporte, (2019). Objetivos. [online]. Ministério do Esporte. Available at: http://portal.esporte.gov.br/snee/segundotempo/objetivos.jsp [Accessed 2 Oct. 2019].

Müller, M. (2017). Approaching paradox: Loving and hating mega-events. *Tourism Management*, 63, pp. 234–241.

National Coalition of Local Committees for a People's World Cup and Olympics, (2012). *Mega-events and human rights violations in Brazil: Executive summary* [pdf]. Available at:http://rioonwatch.org/wp-content/uploads/2013/05/2012-World-Cup-Olympics-Dossier-English.pdf [Accessed 29 Oct. 2019].

Penglase, R.B. (2016). Pacifying the empire of love: Sport, spectacle, security in Rio de Janeiro. *Brasiliana-Journal for Brazilian Studies*, 4(2), pp. 254–282.

Ratten, V. (2011). Sport-based entrepreneurship: Towards a new theory of entrepreneurship and sport management. *International Entrepreneurship and Management Journal*, 7(1), pp. 57–69. Available at: https://doi.org/10.1007/s11365-010-0138-z [Accessed 3 Jan. 2020].

Reid, G. (2017). A fairytale narrative for community sport? Exploring the politics of sport social enterprise. *International Journal of Sport Policy*, 9(4), pp. 597–611.

Reis, A.C., Sousa-Mast, F.R. and Gurgel, L.A. (2014). Rio 2016 and the sport participation legacies. *Leisure Studies*, 33(5), pp. 437–453.

Resende, C. (2010). O esporte na política externa do governo Lula: o importante é competir? *Meridiano 47*, 11(122), pp. 35–41.

Rivera-Santos, M., Holt, D., Littlewood, D. and Kolk, A. (2015). Social entrepreneurship in sub-saharan Africa. *Academy of Management Perspectives*, 29(1), pp. 72–91. Available at: https://doi.org/10.5465/amp.2013.0128 [Accessed 3 Jan. 2020].

Rolnik, R. (2009). Report of the special rapporteur on adequate housing as a component of the right to an adequate standard of living, and on the right to non-discrimination in this context. [online]. Available at: http://www2.ohchr.org/english/bodies/hrcouncil/docs/13session/A-HRC-13-20.pdf [Accessed 29 Oct. 2019].

Rossi, T. and Jeanes, R. (2018). Is sport for development already an anachronism in the age of austerity or can it be a space of hope? *International Journal of Sport Policy*, 10(1), pp. 185–201. Available at: https://doi.org/10.1080/19406940.2017.1380682 [Accessed 20 Dec. 2019].

Sánchez, F. and Broudehoux, A.M. (2013). Mega-events and urban regeneration in Rio de Janeiro: Planning in a state of emergency. *International Journal of Urban Sustainable Development*, 5(2), pp. 132–153. Available at: https://www.tandfonline.com/doi/abs/10.1080/19463138.2013.839450 [Accessed 03 Feb. 2020].

Silva, O.G.T., Romera, L. and Borges, C.N. (2014). A sociologia pública no âmbito da produção e intervenção em esporte e lazer no Brasil. *Movimento*, 20(sp.), pp. 97–108.

Silvestre, G. and Oliveira, N.G. (2012). The revanchist logic of mega-events: Community displacement in Rio de Janeiro's West End. *Visual Studies*, 27(2), pp. 204–210.

Smith, W.K., Gonin, M. and Besharov, M.L. (2013). Managing social-business tensions: A review and research agenda for social enterprise. *Business Ethics Quarterly*, 23(3), pp. 407–442. Available at: https://doi.org/10.5840/beq201323327 [Accessed 3 Jun. 2019].

Souza, C.H.L. (2012). *A que vieram as conferências nacionais? Uma análise dos objetivos dos processos realizados entre 2003 e 2010.* [pdf] Brasília: IPEA, pp. 1–40. Available at: https://www.ipea.gov.br/participacao/images/pdfs/td_1718.pdf [Accessed 03 Feb. 2020].

Sport for Social Change Network, (2017). *Relatório Anual 2016.* [online]. Sport for Social Change Network. Available at: https://issuu.com/agencia-sassarico/docs/rems-relatorio-final [Accessed 2 Jan. 2020].

Sport for Social Change Network, (2019). *Quem somos?* [online]. Sport for Social Change Network. Available at: http://rems.org.br/br/quem-somos/ [Accessed 2 Jan. 2020].

Todos Pela Educação, (2020). OPNE Indicadores - Meta - Educação integral - Porcentagem de escolas públicas da Educação Básica com matrículas em tempo integral. [online]. Todos Pela Educação. Available at: https://www.observatoriodopne.org.br/indicadores/metas/6-educacao-integral/indicadores [Accessed 14 Jan. 2020].

Trindade, N.V. (2017). *A "caixa-branca" dos projetos sociais esportivos: o caso do Instituto Compartilhar – Curitiba/PR.* M.A. dissertation, Universidade Federal do Paraná. Available at: https://acervodigital.ufpr.br/handle/1884/53491 [Accessed 14 Jan. 2019].

Vico, R.P., Uvinha, R.R. and Gustavo, N. (2019). Sports mega-events in the perception of the local community: The case of Itaquera region in Sao Paulo at the 2014 FIFA World Cup Brazil. *Soccer & Society*, 20(6), pp. 810–823.

Weerawardena, J. and Sullivan Mort, G. (2006). Investigating social entrepreneurship: A multidimensional model. *Journal of World Business*, 41(1), pp. 21–35. Available at: https://doi.org/10.1016/j.jwb.2005.09.001 [Accessed 12 Dec. 2019].

Widdop, P., King, N., Parnell, D., Cutts, D. and Millward, P. (2018). Austerity, policy and sport participation in England. *International Journal of Sport Policy and Politics*, 10(1), pp. 7–24. Available at: https://doi.org/10.1080/19406940.2017.1348964 [Accessed 3 Jun. 2019].

World Bank, (2019). World development indicators. [online]. Available at: https://databank.worldbank.org/reports.aspx?source=2&type=metadata&series=NY.GDP.MKTP.CD# [Accessed 14 Nov. 2019].

Zaluar, A. (1994). *Cidadãos não vão ao paraíso*. São Paulo: Escuta.

Chapter 3

Sport and development in China

Professional football as wealth generator and national dream bearer

Huan Xiong and Yang Ma

Introduction: historical background to the rise of professional sport in China

Sport as a subsystem of society has played its part, in the same manner as education, the economy and other social institutions, in reflecting and stimulating the transformation of China from a cultural-bound empire to a modern nation state (Lu and Hong, 2013). When modern sport was initially introduced to China in the mid-19th century, Chinese reformists believed that sport and physical education was the best way to cultivate new citizens for a new China by improving people's physical strength, enlightening their intelligence and promoting their morality (Kang, 2005). They declared that the power of a nation state was based on people's physical strength, and sport is a crucial way to "preserve the nation" and "preserve the race" (Liang, 2002, p. 92). Chinese politicians, educationalists and nationalists hoped to achieve national salvation, revival and prosperity through sport. However, due to a long period of chaos, upheaval and wars (such as the Opium Wars of 1840 and 1860; the collapse of Qing dynasty and rise of the Republic of China, 1911–1912; Warlord periods, 1916–1928; Anti-Japan Wars, 1931–1945; and Chinese Civil Wars, 1946–1949), Chinese society was torn apart, in which circumstance, the majority of people showed no interest in sport. This situation did not change until the establishment of the People's Republic of China (the PRC), especially after economic reform and an open-door policy was endorsed beginning in 1979.

At the beginning of the PRC, in order to re-integrate its members into the socialist order and at the same time re-build its international status, Chinese sport was closely associated with its political objectives: communism and nationalism (Xiong, 2009). On 20 June 1952, Chairman Mao advocated, "developing sport and promoting people's physique" (Xiong and Zhong, 2010, p. 3). This slogan strengthened the main function of sport in this period and contributed to establishing the significance of sport in people's daily lives. Nevertheless, China, at that time, was an impoverished and backward country. The government did not have a large budget to build proper sports venues and facilities. People practised simple physical exercises that did not require professional and high-standard facilities, for example, playing football in the factory compound, jogging in the streets, swimming in lakes or rivers or skipping rope in the fields.

Moreover, in this period, people's sport participation appeared to be more government-led, collective activities to serve communist spirits; therefore, sport was regarded as a political activity rather than a personal choice of life (Wu, 1999, p. 191). By late 1979, the PRC regained her membership of the IOC and many international competitions were open to the Chinese. The success of the Chinese athletes at FIVB Volleyball Women's World Cup in 1981 and the 1982 New Delhi Asia Games brought the buzzword 'competition' to the Chinese. Sport provided the Chinese with a critical arena in which to celebrate national identities. Elite sport competition was also regarded as an effective way to boost China's new image on the international stage. To ensure the success of international competition, the government sought and gained "the whole country's support for the elite sport system" (*Juguo Tizhi*) in the early 1980s (Hu and Henry, 2017). This system channelled the limited resources to fully support elite sport development. It effectively produced hundreds of thousands of young elite athletes in a short time in pursuit of ideological superiority and national status (Hong, Wu and Xiong, 2005). Its main characteristics were centralised management and administration and guaranteed funds and human resources from the whole country to ensure its maximum support (Hao, 2004).

In the 1980s, the Chinese Communist Party (CCP) broke away from the long-standing bondage of 'leftist' practice and embraced pragmatic economic and social reform. Since then, Chinese society itself has undergone a startling transformation, as diversity, consumerism, enhanced personal autonomy, and cultural creativity have begun to appear forcibly (Li, 1996). These social changes have influenced the development of Chinese sport in two significant ways. First, they have stimulated an institutional reconstruction of the sport system through the reform of sports strategy, policy, administrative structures and functions. Sport is not only perceived as a political tool but also as an economic booster. This has been a top-down process on the part of the state, aiming to satisfy the increasing economic and social demands for sport. Second, these social changes launched social and cultural re-building of sport with developments in sports infrastructures, participation models and sports values. It has been a bottom-up process driven by the complex demands of Chinese people and the ever-growing market. With integral forces initiated from the economic reform, Chinese sport has been transformed by the introduction of privatisation, diversification and commercialisation. By transcending the political dominance of sport, the sport industry has been enriched and accelerated under President Xi Jinping's leadership since the 2010s (Zheng and Tan, 2019).

The consensus among researchers is that the Chinese economic success story was actuated by the manufacturing industry and massive exports during the past three decades (Ma and Kurscheidt, 2019; Sullivan, Chadwick and Gow, 2019). Under the great pressure of the global economic downturn, China has sought to recalibrate the traditional manufacturing-led model (Sullivan, Chadwick and Gow, 2019) and has lent primacy to the service industry (Yu et al., 2019). The sport industry has been identified as a fruitful area for implementing this service-oriented economy policy and hence has been affirmed as a new pillar (Ma and Kurscheidt, 2020). Within this context, professional team sports were distinguished as indispensable parts of a service-oriented national strategy (Liu, Zhang and Desbordes, 2017; Yu et al., 2019). Further corresponding measures were enumerated in the 'Guidelines on Promotion of Sport Industry and Sport Consumption' by the State Council, published in October 2014. The aim of the sport industry policy is to, by 2025, establish a well-configured, multi-functional and comprehensive sport industry system, to enrich the sport goods and service sector, to stimulate the consumption demand and to make the entire scale of the sport industry in China exceed 5,000 billion Chinese RMB, which will become a driving force in promoting the sustainable development of the economy and society (Zheng and Tan, 2019, p. 115). This 5,000 billion RMB ambition will significantly enlarge the scale and increase the revenue of the sport industry in China, fostering a new source of economic growth and employment.

Among team sports, football is at the forefront of the sports reformation and is positioned as a role model for other Chinese sports. The Hongshankou Football Meeting held in 1992 heralded the beginning of the institutional transformation of Chinese football, the impact of which transcended football by providing a template for the other sports (Zheng et al., 2019). The *Jia A* football league was established in the mid-1990s and led to the professionalisation process of Chinese sport. In 2004, the Chinese Football Association Super League (CSL) was established. It was led by the Chinese Football Association and run by the Chinese Football Association Super League Co Ltd. The CSL has become a lucrative business, with its net value rising rapidly (Zheng et al., 2019). There has been an influx of financial investment injected into the CSL, and this has also led to the increased national and international attention on Chinese football, including the attention of Chinese political leader Xi Jinping. Xi Jinping's explicit interest in football has propelled the rapid growth of the football industry (Tan et al., 2016). Football, described as a *lingua franca* (Morrow, 2003), appears to be perceived by Chinese policymakers as one element in China's 'comprehensive rejuvenation' process (National Development and Reform Commission [NDRC], 2016). This chapter will use the development of Chinese professional football as a case to demonstrate how sport has been interwoven with social and economic development in contemporary China.

The commercialisation of professional football in China: China's ambitions

Football's global centre of gravity is shifting eastwards as countries in Asia begin to deliberately and systematically attach great importance to the revitalisation of football (Connell, 2018; Huth, Hähnlein and Kurscheidt, 2018; Sullivan, 2018). Among Asian countries, Qatar and the PRC are considered pioneers, triggering football's *Asianisation* (Sullivan, 2018). The acquisition of the rights to present the 2022 FIFA World Cup finals consolidated Qatar's leading position in all things football within Asia. However, in the economic domain, the PRC has experienced a dramatic turn-around and achieved spectacular economic success.

Chinese professional football has been targeted as a productive area for implementing service-oriented economic policy (Liu, Zhang and Desbordes, 2017; Ma and Kurscheidt, 2019; Yu et al., 2019). The economic development of the PRC has not been immune to the global economic downturn. In 2010, the PRC issued the 13th Five-Year Plan, formulating an annual target rate of growth of 6.5% with the aim of doubling the country's GDP by 2020 (Grix, Brannagan and Lee, 2019). In light of the increasing wages and exchange rates, traditional economic policy, which heavily relies on the manufacturing industry and massive exports, is on the brink of exhaustion (Liu, Zhang and Desbordes, 2017; Ma and Kurscheidt, 2019). To achieve the goals introduced in the 13th Five-Year Plan, the central government is attempting to recalibrate the manufacturing-led model that has facilitated the country's economic boom (Sullivan, Chadwick and Gow, 2019) and prioritise the service industry.

Against this backdrop, the *Guidelines on Promotion of Sport Industry and Sport Consumption*, enacted on 20 October 2014, by the State Council, is commonly considered the cornerstone for the expansion of the Chinese sport industry (Liu, Zhang and Desbordes, 2017; Ma and Kurscheidt, 2019). The most pressing concern is their ambitious target of achieving a gross output of the sport industry exceeding 5,000 billion RMB by 2025 (Zheng et al., 2019). Notably, this document highlights the following goals pertaining to Chinese professional football: (1) to facilitate the organisational reform of professional sport; (2) to accelerate the development of team sports that embrace a mass base such as football, basketball and volleyball; and (3) to draft medium- and long-term plans for underperforming Chinese football (Liu, Zhang and Desbordes, 2017).

In line with international sport marketing, spectator sports can be classified as a hedonic mass service (Stieler and Germelmann, 2016). The PRC has developed into a major consumer market because of its large population, and Chinese consumers are now obtaining enough disposable income to afford entertainment and other non-essential products (Menefee and Casper, 2011). This position is re-affirmed through the latest introduction of *An Outline of Establishing a World Sports Power*, in which the determination to forge the sport industry into an economic pillar was explicitly re-emphasised (State Council, 2019). Echoing the argument of Tan et al. (2016), football plays a bellwether role in the development of the sport industry.

Interestingly, the latest commercialisation process of Chinese professional football, which was mainly triggered by the shift in economic policy, is totally different from the initial commercialisation process, which was driven by the overriding prioritisation of *low investment and quick return* sports or disciplines (Zheng and Chen, 2016) and the *medal intensive* sports or disciplines (Baker et al., 1993; Theodoraki, 2004). Unfortunately, in 1992, the development of Chinese football, a notable representative of 'high investment but slow return' sports or disciplines and a sport that is a strong-hold of Western countries (Zheng et al., 2019), suffered cuts to public funding, forcing Chinese football to follow a more market-based logic and become more self-reliant (Hong and Lu, 2013; Zheng and Chen, 2016; Zheng et al., 2019).

Considering the favourable football development policy enacted in 2014, private (corporate) actors have demonstrated an eagerness to invest in professional football. Compared to the initial commercialisation progress featuring 'restricted capitalism' (Amara et al., 2005; Hong and Lu, 2013; Tan and Bairner, 2010), the Chinese Super League (CSL), the top-flight professional football league in mainland China, has witnessed the penetration of capitalism with respect to the entry of private (corporate) actors (Liang, 2014, 2017; Ma and Kurscheidt, 2019; Sullivan, Chadwick and Gow, 2019; Yu et al., 2019). Local professional football clubs have been acquired by investors mainly from the real estate industry including the Evergrande Real Estate Group and Guangzhou R&F Group.

Guangzhou Evergrande Football Club is the most successful and valuable football team in China to date, with a team value of 282 million US dollars (Forbes, 2017) and revenue of 50 million US dollars (NEEQ, 2019). In March 2010, Evergrande (EREG) took over the Guangzhou Football Club from the Guangzhou Municipal Football Association for a fee of 100 million RMB, changing the club's name to Guangzhou Evergrande Football Club (GEFC). Backed by soft loans of EREG, the GEFC spent an additional 170 million RMB for high-profile talent imports domestically and abroad, including national team players Gao Lin and Sun Xiang, national team captain Zheng Zhi and Luiz Muriqui from Brazil. The GEFC was promoted to the CSL in only 243 days (Ma and Zheng, 2020). In the following seasons, the GEFC further strengthened its squad with players and coaches of great reputation.

Moreover, China's largest e-commerce firm, Alibaba, bought a 37.81% stake in the GEFC, leading to the change of the club name to Guangzhou Evergrande Taobao FC (Ma and Kurscheidt, 2019). As a result, the GEFC was able to further develop their professional standing and they won the top-tiered league title every year from 2011 to 2017. The GEFC has also achieved remarkable success in competition against other Asian professional football clubs, particularly the Japanese and Korean counterparts. Notably, the GEFC is the only Chinese professional football club that has ever won the Asian Football Confederation (AFC) Champions League (twice, in 2013 and 2015). In light of the continuing underperformance, *inter alia*, the humiliating failures against the Japanese and the South Koreans, the Chinese men's national team has been frequently criticised by the domestic mainstream media as 'cowards' or the nation's 'chronic illness'. Victory for the GEFC stimulated intense nationalism among Chinese people to a great extent, compensating for the embarrassment triggered by the consistent underperformance of the men's national team.

However, the CSL found itself confronted with diverse governance challenges, such as divergent goal settings and problems of compliance (Ma and Kurscheidt,

2019). More specifically, as a government agency, the Chinese Football Association (CFA) was under high pressure to promote the underperforming Chinese national team. Thus, at the end of each financial year, the majority of the funds sourced from the CSL, for instance, from the sales of sponsorship, broadcasting, advertising and jersey rights, were reallocated for the objective of national football team development. The default strategy for promoting the performance of the national football team is to strengthen the 'inviting in' and 'sending out' policies (i.e., inviting internationally renowned coaches and sending promising players or the entire team to take part in lower-tiered Western football leagues). As a result, only partial revenues have been allocated for the sustainable development of the CSL. Regarding the compliance issue, there is substantial evidence that the Jia-A League was puzzled by an outbreak of corruption and match-fixing, for which more than 100 people were arrested (Hong and Lu, 2013).

Comparing the commercialisation process of Chinese professional football with the commercialisation process of western professional football, China adheres to an approach that was induced by an exogenous policy shift rather than an endogenous shift regarding market structures. Within the context of western countries, after the Industrial Revolution, the increased wages and reduced workloads greatly stimulated the demand side (i.e., fans) to pay for full-time professional football players (Andrews, 2004; Gerrard, 2004; Morrow, 2003). In contrast, we can conclude that Chinese professional football follows a commercialisation pattern with Chinese characteristics. Alternatively, it is perhaps much more accurate to say that Chinese professional football has developed based on a politically led logic.

The *status quo* of the professional football industry in China: wealth generator

International football expansion

Along with the globalisation of football, Chinese private companies have started to invest in global football. From 2015 to the end of 2016, Chinese private (corporate) actors invested over 2 billion US dollars in international professional football (Yu et al., 2019) as shown in Table 3.1.

Although the State Council of the PRC has initiated a large-scale crackdown on capital outflow, which indicates that the acquisitions of international professional football clubs have been severely restrained, the acquisitions have revealed the PRC's bold ambition concerning greater commercialisation (Sullivan, Chadwick and Gow, 2019). In addition to the international professional football clubs, the emphasis has also been placed on related international sports marketing companies. For example, in terms of sport and media, a Swiss company that deals with media and marketing rights for international sports organisations was acquired by the Wanda Group (Sullivan, 2018). The CSL clubs are also spending huge sums of money buying football superstars from the international market, e.g., Jiangsu Suning paid a record high of 50 million Euros to sign up Shakhtar

Table 3.1 The acquisitions of international professional football clubs

Investors	Clubs	Leagues	Expenditures	Shares (%)
United Vansen	ADO Den Haag	Eredivisie	€8 million	100
Wanda Group	Atletico Madrid	La Liga	€45 million	20
Roydx Group	FCSM	Ligue 2	€7 million	100
CEFC China	SK Slavia Praha	Czech First League	€10 million	60
Rastar Group	RCD Espanyol	La Liga	€17 million	56
Shanghai Genbao	Lorca FC	The Segunda Division	Unknown	51
Chinese Culture Group	Manchester City FC	English Premier League	US$400 million	13
Zhejiang Ruikang	Aston Villa	Football League Championship	¥ 570 million	100
Desports	Granada Club	La Liga	€37 million	98
Plateno Group	OGC Nice	Ligue 1	€40 million	40
Sunning Holdings Group	Inter Milan	Serie A	€270 million	70
Ledman	Newcastle Jets Football Club	A-League	A$5.5 million	100
Fosun Group	Wolverhampton Wanderers FC	Football League Championship	£45 million	100
ORG Technology	AJ Auxerre	Ligue 2	€7 million	59.95
Sino-European Sport	AC Milan	Serie A	€520 million	99.93
Palmsports	West Bromwich Albion FC	Football League Championship	¥ 300 million	88
Rheinsports	Southampton FC	English Premier League	£45 million	80

Source: Edited by the authors based on Huang et al. (2019).

Donetsk forward and Brazilian midfielder Alex Teixeira on 5 February 2016. In total, during the January–February transfer window of 2016, the CSL teams' overall spending was worth a world-beating 334 million Euros, outstripping the English Premier League's 253 million Euros for the same period (CCTV, 2016).

In addition, the PRC is actively engaged in international football stadium construction projects. For example, the Wanda Group acquired a 20% stake in the Spanish professional football club Atletico Madrid and constructed the grand Wanda Metropolitano Stadium (Sullivan, Chadwick and Gow, 2019). Currently, the PRC is co-operating with Qatar on stadium construction for the World Cup finals. Such projects are considered *stadium diplomacy*, in which the PRC participates in such co-operations in return for access to raw materials, mineral resources and markets (Sullivan, 2018).

The income structure of the professional Chinese football league (CSL)

CSL is one of the most popular professional sports leagues in China, with an average attendance of 24,107 for league matches in the 2018 season. This is the twelfth highest of any domestic professional sport league in the world and the sixth highest of any professional association football league in the world (Upton, 2019). The League is now running under the authorisation of the CFA. The CSL Company, which is currently the commercial branch of the League, is a corporation in which the CFA and all the member clubs act as shareholders. CSL revenues grew from 17.53 million US dollars in 2012 to 225 million US dollars in 2018 (Sina Finance, 2019), and net profits increased from 9.5 million US dollars to 80 million US dollars. The skyrocketing increase was largely triggered by the new broadcasting contract, which is 26 times higher than the previous one (Ma and Kurscheidt, 2019). It has made a great contribution to China's football industry. Sponsorship, broadcasting rights and ticket sales, which together constitute the main revenue streams of the CSL, are introduced below.

Sponsorship

Football draws substantial attention from the entire nation, and it naturally has a highly prominent exposure rate for advertisements. From 2012 to 2016, the sponsorship revenues of the CSL grew from 186 million US dollars to 235 million US dollars (Yu et al., 2019). Specifically, there are three levels of sponsors in the CSL. As shown in Table 3.2, regarding the naming sponsorship of the CSL, the annual value grew from 8 million euros in 2004 to 200 million RMB in 2019 (Sullivan, 2018; Zheng et al., 2019). More importantly, in stark contrast to the frequently changing naming rights of previous seasons, the naming sponsorship between Ping An insurance and the CSL has become increasingly stable since 2014. The latest contract, which runs from 2018 to 2022, pays 200 million RMB per year (Sullivan, 2018). This stable sponsorship is vital for the sustainable commercialisation and development of the CSL in the long term.

Table 3.3 below shows that the second-level sponsors are generally identified as official commercial partners, incorporating companies from various sectors. The third-level sponsors are equipment suppliers such as TAG Heuer and Absen LED. The annual sponsorship value ranges from 15 million RMB to 50 million RMB (Sullivan, 2018).

Sports media and broadcasting

The first broadcast rights holders of the CSL was the Shanghai Media Group (SMG). In September 2003, they signed a contract for the 2004–2006 seasons.

Table 3.2 Annual sponsorship value of the CSL from 2004 to 2019

Season	Sponsor	Annual value	Official title-sponsored league name
2004	Siemens Mobile	€8 million	Siemens Mobile Chinese Super League
2005	No sponsor		Chinese Football Association Super League
2006	Iphox	€6 million	Iphox Chinese Super League
2007	Kingway Beer	¥ 36 million	Kingway Beer Chinese Super League
2008	Kingway Beer	¥ 38 million	Kingway Beer Chinese Super League
2009	Pirelli	€5 million	Pirelli Chinese Super League
2010	Pirelli	€5 million	Pirelli Chinese Super League
2011	Wanda Plaza	¥ 65 million	Wanda Plaza Chinese Super League
2012	Wanda Plaza	¥ 65 million	Wanda Plaza Chinese Super League
2013	Wanda Plaza	¥ 65 million	Wanda Plaza Chinese Super League
2014	Ping An Insurance	¥ 150 million	China Ping'an Chinese Super League
2015	Ping An Insurance	¥ 165 million	China Ping'an Chinese Super League
2016	Ping An Insurance	¥ 181.5 million	China Ping'an Chinese Super League
2017	Ping An Insurance	¥ 199.65 million	China Ping'an Chinese Super League
2018	Ping An Insurance	¥ 200 million	China Ping'an Chinese Super League
2019	Ping An Insurance	¥ 200 million	China Ping'an Chinese Super League

Source: Edited by the authors based on Sullivan (2018) and Zheng et al. (2019).

The second SMG contract was signed in February 2007 for a five-year period (2007–2011). China Central Television (CCTV) acquired the CSL Television rights in 2012, and they held the rights until 2015 under an annual contract, with CSL broadcast on CCTV's public cable TV channel CCTV5 and CCTV5+. In 2015, the CSL sold its five-year (2016–2020) broadcasting rights for a record-breaking price of 1.25 billion US dollars, an amount 26 times higher than that of the previous 2015 season, to Ti'ao Dongli Sports Communications (Liu, Zhang and Desbordes, 2017). When the latest broadcasting rights deal was signed, it was extended from five to ten years and commanded an extra broadcasting fee of 3 billion RMB (Sullivan, 2018). This amount of money is divided into three parts: 10% reserved for the CFA and CSL company, which is paid out as facilities fees and management expenses. For the remaining 90%, 81% of this is divided equally between the clubs and 9% is awarded to clubs on a merit basis based on their final league position.

Table 3.3 Other sponsors of CSL in recent seasons

Type	Sponsor	Length	Annual value
Commercial Partner	Nike	2009–2019	US$15 million
	Ford	2014–2017	¥ 40 million
	JD	2014–2018	¥ 35 million
	Shell	2017–2020	¥ 50 million
	DHL	2018–2020	¥ 20 million
	Laoshan	2017–2021	¥ 40 million
	Redbull	2016–2017	¥ 20 million
	Yanghe	2017	¥ 20 million
	Dongpeng	2018	¥ 30–40 million
	East IC	2017–2019	¥ 18 million
	Jinritoutiao	2017–2020	¥ 20 million
Equipment Supplier	TAG Heuer	2016–2019	¥ 40 million
	Absen	2018	LED Board Provider and ¥ 20 million

Source: Edited by the authors based on Sullivan (2018).

With the rapid development in the Internet industry, the emergence of Internet-based TV and platforms finally terminated CCTV's traditional monopoly on sports broadcasting in mainland China (Zheng et al., 2019). Of course, the broadcasting rights of the CSL are thought to be a scarce resource. Internet-based sports TV, represented by LeSports and PPTV, has been aggressively obtaining all online streaming rights of CSL matches. LeSports spent 2.7 billion RMB purchasing the broadcasting rights for two seasons (2016 and 2017) from Ti'ao Dongli Sports Communications. Subsequently, PPTV bought broadcasting rights for 1.35 billion RMB per year.

In addition, the CSL expanded into the global media football landscape (Yu et al., 2019). Currently, the International Management Group (IMG) holds the global media rights to the CSL. The first contract was signed in 2016 for two seasons, and in 2018, IMG and CSL sealed a three-year extension. The CSL is now broadcasting in 96 countries across the world (Sullivan, 2018).

Ticket sales

Relying on massive investment in high-profile international players, such as the Brazilians Oscar dos Santos Emboaba Júnio ("Oscar") and Givanildo Vieira de Sousa ("Hulk") from Chelsea FC and Zenit St. Petersburg, respectively (Sullivan, 2018), the popularity of the CSL has gradually increased. As a comparison, the number of Chinese football fans is equal to the population of the United States (Yu et al., 2019). From 2004 to 2018, average attendance at CSL matches increased from 10,838 to 24,107 (see Table 3.4) with the League consequently ranking among the top five globally in terms of highest attendance (Yu et al., 2019). Ticket income grew from 13 million US dollars in 2012 to 42 million US dollars in 2018 (Chinese Super League, 2019).

Table 3.4 Attendance of CSL (2004–2018)

Season	Total attendance	Games	Average
2004	1,430,600	132	10,838
2005	1,871,700	182	10,284
2006	2,228,300	210	10,611
2007	3,173,500	210	15,112
2008	3,065,280	228	13,444
2009	3,854,115	240	16,059
2010	3,499,304	240	14,581
2011	4,236,322	240	17,651
2012	4,497,578	240	18,740
2013	4,456,977	240	18,571
2014	4,556,520	240	18,986
2015	5,326,304	240	22,193
2016	5,798,135	240	24,159
2017	5,703,871	240	23,766
2018	5,785,766	240	24,107

Source: Edited by the authors based on data from the official site of the Chinese Super League (http://csl-china.com/).

Conclusion: China's football dreams and the socio-economic development of the nation

For China, football is not just an economic booster but also an indicator of social development. At an official meeting with the president of the Korea Democratic Party in 2011, Xi Jin-Ping, the then Vice-President of the PRC, highlighted his three World Cup dreams of "participating in the World Cup", "hosting the World Cup" and "being the World Cup champions" (Xi, 2011, p. 1). It is a striking historical resemblance to the Chinese Olympic dreams of "sending athletes to the Olympic Games", "winning an Olympic gold medal" and "hosting Olympic Games", invoked in *Tiantsin Young Men* in 1908. After 100 years, China has accomplished these three Olympic dreams. If Olympic dreams, as a political objective, have shown China's ambitions and determination to be a leading sports power (Hong, Wu and Xiong, 2005), what do the football dreams mean to China and Chinese people in the new decade?

From the founding of the PRC, football was "a symbol of modernity; a talisman of topicality; a statement of intent" (Dong and Mangan, 2001, p. 79). The contemporary party-state has reanimated football as a vehicle for its nation-building projects. A flourishing domestic football industry, combined with internationally competitive performance, has a role to play in the New Era (post-socialism) through the promotion of domestic consumption, civic participation, cultural engagement and national pride (Sullivan, Chadwick and Gow, 2019). China's football dreams are also the carriers of economic, political, cultural and educational integration of the post-socialist society. As Sullivan et al. (2019) indicated, the discourse of the Chinese football dream is a precondition for the activity which leads to its reproduction and transformation and propels development along a trajectory deemed desirable by the state. Sport policies, such as the ones highlighted below, have formalised the pathways of China's football dreams step by step. "Accelerating the Development of the Sports Industry to Promote Sport Consumption" issued in 2014 set out an industrial vision for Chinese Sport (The State Council of PRC, 2014); "The Overall Reform Plan for the Reform and Development of Chinese Football" (2015) started the professionalisation of Chinese football and designed the institutional reformation with greater autonomy in planning and operations for the CFA. Along with the institutional reformation of Chinese football, in "Football Development Plan 2016–2050", the government sets out targets, means and benchmarks for a projected world-class football power (NDRC, 2016).

Chinese football policies primarily emphasise that the development of football should be integrated into the economic and social development plan of the nation and require the reformation of the football administrative system by establishing new governance (The State Council of PRC, 2015). Grassroots initiatives are manifest in the establishment of football as a key component in compulsory education, the increase of people involved in football and the construction of national football facilities nationwide (NDRC, 2016). In terms of the medium-term phase, the emphasis is on developing infrastructure for campus football, amateur participation and consolidating professional leagues. The ambition for the national men's team is to become a leading force in Asian football by 2030. The overarching goal for the long-term phase is to establish China as a "world-class football power", aligning with broader national objectives to establish a nation characterised as powerful, civilised and harmonious by the 100th anniversary of the founding of the PRC in 2049 (Gow, 2017).

As Yu et al. (2019) argued, the business of football – and success thereof – is framed within the national imaginary as productive to the nation, the state and the people therein. It is exemplified in narratives and praxes formed around: (1) economic development through football, (2) football's function in promoting the overall health and productivity of the nation, (3) seizing the productive capacities of the national population to grow the status of the modern nation and pacify social unease and (4) using football to make capital more 'fluid' within and outside of the domestic marketplace (Yu et al., 2019). What becomes clear in these concurrent initiatives is that football itself has emerged as an important commodity form and 'scape' through which the nation-state can be assembled, articulated, imagined and put into praxis. More importantly, it will establish a space for citizens to actively participate in the 'Chinese dream' through non-political activity, allow citizens to express their identity in a manner approved by the state and continue to develop a new sector to facilitate China's shift to a consumer-driven economy (Sullivan, Chadwick and Gow, 2019).

Nevertheless, the fact is that the process of China's football reform lags far behind the transformation and development of Chinese society. To date, its governance structure is still considered to be the relics of the planned economy. There is substantial evidence that the long-standing governance structure featuring governmental control continues to act as an impediment to the commercialisation of Chinese professional football. The clashes between traditional government influence and the emerging commercial and market elements in professional sports and sports consumption remain a big challenge. To achieve a greater development as a socio-economic booster, a further reformation of Chinese football governance structure is needed. The good omen is that the latest policy mix of national macroeconomic policy and football policy is leading a new model of governance, which hopefully will revolve around an intensified marketisation of football, greater autonomy for sports organisations and less governmental control, permitting the market to play the predominant role in determining resource allocation. Only then will Chinese football become a key feature of Xi's "New Era of Socialism with Chinese characteristics" as both a driver of China's shift to a consumer-driven economy and as a potentially significant source of cultural power aimed at fostering national pride and citizenship identity (Sullivan, Chadwick and Gow, 2019).

References

Amara, M., Henry, I., Liang, J. and Uchiumi, K. (2005). The governance of professional soccer: Five case studies – Algeria, China, England, France and Japan. *European Journal of Sport Science*, 5(4), pp. 189–206.

Andrews, D.L. (2004). Sport in the late capitalist moment. In: T. Slack, ed., *The commercialisation of sport*. New York: Routledge, pp. 2–28.

Baker, J.A.W., Cao, X. -J., Pan, D. W. and Lin, W. (1993). Sport administration in the People's Republic of China. *Journal of Sport Management*, 7(1), pp. 71–77.

CCTV, (2016). *Chinese Super League on record spending.* [online]. Available at: http://english.cntv.cn/2016/02/29/VIDE69rPejl9GV5QYeDc7d9y160229.shtml [Accessed 25 May. 2020].

Chinese Super League, (2019). *Archive statistics.* [online]. Available at: http://csl-china.com/ [Accessed 26 Dec. 2019].

Connell, J. (2018). Globalisation, soft power, and the rise of football in China. *Geographical Research*, 56(1), pp. 5–15.

Dong, J. X. and Mangan, J. A. (2001). Football in the New China: Political statement, entrepreneurial enticement and patriotic passion. *Soccer & Society*, 2(3), pp. 79–100.

Forbes Report, (2017). *Chinese soccer's most valuable teams 2017.* [online]. Available at: https://sports.phb123.com/football/15827.html [Accessed 16 Feb. 2019].

Gerrard, B. (2004). Media ownership of teams: The latest stage in the commercialisation of team sports. In: T. Slack, ed., *The commercialisation of sport*. New York: Routledge, pp. 240–257.

Gow, M. (2017). The core socialist values of the Chinese dream: Towards a Chinese integral state. *Critical Asian Studies*, 49(1), pp. 92–116.

Grix, J., Brannagan, P. M. and Lee, D. (2019). *Entering the global arena: Emerging states, soft power strategies and sports mega-events*. Singapore: Palgrave Macmillan.

Hao, Q. (2004). The definition, characteristics and functions of the Chinese elite sport system [In Mandarin]. *Journal of Chengdu University of Sport*, 30(1), pp. 7–11.

Hong, F. and Lu, Z. (2013). The professionalisation and commercialisation of football in China (1993–2013). *The International Journal of the History of Sport*, 14(30), pp. 1637–1654.

Hong, F., Wu, P. and Xiong, H. (2005). Beijing ambitions: An analysis of the Chinese elite sports system and its Olympic strategy for the 2008 Olympic Games. *The International Journal of the History of Sport*, 22(4), pp. 510–529.

Hu, X. and Henry, I. (2017). Reform and maintenance of Juguo Tizhi: Governmental management discourse of Chinese elite sport. *European Sport Management Quarterly*, 17(4), pp. 531–553.

Huang, D., Guo, S., Yang, Q., Chen, C. and Cai, G. (2019). Risk identification of Chinese capital M & A of overseas football clubs: An exploratory analysis based on grounded theory [in Mandarin]. *Journal of Shenyang Sport University*, 38(6), pp. 42–49.

Huth, C., Hähnlein, J. and Kurscheidt, M. (2018). Internationale Zielmarktauswahl im Profifußball: Ein Scoring-Modell zur Deutschen Fußball Liga [Selection of international target markets in professional football: A scoring model for the German Bundesliga]. *Sciamus – Sport und Management*, 9(1), pp. 32–49.

Kang, Youwei (2005). *Datongshu*. Shanghai: Shanghai Guji Press.

Li, Y. (1996). *Jingji, wenhua yu fazhan* [Economics, culture and development]. Beijing: Sanlian shudian.

Liang, Q. (2002). *Bianfa Tongyi* [Changes of the laws]. Beijing: Huaxia chubanshe.

Liang, Y. (2014). The development pattern and a clubs' perspective on football governance in China. *Soccer and Society*, 15(3), pp. 430–448.

Liang, Y. (2017). Marketisation impact on the relationships between supporters and football clubs. *The International Journal of the History of Sport*, 34(17–18), pp. 1–19.

Liu, D., Zhang, J. J. and Desbordes, M. (2017). Sport business in China: Current state and prospect. *International Journal of Sports Marketing and Sponsorship*, 18(1), pp. 2–10.

Lu, Z. and Hong, F. (2013). *Sport and nationalism in China*. London: Taylor and Francis.

Ma, Y. and Kurscheidt, M. (2019). Governance of the Chinese Super League: A struggle between governmental control and market orientation. *Sport, Business and Management: An International Journal*, 9(1), pp. 4–25.

Ma, Y. and Kurscheidt, M. (2020). Doing it the Chinese way: The politically-led commercialisation of professional football in China. *Journal of Global Sport Management*, pp. 1–17.

Ma, Y. and Zheng, J. (2020). Commercialisation of sport in China. In: H. Fan and Z. Lu, eds., *Routledge Handbook of Sport in Asia*. Abingdon: Routledge.

Menefee, W. C. and Casper, J. M. (2011). Professional basketball fans in China: A comparison of National Basketball Association and Chinese Basketball Association team identification. *International Journal of Sport Management and Marketing*, 9(3/4), pp. 185–200.

Morrow, S. (2003). *The people's game: Football, finance and society*. New York: Palgrave Macmillan.

National Development and Reform Commission of the PRC (NDRC), (2016). *Notice on printing and distributing the national construction plan for football pitches and facilities*, (2016–2020). [online]. Available at: www.ndrc.gov.cn/zcfb/zcfbtz/201605/t20160510_801118.html [Accessed 1 Oct. 2018].

National Equities Exchange and Quotations (NEEQ), (2019). *Half year report of Guangzhou Evergrande Taobao Football Club Co.* [online]. Available at: http://www.neeq.com.cn/index/searchInfo.do [Accessed 18 Apr. 2020].

Sina Finance, (2019). *2018 Zhongchao shangye baogao chulu, zhongchao gongsi quannian shouru chao 15yi* [The commercial report of 2018 CSL is out, total revenues exceed

1.5 billion RMB). [online]. Available at: https://finance.sina.com.cn/roll/2019-03-21/doc-ihsxncvh4335133.shtml [Accessed 12 Apr. 2020].

Stieler, M. and Germelmann, C.C. (2016). Fan experience in spectator sports and the feeling of social connectedness. In: K.K. Kim, ed., *Celebrating America's pastimes: Baseball, hot dogs, apple pie and marketing?* Switzerland: Springer, pp. 911–918.

Sullivan, J. (2018). *China's football dream.* [ebook] Nottingham: University of Nottingham Asia Research Institute. [online]. Available at: https://www.nottingham.ac.uk/asiaresearch/documents/cso-ebook.pdf [Accessed 26 Dec. 2019].

Sullivan, J., Chadwick, S. and Gow, M. (2019). China's football dream: Sport, citizenship, symbolic power, and civic spaces. *Journal of Sport and Social Issues,* 43(6), pp. 493–514.

Tan, T.-C. and Bairner, A. (2010). Globalisation and Chinese sport policy: The case of elite football in the People's Republic of China. *The China Quarterly,* 203, pp. 581–600.

Tan, T.-C., Huang, H.C., Bairner, A. and Chen, Y.W. (2016). Xi Jin-Ping's World Cup dreams: From a major sports country to a world sports power. *The International Journal of the History of Sport,* 33(12), pp. 1449–1465.

The State Council of People's Republic of China, (2014, 20 October). *Guowuyuan guanyu jiakuai fazhan tiyu chanye cujin tiyu xiaofei de ruogan yijian* [State council opinions concerning the acceleration of sports industry development and promotion of sports consumption]. [online]. Available at: http://www.gov.cn/zhengce/content/2014-10/20/content_9152.htm [Accessed 22 Jan. 2020].

The State Council of the People's Republic of China, (2015). *Zhongguo zuqiu gaige fazhan zongti fang'an* [The overall reform plan for the reform and development of Chinese football). [online]. Available at: http://sports.people.com.cn/n/2015/0316/c22176-26699805.html [Accessed 22 Jan. 2020].

The State Council of the People's Republic of China, (2019). *An outline of establishing a world sports power.* Beijing: The State Council of the People's Republic of China.

Theodoraki, E. (2004). Sport management reform, national competitiveness and Olympic glory in the People's Republic of China. *Managing Leisure,* 9(4), pp. 193–211.

Upton, P. (2019). Opportunity for big growth in China's sports industry. *China Briefing.* [online]. Available at: https://www.china-briefing.com/news/opportunity-big-growth-chinas-sports-industry/.

Wu, S. (1999). *Zhonghua renmin gongheguo tiyu shi* [Sport history of People's Republic of China 1949–1998]. Beijing: zhongguo shuji chubanshe.

Xi, J. (2011). *Xi meets with South Korean guests on Chinese football hopes for World Cup.* [online]. People Available at: http://gx.people.com.cn/GB/179479/15082835.html [Accessed 18 Apr. 2020].

Xiong, H. (2009). *Urbanisation and transformation of Chinese Women's Sport since 1980: Reconstruction, stratification and emancipation.* London: VDM Verlag Dr. Muler.

Xiong, X. and Zhong, B. (2010). *Xin Zhongguo tiyu 60 nian* [Sport in the New China for 60 years]. Beijing: Beijing Sport University Press.

Yu, L., Newman, J., Xue, H. and Pu, H. (2019). The transition game: Toward a cultural economy of football in post-socialist China. *International Review for the Sociology of Sport,* 54(6), pp. 711–737.

Zheng, J. and Chen, S. (2016). Exploring China's success at the Olympic Games: A competitive advantage approach. *European Sport Management Quarterly,* 16(2), pp. 148–171.

Zheng, J., Chen, S., Tan, T. and Houlihan, B. (2019). *Sport policy in China.* Abingdon: Routledge.

Zheng, J. and Tan, T. (2019) Emerging eras and their trends: Professionalisation, commercialisation, sports industry and sports media. In: J. Zheng et al., eds., *Sport policy in China.* Abingdon: Routledge, pp. 100–129.

Chapter 4

Sport and development in the Czech Republic

Sport as a tool for social and cultural transformation

Simona Šafaříková and Arnošt Svoboda

Introduction

In the Czech Republic, and formerly in the Czech countries, sport has been associated with numerous significant historical events. Except for several international competitive results in tennis, ice hockey, football and many other disciplines, there were several instances in history when sports not only enhanced the picture of the Czech Republic abroad but also served as a tool for achieving other goals. Such goals may lie in the political, cultural and social area.

The main goal of this chapter is to present sport activities in the Czech national context not as an end in itself but as a dynamic instrument which may be used for reaching goals both on the national level and internationally. Specifically, the theoretical conception of *sport plus* and *plus sport* introduced by Coalter (2009) and further elaborated by Astle (2014) will be used. In this regard, an overview of the historical role of the sporting movements in Czech countries oscillates between Astle's *sport and development, sport for development,* and *development through sport* (see Chapter 1 for descriptions of these terms) as processes where the subject of development lies in a societal sphere. In other words, the establishment of the modern sport movement in the Czech countries in the 19th century is not strictly observed as a process of structural and organisational development of sporting bodies but as a series of steps in which sport gains a significant position within the developing Czech society. Moreover, as Darnell, Field and Kidd (2019) argue, political agents often use sport and sporting practices as a source of *soft power* (see Nye, 2004) and, thus, help strengthen the position of regimes or build a sense of citizenship. By the same token, the description of selected current sporting initiatives in the Czech Republic refers not only to the three above-mentioned models but also to the *development of sport* where the sport itself is the outcome being developed.

First, the chapter presents a brief overview of the role that evolving modern sport played in the process of gaining independence of the Czech lands in the context of Central Europe during the turbulent 19th century. Furthermore, the chapter follows the prominent emergence of another facet of Czech sport history, mass participation exercises called *Spartakiády* – a tool used by the Communist regime for ideological representation since its beginning in 1948. After the fall of the Communist government, the civil society burgeoned and soon started to re-flect significant social problems within the newly formed democratic state. Finally, the chapter concludes with a description of various contemporary interventions by non-profits and other organisations using sport as a tool for mitigating and solving a variety of social problems at the national level.

The rise of modern sport under the Austro-Hungarian empire (19th century)

After political reforms within the Austro-Hungarian empire in the 18th century, social and cultural conditions relaxed. Against this backdrop, the legislative and state control became less strict and, hence, enabled a moderate growth of public life. Later in the 19th century, together with other civil activities, physical exer-cises and newly established modern forms of sport gained in popularity. Yet, the organised physical activities were first confined to the private houses of wealthy citizens and primary and secondary schools. These first decades of the develop-ment of Czech modern sport resemble Astle's *sport and development* model, where sporting practices are spread throughout the society without a utilitarian link to nationalist movements proliferating throughout the north-western part of the Austrian empire (Kössl, Štumbauer and Waic, 2018; Waic, 2013).

Over time, organised modern sport became a deliberate vehicle to support and enhance national awareness within the Czech countries. This role was further enhanced by the first sporting successes of Czech athletes such as the victory of Žemla brothers at the Tennis Austrian Championship in 1906 (Svoboda and Numerato, 2019). Thus, together with other civic initiatives and the popularity of new public associations active in many spheres of the Czech society, numerous new sporting clubs and associations came under the surveillance of Austrian au-thorities since they were considered a security threat (Kössl, Štumbauer and Waic, 2018; Waic, 2013).

Sokol and the rise of nationalism (1862–1938)

Similar to other Central European countries, a specific status was achieved by sports associations where the primary role was attained by *Sokol* [Falcon] founded in 1862. The first member base was constituted mainly by the petite bourgeoisie and working class as a dynamic stratum of the newly forming civil society. Con-trary to similar initiatives in Prussia, France or the United Kingdom where such organisations originated mainly as a response to military tensions, Sokol was es-tablished in close connection to the Czech nationalist movement (Nolte, 2002). Soon, many public ceremonies of Sokol turned to symbolic anti-establishment demonstrations which foreshadowed sharpened relationships between Sokol and the state administration until the end of the Austrian empire in 1918. More and more, Sokol's activities and its public perception entered the model which theoretically falls into the Astle's (2014) category *sport for development* with an increasing international aspect. Sokol members travelled abroad spreading the image of Czech countries as a peculiar territorial, cultural and social unit (Nolte, 2002). Also, Sokol's gatherings that featured mass gymnastic exercises, *Slety*, taking place every six years, attracted increasing numbers of participants. In the years just before World War I, military aspects of physical training were emphasised, and the role of Sokol as a "national army" of a non-existent state was widely acknowledged (Nolte, 2002).

The symbolic capital of Sokol accelerated during World War I. Many of its gyms were changed into hospitals, and Sokol actively raised funds for families of wounded and dead soldiers. Many members of Sokol were also active in legions outside the Austrian army. Also, during the first months of the newly established Czechoslovakia in 1918, members of Sokol were highly visible as patrols during the taking over and securing of key state offices and, later, as members of the para-military units intervening at conflict sites on the state borders (Kössl, Štumbauer and Waic, 2018; Nolte, 2002).

During the first 20 years of the newly established Czechoslovak state, Sokol continued representing nationalism. As Roubal (2016) remarked, it helped with creating the "imagined" picture of the state in people's minds. Perhaps the most visible image of the connection between Sokol and the nation came in 1938, under the acute danger from Nazi Germany. The last pre-war Slet (singular of Slety) took place in Prague at the newly built Strahovský stadium, the largest exercise area in the world at 310 by 202 meters (Nolte, 2002). In front of the then-President Edvard Beneš, members of the cabinet, parliament and diplomats, 30,000 men demonstrated a routine named *Přísaha republice* [Oath to the Republic], set to a medieval Hussite chorale *Ktož jsú boží bojovníci* [You who are Warriors of God] (Burian et al., 2012). The famous Czech novelist Karel Čapek wrote, "People paid tribute to people. The nation celebrated itself" (Čapek, 1938, p. 1).

The Olympic movement reborn (1894–1918)

Another apt example of the role of sport as a deliberate catalyst for cultural and political development, or *sport for development* (Astle, 2014), is the establishment of the Olympic movement in the Czech countries. It can be also considered as *sport plus* in the model by Coalter (2009) because the Czech Olympic movement also served as a tool to fight for independence within the Austro-Hungarian empire. Formed in 1894, the International Olympic Committee (IOC) had 12 founding members including Czech Jiří Guth. Paradoxically, he represented a nation without its state. As Waic (2013) comments, it was only a matter of time before Austrian authorities would start concentrating on such activities as another possible threat to the unity of their empire. At the first Olympics in 1896, Guth realised the potential of national representation on the international stage, all the more because the IOC decided that its members should stand for specific nations instead of states (Kolář, 2018).

In 1900, the new *Czech Olympic Committee* (established a year earlier) began with preparation for the next Olympic Games. The Czechs wanted to take full advantage of the international visibility of the Games and "wanted to make possible the sending of the Czech athletes…regardless the chance for success" (Waic, 2013, p. 151). As the renown of the Olympics grew, the vigilance of Austrian authorities focused more on the separate Czech representation at the Games. Ultimately, the 6th Olympic Congress in Paris in 1914 marked the end of independent Czech representation under Austrian rule (Kolář, 2018; Waic, 2013). Nevertheless, the Great War resulted in radical changes, including the end of the Austrian empire that brought about the formation of the Czechoslovak Republic, the first independent Czech and Slovak state after almost 400 years.

Soft power and Spartakiády (1955–1985)

As a third example of the significant role of sport as a tool for cultural transformation, we will describe *Spartakiády* [Spartakiads] – sporting events that took place every five years (from 1955 to 1985) during the Communist regime in former Czechoslovakia. After the takeover of power by the Communist party in 1948 and the installation of the totalitarian regime for the next 41 years, the new political leaders sought tools not only for maintaining the government rule but also for adjusting attitudes of citizens towards the new political system. In this regard, using cultural events for shaping preferences of the public is an example of utilising *soft power* (Nye, 2004) as opposed to other methods using direct, armed or economic force. In particular, Communists tried to establish a new cultural tradition without strong historical ties to specific social groups (Roubal, 2016). In contrast to previously described historical instances, Spartakiády was an intentional tool used from the beginning to support the status of the Communist party. As such, it falls into the category of *development through sport* of Astle's (2014) typology.

As we already mentioned, the Czech organisation Sokol established the tradition of mass gymnastic exercises in the 19th century – Slety. After the onset of the Communist regime, together with many associations stemming from the civic society, Sokol was persecuted and finally disbanded in 1952 (Roubal, 2016). Still, Sokol's tradition of mass participation exercises seemed to be the right instrument for uniting the nation and presenting it as a solid mass (Thorne, 2011). Inspired by Slety, the Communist regime established new mass participation exercise events: *Spartakiády*. Its visual conception was remarkably similar to Slety, while the ideological background was different (Roubal, 2006).

In the years following the first, rather criticised, Spartakiáda, the events came closer to natural gymnastic activities, and participation was not enforced as strongly as it was in the first years. In the so-called "normalisation period", following the military occupation of Czechoslovakia in 1968 and lasting until the 1980s,[1] the general presentation moved even more to family and national topics. At the same time, specific age and gender groups were displayed instead of routines based on various professions. Furthermore, as of Spartakiáda in 1975, the

Soviet Union flag was no longer hung, and the Soviet anthem was not played, partly due to concerns about spontaneous reactions from the gymnasts and audience. According to Roubal (2016), the adapted conception and stalled development of Spartakiády reflected the attempted stability in society after the social and political turbulence escalated in 1968 and ended with the invasion of Warsaw Pack armies. The regime further tried to form Spartakiády into a state of compromise that would be acceptable for participants and, simultaneously, still serve as a tool for presenting a socialist order and harmony between people united under the Communist regime (Thorne, 2011).

Sport and social transformation (post-1989)

The revolutionary year 1989 meant a big change for the Czechoslovak society, culture and, predominantly, political system. The *Velvet Revolution*, the non-violent end of the Communist regime initiated by student demonstrations in Prague, 17 November 1989, brought an end to more than 40 years of the Communist party's rule. During those several decades, sport was often used as a tool to strengthen the political regime but at the same time also as a tool to resist it. Amongst the well-known examples of resistance are ice-hockey matches between Czechoslovakia and the Soviet Union. After the military invasion in 1968, these events were full of escalated symbolic defiance against the Soviets (Jakubcová, 2012; Pacina, 2004). However, these public acts of resistance were ambiguous and were utilised by different parties for different purposes (Marada, 2003). As we indicated previously, the Communist regime also utilised sport to display itself positively to both domestic and foreign audiences. Such a blending of institutions of state and those of the civil sphere was a significant facet of Communist Czechoslovakia. For that reason, civil society as a partner and opponent for the political sphere could not develop under such conditions at all. The preferred model of state administration was a centralised hierarchy enforced by repression and new legislation which precluded establishment of new civil initiatives or subsumed them into the state unions. Even so, several sectors were controlled less strictly such as environmental organisations, some scientists' groups or activities of recognised churches. The rest of the non-state sector was more or less illegal and intensively oppressed (Skovajsa, 2010).

It was only after 1989 when the civil society began to fully burgeon in Czechoslovakia and, since 1993, in the Czech Republic. The legislative framework was amended, and independent and voluntary initiatives could be founded. From the beginning, they had a strong supporter in the then-President Václav Havel. But simultaneously, the post-communist tradition often brought a tense attitude to the relationship between state and civil society which was perceived as opposition to the state. Apart from Havel, numerous prominent Czech politicians have strongly opposed the civil society. As a concept, civil society is often mixed up with NGOs (Rakušanová, 2007), which are repeatedly criticised as exceeding their "place" in politics.

Initially, many non-governmental organisations were funded by foreign donors' embassies of Western governments or private funds, such as the Open Society Fund, the German Marshall Fund or the Rockefeller Foundation. Towards the end of the 1990s, EU funds began to take over the leading role and, gradually, became the primary source of international funding for Czech NGOs (Navrátil and Pejcal, 2014). Currently, we can see various types of Czech sporting non-profit organisations. Some of the biggest are, however, big sporting unions such as the Football Association of the Czech Republic or the Czech Athletics Union, which regularly place amongst the largest recipients of public subsidies (Břešťan, 2018).

In 2011, Numerato (2011) concluded that the willingness of Czech sports associations to adopt a *sport plus* (Coalter, 2009) approach was rather limited, even though the Czech Association Sport for All (see later) might seem to proclaim it in its vision. Still, the current strategic plan, Sport Support Conception 2016–2025, introduces strategic objectives for the Czech sport which leaves quite a lot of space for grassroots activities and for initiatives using sport for social and cultural goals. Amongst others, these goals include utilising the integration potential of sport for all the social groups of children and youth, supporting sport for the development of local communities or ensuring accessibility of sport for disabled people. The plan also clearly states the pillars for its goals as: sport as a tool for spreading values of fair-play and justice; for self-fulfilment or for supporting national pride (MŠMT, 2016). Concerning the implementation of the objectives, the projects and activities administered by Czech NGOs, sport clubs and associations or public bodies cover the broad spectrum of development practices, both involving *sport plus* and *plus sport* approaches. Yet, the developing Czech SDP sector still lacks a thorough critical review focused not only on the reasons behind the activities but also on the evaluation of the operations (see also Coalter, 2009).

To demonstrate some of the activities, the following sections present examples of three initiatives that have played a significant role in the modern Czech SDP/ SFD field: the Football for Development project, the Every Basket Counts initiative and the Czech Association Sport for All. These initiatives use sport as a tool to achieve different aims and can also contribute to levelling the inequalities existing in sport participation (Slepičková, 2007; Špaček, 2011). They cover different models as defined by Astle (2014) in the sport development continuum.

Football for development

The topic of *sport for development (and peace)*, as understood internationally within the *Sport for Development and Peace* and *Sport for Development* (SDP and SFD) concepts (see e.g., Levermore and Beacom, 2009; Schulenkorf, Sherry and Rowe, 2016), is pretty new in the context of the Czech Republic concerning specifically focused social programmes. Taking into account Astle's proposed conceptualisation (2014), we are focused especially on *development through sport* and *sport for development* (see Chapter 1 for explanations of these terms).

One of the first projects within these categories (as defined by Astle, 2014) implemented in this country since 2005 was *Football for Development (FFD)*. Until now, this project has been unique in how it uses football as a tool to tackle social problems within the Czech Republic. Thanks to this project, football started to be gradually used by several social workers in their everyday work with children and youth in drop-in centres, and its image as a purely professional and competitive sport is changing.

FFD is a Czech sport educational project whose structure, aims, methods and regional focus within the Czech Republic have evolved a lot over its lifetime until the present day. Since its beginning in 2005, it has been part of the Czech Development Cooperation, with its aim "to contribute to increasing participation and global responsibility of young people through connection of local and global problems while using the potential of football as an effective tool in raising awareness" (INEX-SDA, 2012, p. 3). We argue that FFD falls under both the *development through sport* and *sport for development* categories because it brings together communities from developed as well as developing countries through an international youth exchange and tackles non-sporting issues at the same time. It has been financed through the Global Development Education programme, supported officially by the Czech Development Agency and the Czech Ministry of Foreign Affairs (Šafaříková, 2012). Since 2005, the project has been administered by INEX-SDA, the Czech NGO that organises international voluntary work and through that work contributes to intercultural education. According to Coalter's (2007) definition, INEX-SDA falls under the *plus sport* approach as sport is just one of the innovative tools the NGO has been using in its everyday work.

The FFD project aimed to address global and local problems through playing football and contribute to their solutions. From the beginning, the main partner of INEX-SDA was MYSA (Mathare Youth Sport Association from Nairobi, Kenya), one of the oldest sport-for-development NGOs on the African continent with many years of experience in using football as a tool to work with marginalised youth populations, especially in Nairobi slums. The aim of joint seminars and workshops was to introduce football as a tool to promote *development through sport* (as defined by Astle, 2014) in the Czech Republic and contribute to the aims of global development education (as defined by Czech Ministry of Foreign Affairs, MZV ČR, 2011). Until 2011, the project mainly focused on formal education and enabled the Czech youth from secondary schools to meet their Kenyan counterparts, discuss current issues, share their life problems and challenges and spend time together. Football tournaments were always the main activity, but the whole project would have been pointless without the formal workshops/seminars focusing on the global topics and informal meetings organised around football tournaments and provided by the Kenyan youth. This part of the FFD project emphasised the *sport for development* approach (Astle, 2014), as it used sport as part of the international development programme to spread social messages and tackle educational issues bringing youth from developing (Kenya) and developed/ emerging (Czech Republic) countries together. Football matches were played in three halves without referees (at that time, the label "fair play football" was used instead of "football3" that is used currently). The tournaments were organised in big and small cities and sometimes the MYSA youth were the first foreigners with different skin colour to visit a specific region of the Czech Republic. Each time, the whole team stayed around three to five days in this specific Czech city or region. At that time, INEX-SDA was not yet a member of the international platform *streetfootballworld*, mainly because the activities of the project at that stage were not organised throughout the whole calendar year. However, INEX-SDA was trying to become part of this bigger network and already participated in several seminars and events organised by *streetfootballworld* (Šafaříková, 2012).

From 2011 onwards, the project changed its focus. MYSA started to send one young leader for a three-month internship, which strengthened its role in the project. This also fostered the *sport for development* model within this project. At the same time, the concept of using football as a tool for development was more thoroughly introduced to cooperating organisations in different Czech cities and regions. There, the project's goal was to tackle a mix of social welfare issues, such as exclusion or anti-social behaviour, which is a common scope of work for Czech NGOs in the social work field. Therefore, the leader visited all the centres and shared the MYSA experience with the social workers. The team of so-called "ambassadors" was created every year from Czech volunteer participants (mainly university students with interest in football) and MYSA youth leaders. This team, formed by six Czech and six Kenyan members, together prepared the whole one-month awareness-raising campaign ("Action Days") and implemented all the activities (e.g., workshops, discussions, exhibitions and tournaments) in different Czech cities and regions.

Consequently, the project moved from the formal educational sector to the informal one. Secondary schools were abandoned, and the activities around football were instead introduced to more underprivileged areas and places of the Czech Republic (e.g., juvenile homes, socially excluded places and youth drop-in centres) that might be more comparable to those youth MYSA works with in Nairobi. This change also fostered the *development through sport* aspect of the whole FFD project as it brought football and other related activities to marginalised communities within the Czech Republic and contributed to mutual learning and intercultural exchange within the Czech/Kenyan ambassadors' team, public and clients of the juvenile homes and drop-in centres. The ambassadors' team also used the methodology of the "Theatre of the oppressed", developed by Augusto Boal, who was influenced by Paulo Freire's work (Barak, 2016), when discussing problematic issues with the local populations. The social workers started to get to know the concepts of *sport for development and peace* and *development through sport* and were introduced to the football3 methodology. Several manuals about the use of football were prepared. Even though the most visible part of the whole project was still a one-month campaign ("Action Days"), in each selected city or region, the partner organisations started to implement the year-long street football league that is organised on a regular basis. These leagues currently work with marginalised youth and provide organised football tournaments and trainings during the whole year. Based on these changes, Football for Development/ INEX-SDA became a member of *streetfootballworld* world-wide network in 2016.

Furthermore, in 2016, the project stopped working exclusively with MYSA, and other SFD NGOs were invited to take part in the "Action Days" in the Czech Republic (e.g., Tiempo de Juego from Colombia, Football for Life from Cambodia and Kickfair from Germany) and share their experience in using football as a tool in *development through sport* and *sport for development*. FFD ambassadors represent one of the project's target groups where the impacts are most visible. Due to the one-month intensive programme during the Action Days, the ambassadors can acquire new knowledge and skills and to think about their attitudes and values (Čížmáriková et al., 2013). However, until now, project evaluation has not been the main aim of the participating NGOs, and their capacities in this area are also limited.

During the FFD project lifetime, different stakeholders became involved in its implementation, including the Football Association of the Czech Republic and Czech football club FC Slovan Liberec. This initiative has been supported through the Czech Development Agency and has also become part of several EU-funded projects. Famous Czech football players, such as Tomáš Ujfaluši and Vladimír Darida, became the media faces of the project. Since its inception in 2005, FFD has come a long way and is regarded as a pioneer SDP/SFD initiative in the Czech Republic.

Every basket counts

Každý koš pomáhá [*Every Basket Counts*] started in 2007 as a small initiative to link the sport of basketball with charities. With this money, the initiative aims to support different non-sporting issues. Due to its specific focus on fundraising specifically directed at support of social welfare, gender or healthcare initiatives, it falls under the *development through sport* approach (as defined by Astle, 2014). The main partners of this initiative at its beginning were the Czech Basketball Association (with all the professional clubs of the Czech National Basketball League) and the Sport Newsroom of Czech Television (Každý koš pomáhá, 2020). The agreement between these two entities led to the organisation of a financial collection within a selected round of basketball league where different Czech basketball clubs, players, spectators and other partners contributed financially. In 2009, during the 42nd round of the league, the clubs decided to assist with 100 CZK (approximately 4 €) per basket point scored, and the players agreed to contribute 10 CZK per basket point scored (ČT24, 2020). Spectators could participate through the donation SMS (called DMS). During the first three years of this initiative (2007, 2008 and 2009), 850,000 CZK (approximately 32,700 €) was raised. Every year this money (raised through the basketball matches during one specific round of the basketball league) has been used to support different causes (e.g., supporting several halfway houses and a mobile hospice).

Since this beginning, the association has evolved into a much broader initiative where athletes from different disciplines (now including handball, swimming, volleyball, shooting, ice hockey and athletics) contribute financially, each according to their own decision. Therefore, in future years, the money collected from the different sport codes might be based on goals scored, smashes made, meters swam, targets hit, etc., as decided by the particular sport teams or athletes (Každý koš pomáhá, 2020). The charity fundraising is supported by the Sport Newsroom of Czech Television, which has handled the media coverage since the beginning of the initiative.

In 2020, the association launched a project, "Athletes for women in need", that aims to support single mothers. The support is organised and distributed in cooperation with an NGO that has been working with single mothers since the 1990s. Each sport team and athletes can freely decide how they want to contribute (e.g., goals and kilometres run) and with what means (e.g., money and clothes). The public can participate through DMS (donation SMS), sending amounts of 30, 60 or 90 CZK.

Czech Association Sport for All

The Czech Association Sport for All (ČASPV) has its origins at the beginning of the 19th century with the foundation of the Sokol movement. However, ČASPV was newly established as a non-government, independent organisation in 1992 (Sekot, 2010) after the fall of the Communist regime. It is a member of ISCA (International Sport and Cultural Associations) and thanks to that, it was able to participate in several international projects such as Sport for All and the Environment, NowWeMOVE and MOVE Week. It currently has more than 60,000 members throughout the Czech Republic. The aim of ČASPV is to make sport and physical activity available to all, regardless of their socio-economic status. It promotes mass sport participation through the use of a variety of different sport disciplines (ČASPV, 2020; Špaček, 2011). The association also aims to use sport to counter the many negative social issues that threaten modern Czech society (e.g., drug abuse and anti-social behaviour) (ČASPV, 2020). In this proclamation, we can see a possible connection to the SDP/SFD movement (as understood by e.g., Coalter, 2019; Schulenkorf, Sherry and Rowe, 2016). When taking into consideration Astle's (2014) conceptualisation, ČASPV oscillates between two categories on the proposed continuum. The focus on encouragement of mass participation in different sport disciplines places ČASPV in the *development of sport* category. As such, it is unique amongst the initiatives mentioned here with the goals being set even in the sporting field. At the same time, the education projects it delivers aim to promote values supposedly inherent to sport, moving ČASPV also to the *development through sport* category.

One of the ČASPV projects that used sport to educate about the environment and sustainable development was Sport for All and the Environment (SforAE) organised by four NGOs from Visegrad countries (Czech Republic, Poland, Slovakia and Hungary) and financed through the ERASMUS+ programme. Its aim was to promote environmental protection and raise awareness of the importance of a clean and safe environment that can also be used for sport activities. The project prepared several recommendations on how to organise sustainable sporting events accompanied by examples of best practice (SforAE, 2019).

Based on the materials and information available, one of the goals of ČASPV is to encourage mass sport participation (*development of sport*). Furthermore, it uses sport as a tool to tackle non-sporting issues and to fight social problems mainly through specific projects, as seen in the case of SforAE, and through an assumption that the mere participation in different sporting activities during leisure time might help to stop risky social behaviour.

Conclusion

We can see that sport and physical activities have been used in many different ways throughout the Czech history and even today. The examples provided demonstrate that, historically, there has been a shift from Astle's (2014) model of *sport and development* as a practice of relatively independent evolution of sport and other cultural or political spheres over *sport for development* with a freshly institutionalised sport affecting international diplomatic relations to the *development through sport* where the political regime uses sport to support its position.

Even though several researchers (Levermore and Beacom, 2009) said that sport is an apolitical instrument (comparing it to other tools used in development cooperation), we propose that the Czech history and reality prove that this cannot be stated explicitly. Only the first historical example, the very beginning of the establishment of modern sport in the Czech lands in the 19th century resembles rather apolitical settings of sports. In other words, there was, as Astle argues, sport *and* development. Further stages of historical progress are heavily interwoven with goals set by the political actors or, at least, by actors whose goals closely touch the public affairs such as the fight for national independence. These actors use the sport *for* achieving their development goals. In the Czech history, it was the foundation and expansion of Sokol and its influence on the Czech nation's self-determination under the Austrian empire that was, on the other side, strongly suppressed by Austrian authorities. Even the latter establishment of the Olympic movement purposely linked international relations with promoting the Czechs as a nation without an existing state. The last historical example, the mass gymnastic events Spartakiády, demonstrated how a totalitarian political regime can spread its values and ideology *through* sporting practices. Over the years, the Communist party was quite successful in shifting from forced participation to inclusion of Spartakiády into mainstream culture.

In the same vein, current SDP/SFD initiatives in the Czech Republic oscillate between categories in the societal part of Astle's continuum (2014). These are mainly *development through sport* and *sport for development* models. As the Football for Development project indicates, such actions work well with addressing problematic social issues by motivating people *through* the popularity of movement activities and, at the same time, bringing different cultures together via sporting projects *for* exchanging best practices and life experience. Stemming from the professional sporting field, Every Basket Counts builds on the popularity of the spectator sport, and the *sport plus* activity focused on specific social topics is put into practice *through* fundraising amongst professional teams and athletes and wide spectator public. Finally, motives of Czech Association Sport for All exceed the strictly societal sphere where it addresses negative social phenomena *through* the educational and preventive potential of grassroots sport. Moreover, the main goal of the association is to attract more people to sports and movement activities on an amateur or leisure level and, thus, to assist in strengthening *of* sporting field itself by providing methodical support for clubs and coaches, body diagnosis or information service.

Sport itself is quite a versatile tool without any inherent value-laden meaning (Levermore and Beacom, 2009). Yet, the Czech tradition of grassroots and mass movement activities provide a public picture of sport as a positively perceived practice with the potential to effectively deal with numerous social risks or even political goals. Even though a comprehensive critical reflection on the Czech SDP/SFD initiatives has not been made so far, current academic debates highlight potential weak points of such programmes, similar to those mentioned in literature, such as limits of monitoring and evaluation of the outcomes, use of appropriate academic theoretical background for SDP, inclusion of the voices from the field into the research and the unstable position of NGOs working within the SDP field in the context of neoliberalism (Engelhardt, 2019; Levermore and Beacom, 2009; Massey and Whitley, 2019; Nicholls, Gilda and Sethna, 2011). Future studies of Czech SDP/SFD should therefore include a joint work of academic and non-profit organisations to reveal a better understanding of this topic.

Note

1   The invasion ended the period called Pražské jaro [Prague Spring] known for a significant rise of social and political liberalisation with some key posts in the Communist Party held by reform politicians such as Alexander Dubček. In the first months of 1968, people especially expected a loosening of travel restrictions, censorship and a general democratisation of the politics and society. During the night between 20 and 21 August 1968, armies of the Socialist countries united in the Warsaw Pact and led by the Soviet Union invaded Czechoslovakia. In the following years (up to 1987 when the Soviet leader Gorbachev declared broad liberal reforms), the hoped-for reforms were cancelled, conservative Communist politicians took the lead and the approved goal was to conserve the political and social status quo (Kössl, Štumbauer and Waic, 2018).

References

Astle, A.M. (2014). *Sport development – Plan, programme and practice: A case study of the planned intervention by New Zealand Cricket into cricket in New Zealand.* Unpublished PhD thesis, Massey University, Palmerston North, New Zealand.

Barak, A. (2016). Critical consciousness in critical social work: Learning from the theatre of the oppressed. *British Journal of Social Work*, 46, pp. 1776–1792.

Břešťan, R. (2018). *Peníze pro neziskovky. Největší dotace jdou na sport a sociální politiku, vede Fotbalová asociace, HlídacíPes.org.* Available at: https://hlidacipes.org/penize-pro-neziskovky-nejvetsi-dotace-jdou-na-sport-a-socialni-politiku-vede-fotbalova-asociace/ [Accessed 3 Mar. 2020].

Burian, M. et al. (2012). *Výstava pod křídly Sokola – Přísaha republice.* Ústav pro studium totalitních režimů. Available at: https://www.ustrcr.cz/data/pdf/vystavy/sokol/panel23.pdf [Accessed 22 Feb. 2020].

Čapek, K. (1938). Cesta květů a slávy, *Lidové noviny.* 7th July; issue 335, year 46. Available at: http://www.digitalniknihovna.cz/mzk/view/uuid:bebaff70-48cb-11dd-a240-000d606f5dc6?page=uuid:84f81fc0-3d04-11dd-9e26-000d606f5dc6 [Accessed 22 Feb. 2020].

ČASPV (Česká asociace Sport pro všechny). (2020). Česká asociace Sport pro všechny - základní informace. Available at: http://www.caspv.cz/cz/o-nas/zakladni-informace/. [Accessed 27 Feb. 2020].

Čížmáriková, P., Dušková, L., Hejzlarová, K., Krylová, P., Novotná, K., Šafaříková, S. and Švajgrová, Z. (2013, unpublished). Evaluační zpráva pro interní potřeby organizace INEX-SDA k projektu Fotbal pro rozvoj pro rok 2013. Olomouc: Katedra rozvojových studií.

Coalter, F. (2007). *Sport a wider social role: Who's is keeping the score?* London: Routledge.

Coalter, F. (2009). Sport-in-development: Accountability or development? In: R. Levermore and A. Beacom, eds., *Sport and international development.* Basingstoke: Palgrave Macmillan, pp. 55–75.

ČT24, (2009). *Každý koš pomáhá už třetí rok.* [online]. Available at: https://sport.ceskatelevize.cz/clanek/basketbal/kazdy-kos-pomaha-uz-treti-rok/5bdf8ee10d663b6fe807545f. [Accessed 1 Feb. 2020].

Darnell, S.C., Field, R. and Kidd, B. (2019). *The history and politics of sport-for-development. Activists, ideologues and reformers.* London: Palgrave Macmillan.

Engelhardt. J. (2019). SDP and monitoring and evaluation. In: H. Collison, S.D. Darnell, R. Giulianotti and P.D. Howe, eds., *Routledge handbook of sport for development and peace.* London: Routledge, pp. 128–140.

INEX-SDA. (2012). *Project documentation.* Praha: INEX-SDA.

Jakubcová, K. (2012). *Sport a olympijské hnutí v zemích Visegrádu. Jejich vývoj a transformace v postkomunistické éře.* Praha: Karolinum.

Každý koš pomáhá. (2020). *Každý koš pomáhá.* Available at: http://kazdykospomaha.cz/. [Accessed 6 Feb. 2020].

Kolář, F. (2018). Vývoj olympijského hnutí v Česku. Český olympijský výbor. Available at: https://www.olympic.cz/docs/osmus/vyvoj_olympijskeho_hnuti_v_cesku.pdf [Accessed 21 Feb. 2020].

Kössl, J., Štumbauer, J. and Waic, M. (2018). *Kapitoly z dějin tělesné kultury.* Praha: Karolinum.

Levermore, R. and Beacom, A. (2009). Sport and development: Mapping the field. In: R. Levermore and A. Beacom, eds., *Sport and international development.* New York, NY: Palgrave MacMillan, pp. 1–25.

Marada, R. (2003). *Kultura protestu a politizace každodennosti.* Brno: Centrum pro studium demokracie a kultury.

Massey, W.V. and Whitley, M.A. (2019). SDP and research methods. In: H. Collison, S.D. Darnell, R. Giulianotti and P.D. Howe, eds., *Routledge handbook of sport for development and peace.* London: Routledge, pp. 175–184.

MŠMT, (2016). Koncepce podpory sportu 2016–2025, MŠMT ČR. Available at: http://www.msmt.cz/sport-1/koncepce-podpory-sportu-2016-2025 [Accessed 3 Mar. 2020].

MZV ČR. 2011/Národní strategie globálního rozvojového vzdělávání pro období 2011–2015. Praha: MZV ČR. Available at: http://clanky.rvp.cz/wp-content/upload/prilohy/11559/narodni_strategie_globalniho_rozvojoveho_vzdelavani_pro_obdobi_2011_2015.pdf [Accessed 20 Apr. 2017].

Navrátil, J. and Pejcal, J. (2017). Country report: Czech Republic. In: P. Vandor et al., eds., Civil society in central and eastern Europe: Challenges and opportunities. ERSTE Foundation, pp. 43–57.

Nicholls, S., Gilda, A.R. and Sethna, C. (2011). Perpetuating the 'lack of evidence' discourse in sport for development: Privileged voices, unheard stories and subjugated knowledge. International Review for the Sociology of Sport, 46(3), pp. 249–264.

Nolte, C.E. (2002). The Sokol in the Czech Lands to 1914. Training for the nation. Basingstoke: Palgrave Macmillan.

Numerato, D. (2011). Czech sport governance cultures and a plurality of social capitals. Politicking zone, movement and community. In: M. Groeneveld, B. Houlihan, and F. Ohl, eds., Social capital and sport governance in Europe. New York: Routledge, pp. 41–62.

Nye, J.S. (2004). Soft power. The means to success in world politics. New York: PublicAffairs.

Pacina, V. (2004). Hokejová pomsta za okupaci, iDNES.cz. Available at: http://hokej.idnes.cz/hokejova-pomsta-za-okupaci-d0y-/hokej_ms2004.aspx?c=A040325_111628_reprezentace_rav [Accessed 19 September 2015].

Rakušanová, P. (2007). Povaha občanské společnosti v České republice v kontextu střední Evropy. Praha: Sociologický ústav AV ČR.

Roubal, P. (2006). Jak ochutnat komunistický ráj: dvojí tvář československých spartakiád. Dějiny a současnost, 28(6), pp. 28–31.

Roubal, P. (2016). Československé spartakiády. Praha: Academia.

Šafaříková, S. (2012). Sport a rozvoj – koncept a potenciál pro vzdělávání. Česká kinantropologie, 16(4), 11–28.

Schulenkorf, N., Sherry, E. and Rowe, K. (2016). Sport-for-development: An integrated literature review. Journal of Sport Management, 30(1), pp. 22–39.

Sekot, A. (2010). Sport and physical activities in the Czech Republic. Physical Culture and Sport Studies and Research, 48(1), pp. 44–65.

SforAE (Sport for All and Environment), (2019). NEJLEPŠÍ DOPORUČENÍ - Projekt "Sport pro všechny a životní prostředí". Available at: http://sforae.eu/pdf/sforae_nejlepsi_doporuceni.pdf [Accessed 5 Feb. 2020].

Skovajsa, M. (2010). Organizovaná občanská společnost: teorie a vývoj. In: M. Skovajsa et al., eds., Občanský sektor: Organizovaná občanská společnost v České republice. Praha: Portál, pp. 30–58.

Slepičková, I. (2007). Sport for everyone. New Presence: The Prague Journal of Central European Affairs, Winter, pp. 39.

Špaček, O. (2011). Sport pro všechny? Sociální nerovnosti a sportovní aktivity. Sociální studia, 8(1), pp. 53–78.

Svoboda, A. and Numerato, D. (2019). Socio-cultural transformations of tennis in the Czech Republic. In: R.J. Lake, ed., Routledge handbook of tennis. History, culture and politics. Milton Park: Routledge, pp. 130–140.

Thorne, V. (2011). Těla v pohybu: Masová gymnastika jako kolektivní sociální představení, Sociální studia, 8(1), pp. 99–117.

Waic, M. (2013). Tělovýchova a sport ve službách české národní emancipace. Praha: Karolinum.

Chapter 5

Sport and development in Hungary and the Central and Eastern European region

The development of the leisure sport industry

Zsolt Havran, Ágnes Szabó and Tünde Máté

Introduction

Leisure activities are gaining an increasingly prominent position in the social landscape, recognised as a crucial component of a healthy lifestyle. The leisure industry is a significant part of the global economy and is experiencing rapid expansion (KPMG, 2019). An important subsector is the leisure sport industry. It includes all the products and services concerning leisure sport activities and the total operational activities related to these products and services.

In this chapter, we will focus on the leisure sport industry in the Central and Eastern European (CEE) region. Over the past 30 years, CEE living standards and its service sector have seen significant improvements due to the transition from state socialism to a market economy and the benefits of European Union membership. Forecast revenues for 2020 from sport and outdoor activities in CEE amount to USD 953.4 million, 5% of the European total (Statista, 2020).

The aim of this chapter is to analyse the development of the leisure sport business from the perspective of consumer participation, consumer spending and corporate revenues in the CEE region from 2010 to 2019. Eight countries are involved in this investigation: Bulgaria, Croatia, the Czech Republic, Hungary, Poland, Romania, Slovakia and Slovenia. Our target countries have very similar historical, economic and social backgrounds. We present data on the development of market activity (supply and demand) in these countries' leisure sport sectors.

We pay special attention to the economic opportunities for leisure sport companies. In addition, we offer suggestions to governments on how they might help increase public participation and spending in the leisure sport sector. The academic relevance of this research lies in the fact that there has been no serious regional examination of the topic to date. Since international firms usually make investment decisions based on regional data, private business leaders stand to benefit from a detailed investigation of supply and demand for leisure sport in emerging markets. CEE is a relatively fast-developing area of the world economy. As in other developed and developing countries, the region's service sector saw a significant increase in revenue between 2015 and 2019, according to Eurostat

(2020) data: Expenditures on services increased by about 25% in Slovakia, Croatia and Bulgaria, by 43% in Romania and by 64% in Hungary. Sport – specifically leisure sport – is essentially a service-oriented area that is experiencing intense growth, thanks to an increase in people's free time and disposable incomes. Due to low baselines, growth in the CEE leisure sport industry is particularly rapid. Using regional and national data, we examine trends in physical activity along with supply and demand for leisure sport. We pay special attention to Hungary.

We have found seemingly paradoxical data with respect to private spending on leisure sport and physical activity and the health of the society. Cornia and Paniccia (2000) described this Central European health paradox, arguing that the region's poor health status cannot be explained solely by economic performance – mental, and especially historical factors, play a decisive role. The following sections review the key issues in the development of leisure sport activities in Hungary and CEE.

Short historical and social background

In the Eastern Bloc countries, the political elite strictly controlled politics and the economy. In the same way as other subsystems, sport also lost its autonomy. Elite sport was in a privileged position during state socialism, while other areas of sport were very much neglected. After the change in political systems, all Hungarian governments between 1990 and 2004 also supported elite sport to a greater extent than leisure sport, and the situation has not changed considerably since. Over-politicisation gained ground in Hungarian sport and in the CEE region because neither civil society nor the market could counterbalance the over-dominance of the state (Földesi, 2008).

In socialist Central and Eastern Europe, there was a lack of individual responsibility and self-care, thanks to the regime's "welfare policy", which provided a wide range of "free" services to citizens. That was one of the main reasons why it was difficult for providers to start operating health or fitness services at the time of the political system change (Neulinger, 2007; Simonyi, 2015). In the middle of the 2000s, in Hungary, the business sector was not strong enough, even 15 years after the change of political systems (Földesi, 2008). But after 2005, the business sector gained more strength and significance and could contribute to the development of sport.

Concepts, markets and value creation through leisure sport

The separation of leisure and professional sport happened in the 20th century. There are several reasons for the emergence of leisure sport in societies and also in the economy: (1) the amount of leisure time in society has increased, (2) people have become more health-conscious, (3) people are recognising the importance of a healthy lifestyle, (4) instead of competition and records, active people's main goal is recreation and fitness, (5) some parts of society have some discretionary income for leisure sport (in more immature markets, including Eastern Europe, the growth has actually been driven by an increase in real disposable income), (6) leisure sport could become a branch of the service industry and (7) the growing involvement of a corporate sector that considers employees' well-being.

In our understanding, any physical recreational activity may be considered leisure sport if done regularly or irregularly in our free time, and if the goal is maintenance or restoration of health, recreation, amusement or a feeling of physical and spiritual well-being, both during and after the exercise (Szabó, 2012). We can identify the following prerequisites for leisure sport consumption (Budai, 1999; Laki and Nyerges, 2004): sufficient free time, adequate living standards and money and the right attitude. In our opinion, the most important element is the right attitude, since leisure sport is not a basic need. Consumer-oriented services and satisfied customers could be key factors (Szabó, 2012).

Based on the models of Gratton and Taylor (2000), Parks, Quarterman and Thibault (2007) and the works of András (2003, 2006) on professional sport markets, Szabó (2012) gave a description of leisure sport markets. The consumer, sponsorship and merchandising markets are relevant not only for professional sport but also for leisure sport. In addition, leisure sport includes markets for sports equipment, sportswear and sport professionals. Consumers, sponsors and merchandising markets are the direct sources of income (Szabó, 2014). Most research claims that men, younger people, those with higher income, those living in big cities and the better educated do more sport in their leisure time (Neulinger, 2007; Paár, 2013; Szabó, 2012). An increase in the consumer market would bring growth in the markets of sports equipment, sportswear and sport professionals, sponsorship and merchandising markets (Szabó, 2012).

There is big potential in leisure sport to create value on the micro- and macro-level. The most important micro-level factors are the development of health, abilities and skills, feelings of excitement and lower health-care expenses, both for individuals and companies. The main macro-level factors are lower health-care and sick-pay expenses, lower mortality and disability rates, increased life-expectancy, new jobs and new tax revenues. Micro- and macro-level factors could contribute to national economic competitiveness through the development of human capital, improved health conditions, productivity and the development of social capital (Szabó, 2012).

The development of leisure sport in Hungary and the CEE

Most studies on global sport economics deal with professional sport, while leisure sport does not receive the same attention. The current situation in Hungary is the same as it was in the 1990s when the first 'economic' or 'business' studies typically dealt with various issues of professional sport, with a particular focus on football (András et al., 2019). András et al. (2019) examined 116 peer-reviewed Hungarian sport management articles written from 2003 to 2018 and only 30% of the articles dealt with leisure sport, mostly within the consumer market.

Szabó (2012) introduced the operation of leisure sport markets, assessed the value creation of leisure sport and described the characteristics of the three spheres (state, business and non-profit sectors), their tasks and their shortcomings. Based on her research, the key to a well-functioning Hungarian leisure sport sector lies in the formation of attitudes and boosting consumer demand. Service providers' operation was not problem-free in the 2000s. In many cases, they lacked professionalism (i.e., investors with knowledge of the industry, credible, reliable managers and realistic business plans), while the club system did not work either. Fitness centres did not have enough sponsors, money or energy for marketing activities. Many smaller fitness centres did not even have the software to keep clients' records, and only a third of fitness centres were profitable.

Research by Paár (2013) analysed the trends in sport consumption since the political transition. Paár (2013) stated that, in a micro economic sense, sport consumption in Hungary is a luxury good. He found that living in a bigger settlement type (for example in a bigger city), having a higher level of education, a higher number of children and better income lead to Hungarian households' increased possibility and measure of sport expenditures. By international standards, Hungary belongs to the group of countries with poor health status and a low level of sport expenditure (Paár, 2013). Vörös (2019) carried out a cluster analysis based on Eurostat data and had similar results as Paár (2013). According to Vörös (2019), the CEE countries spent much less money and time on exercising than the EU average. Consequently, they had worse HDI-indexes, health conditions and life expectancies. Hungary spent 7% of its GDP on health, which is 3–4% below the EU average. The life expectancy of Hungarian people is six to eight years shorter than that of their Western European counterparts, and their cancer mortality is the highest in Europe. Apart from the Baltic countries, the population of Central and Eastern Europe has the lowest average life expectancy at birth as well as the lowest healthy life expectancy (Vörös, 2017). At the macro-level, an increase in physical activity may contribute to lowering health care expenditures, and a healthier society may potentially have higher productivity. A 10% increase in physical activity would result in savings of more than 28 billion HUF (ca. 73.7 million GBP) for the Hungarian economy (Ács et al., 2011, 2016).

According to Ács et al. (2018) in the V4 (Visegrad) countries (the Czech Republic, Poland, Hungary, and Slovakia), only 21–35% of the population exercise on a weekly basis. However, their results stress that the population of university students provides more favourable data on physical activities than working adults: 43.8% of female and 57.3% of male students can be classified as highly active.

After reviewing the Hungarian literature on the topic, we investigated it in the other seven examined CEE countries. In Bulgaria, Ignatov, Popeska and Sivevska (2015) defined leisure time similarly to Szabó (2012). Ilieva (2016) involved 153 experts from government, municipalities, public and private companies in a study about the engagement and attitude of professionals in the field of the programme Sport for All (SFA). The report stated that, "the priority funding of the sport of excellence by the state, as well as some negative economic trends in our country in the recent years, have led to gaps in the provision of SFA resources" (Ilieva 2016, p. 227). Having reviewed a number of studies in Poland, Sniadek and Zajadacz (2010) concluded that a very important factor determining the so-called "successful ageing" is regular physical activity. Previous studies have shown that Poles belong to the group of the least active EU citizens. The main reasons behind low physical and tourist activity of Polish seniors are their poor financial standing, lack of active leisure habits and – all too often – an insufficient supply and promotion of sport and leisure activities targeted at this age group.

A Croatian study's results showed that engagement in leisure activities contributes to subjective well-being, while the pattern of important leisure activities somewhat varies across different age and gender groups (Brajša-Žganec, Merkaš and Šverko, 2011). Lipovčan et al. (2018) also examined these correlations and found similar results. According to Romanian research, constant and continuous practice of various types of physical exercise represents a significant factor leading to the improvement of social health (Georgian and Lorand, 2016). Sekot (2013) was looking for what Czech society expected from sport. Relevant data reflects a growing tendency of passive attitudes to sport in the Czech population.

In summary, research on leisure sport in the region has focused on the following topics: investigation of leisure sport habits of different consumers (e.g., seniors or college students), the relationship between leisure sport and well-being and the role the state should play in the development of leisure sport.

Relevant leisure sport data in the CEE region

To answer our research question about how the business of leisure sport has developed in the CEE region and in Hungary in the 2010s, we have done the following work. The leisure sport industry developed without relevant state subsidy in the CEE region. We show empirical data on the number of consumers and the level of consumption, considering sporting goods and services and equipment for sports between 2010 and 2019. Table 5.1 contains the collected regional-level data with details about the source and period of data collection. We used comparable data for the eight CEE countries listed in the introduction and, if available, the average EU-28 value. It is a limitation of our research that some data are not available for every year or the entire period.

After the examination of regional trends, we focused on Hungarian data about business trends in leisure sport (see Table 5.2). To discover the development of the Hungarian leisure sport industry, we concentrated on business results of leisure sport organisations (for-profit and non-profit) including service providers, traders and event organisers. In both the regional and the Hungarian case, we sought to link data collection to the leisure sport markets.

Table 5.1 Regional data collection (sample, data, source and period)

Sample	Collected data	Source	Period	Related leisure sport market
Physical activity	Sporting activity per week	Eurobarometer	2006, 2010, 2014, 2018	Consumer
Fitness club attendance	Proportion of athletes	Eurobarometer	2014, 2018	Consumer
Sporting goods and services by COICOP consumption purpose	Mean consumption expenditure of private households	Eurostat	2010, 2015	Consumer and sports equipment and sportswear
Recreational and sporting services	Annual average rate of change	Eurostat	2015–2019	Consumer
Recreational and sporting service	Annual average index	Eurostat	Changes 2015–2019	Consumer
Equipment for sport, camping and open-air recreation	Annual average index	Eurostat	Changes 2015–2019	Consumer and sports equipment and sportswear
Manufacture of sports goods	Number of enterprises	Eurostat	2008, 2013, 2018	Sports equipment and sportswear
Manufacture of sports goods	Turnover - million euro	Eurostat	2008, 2013, 2018	Sports equipment and sportswear

Development of leisure sport in the CEE region

Physical activity and consumer spending on leisure sport

Compared to 2010 and 2014, the proportion of active people has decreased in the region: Figure 5.1 presents the number of those who never do exercise or play sport, indicating that it increased everywhere in 2018, except in Bulgaria where the numbers are the highest (Eurobarometer, 2006–2018). In 2018, 46% of EU-28 people never did sport, with only Slovenia and the Czech Republic below this average. Except for the Czech Republic (15%), the use of health and fitness centres is also below the EU average in this region. However, sport or physical activity at home is popular in Eastern Europe, with more than half of the respondents in Slovakia (62%), Romania (60%) and Hungary (59%) reporting.

Table 5.2 Leisure sport business trends in Hungary

Sample	Collected data	Source	Period	Related leisure sport market
Companies providing fitness services	Number and financial performance	Hungarian Central Statistical Office	2011–2017	Consumer Sport professionals
Sports foundations and non-profit organisations	Number and revenue	Hungarian Central Statistical Office	2011–2018	Consumer Sport professionals
Largest sportswear and sports equipment in Hungary	Net revenue	Financial statements of involved companies	2010–2018	Consumer Sports equipment and sportswear
Biggest leisure sport event organiser company	Net revenue and operating profit	Financial statements of the company	2011–2018	Consumer Sponsorship
Most popular running events in Budapest	Number of runners	Futanet, 2019 (Budapest Sport Office)	2010–2019	Consumer Sponsorship

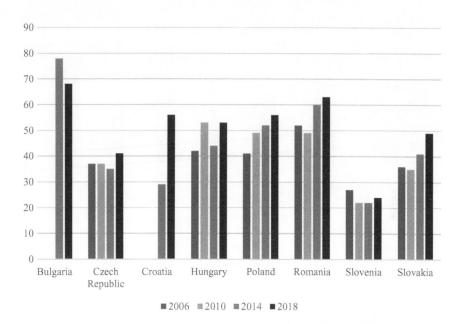

Figure 5.1 How often do you exercise or play sport? – Never (percentage).
Source: Edited by the authors based on Eurobarometer (2006, 2010, 2014, 2018).

According to the Hungarian Central Statistical Office (KSH), sales in sporting goods and equipment increased by 43% between 2010 and 2017. Compared to the Czech Republic and Slovenia, Hungarians spent half as much on sporting goods, sports equipment and sports clothing (Gősi, 2019). Between 2012 and 2016, purchases of sporting goods per capita increased from 30 EUR to 50 EUR in Hungary which is a huge growth in demand considering the development of sport business (Bácsné et al., 2018).

In Poland, the average annual household spending on sport and recreation is PLN 458 (€105), which is an increase of PLN 40 (€9.2) over the last four years. Poles are spending gradually more on sport and recreation, but their physical activity is decreasing (The First news, 2019). The Polish fitness market is one of the top ten markets in Europe and one of the most dynamically developing. The fitness market in Europe and in the CEE region is developing towards the growth of low-cost clubs.

The number of those who attended fitness clubs had increased by 50% from 2014 to 2018 in Hungary and Romania (Table 5.3). The average growth rate in the CEE region was 14%, while in EU-28 there was stagnation, so it suggests a significant development in CEE. Fitness club usage could be one of the most important indicators of business development, people do sports on a business basis, paying for sports service and do not do sports at home or outdoors. However, it is

Table 5.3 Percentage of athletes who attend fitness clubs in CEE

	2014 (%)	2018 (%)	Change (%)
Bulgaria	12	14	+16
Czech Republic	17	15	−12
Croatia	9	7	−22
Hungary	6	9	+50
Poland	9	11	+22
Romania	6	9	+50
Slovenia	6	6	0
Slovakia	13	14	+8
EU28	15	15	0

Source: Edited by the authors based on Eurobarometer (2014, 2018).

a sad fact that only the Czech Republic reaches the EU-28 average of 15% (and in the case of Czech Republic and Croatia there was a decrease). Engagement in leisure sport (especially in fitness clubs) was primarily the domain of young, well-educated urban people who were satisfied with their financial situation. The total number of members of fitness clubs in Poland may increase to a million in a few years, including a large proportion of older people. Fortunately, even more women and older people are attending fitness clubs, and wider sections of society are involved. The fitness services market seems to be becoming more professional and better organised (Cieślikowski and Kantyka, 2018).

The value of the global sports equipment and apparel market is expected to reach USD 619,279 million by 2023, growing at a compound annual growth rate (CAGR) of 7.1% (2017–2023). The equipment segment generated the maximum revenue in 2016. However, the apparel and shoes segments are expected to grow exponentially, especially in running, fitness, bike, team and water sports (Allied Market Research, 2018). There are important factors behind these trends. The market drivers in Europe are as follows: (1) people's increased awareness of a healthy lifestyle and the availability of a growing middle class purchasing power (in more immature markets such as Eastern European countries, the growth is driven by an increase in real disposable income), (2) the expansion of offerings in the value segment (the fitness market in Europe, and in the CEE region is developing towards the growth of low-cost clubs with limited customer support), (3) growing involvement of the corporate sector (concern for employees' well-being) and (4) increased incidence of medical problems.

The Central European home fitness equipment market was expected to grow at a CAGR of 8.2% from 2017 to 2020, with Poland forecasted to experience the highest growth rate of 11.9%, the Czech Republic was in third place behind Slovenia at 11.3%, followed by Slovakia in sixth place with an 8.4% growth. In 2016, the home fitness equipment market in Central Europe was worth $2.14 billion (Cesport, n.a.). Waśkowski (2017) found a massive increase of running events in Poland, going from approximately 500 to 4,000 between 2000 and 2016. The growth of the fitness equipment market could be another good signal of business development on the demand side.

Romania has the fastest-growing health and fitness market in Europe, driven by both penetration and price increases. In Poland, customers, and as a consequence club formats, are rather budget-driven and focused on functionality, while in Romania, customers are more interested in premium offers and are motivated by the overall experience (e.g., the look and feel of the location, and the quality of equipment and trainers) (Kearney, n.a.). As the economy and services improved, so did leisure sport services, and consumer spending could be more significant. The development of the business sector could lead to the development of leisure sport.

In the following section, we analyse the data provided by Eurostat. Figure 5.2 shows the mean consumption expenditure of private households on sporting goods and services in CEE countries between 2010 and 2015, which is a good cumulative indicator of business development on the demand side.

Although there was growth in every country, Bulgaria (34%) and Slovakia (29%) stand out, showing the highest growth rates between 2010 and 2015, while Slovenia has the highest average consumption expenditure of private households on sporting goods and services, with only a 1% growth rate. In Hungary, the growth rate was 14%.

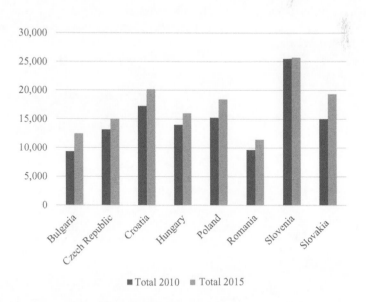

Figure 5.2 Mean consumption expenditure of private households on sporting goods and services by COICOP consumption purpose 2010 and 2015 (PPS).

Source: Edited by the authors based on Eurostat (2019).

Goods manufacturing and service providing in leisure sport

In Figure 5.3, it can be seen that in the region there has been an approximately 2% annual average shift in spending on recreation and sporting services between 2015 and 2019. Four countries in the region also outperformed the EU-28. Slovakia and Hungary show the greatest changes in growth. In Croatia, there was a peak in 2015, followed by a downturn.

Examining the details, compared to 2015, Slovakia, Hungary and the Czech Republic have a more than 10% growth in the annual average index of recreational and sporting services from 2015 to 2019 (EU-28 has 8%), while Croatia is the only one in the region with a decline, due to the peak in 2015 followed by a fall. Considering the annual average index of sports equipment, camping and open-air recreation, there was a 10% growth in Hungary and in Slovenia, a 5% growth in Romania and a 6% decrease in Slovakia (Eurostat, 2019). Just for comparison, according to KPMG (2019), the global fitness industry has shown compound annual growth of 4.8% between 2015 and 2017.

In this region, most manufacturers of sports goods are located in the Czech Republic (around 12% of all the EU-28 manufacturers) and Poland (10% of EU-28), while the biggest increase was seen in Slovakia and Bulgaria (starting from almost zero level). Considering the region as a whole, there was a 35% growth in the numbers of manufacturers between 2008 and 2018 (from 1,057 to 1,428), which shows the development of the supply side of leisure sport industry. As far as the turnover is concerned, the Czech Republic and Hungary have the highest revenues, but they are only around 3% of the turnover of all manufacturers within EU-28 (Figure 5.4). The biggest growth happened in Bulgaria and Romania between

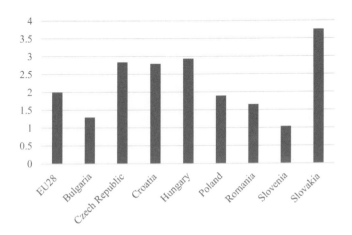

Figure 5.3 Annual average rate (percentage) of change between 2015 and 2019: Recreational and sporting services.

Source: Edited by the authors based on Eurostat (2019).

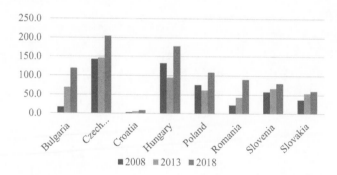

Figure 5.4 Manufacture of sports goods – turnover – million euro.
Source: Edited by the authors based on Eurostat (2019).

2008 and 2018 (Bulgaria is one of the poorest members of the European Union. Revenues of branded sports goods in Bulgaria were around €110 million in 2018, comparatively small for a population of 7.5 million people). In the region, there was an overall 74% growth in the turnover of manufacturers between 2008 and 2018 (from 488.8 to 850.1 million euro).

All the factors examined in the region have shown an increase (Table 5.4). Considering recreational and sporting services, the annual average rate of change between 2015 and 2019 was higher in four countries (Czech Republic, Croatia, Hungary and Slovakia) than the EU-28 average. Considering the annual average index of sports equipment, camping and open-air recreation, there was a 10% growth in Hungary and Slovenia between 2015 and 2019, and most countries show higher increases than the EU-28 average. The number and revenues of manufacturers of sports goods have also increased. The Czech Republic and Poland stand out in numbers, while the Czech Republic and Hungary have record revenues. This significant increase is partly due to the relatively low starting base, but our aim was to present the expected trends in emerging markets, which appear to be very positive both on demand and supply side. Our analysis can also provide many good lessons for investors and provide a strong example to other emerging markets.

The Hungarian case of leisure sport development

After the presentation of CEE data, we will highlight the Hungarian trends of the leisure sport markets. We identified the increase in consumer interest by examining the performance of organisations that operate in the related markets: sport service providers (companies and non-profit organisations), sporting goods retailers and sport event organisers. The numbers and revenues of companies providing fitness services can be seen in Figure 5.5.

According to the data of the Hungarian Central Statistical Office, the number and turnover of companies providing physical exercise services has increased in

Table 5.4 Summary table of regional differences

		The direction of change	"LEADERS" considering changes	"LEADERS" considering values
Physical activity	Sporting activity per week	Decrease	Croatia	Bulgaria, Romania
Fitness club attendance	Proportion of athletes	Increase	Hungary, Romania, Bulgaria, Slovakia	Czech Republic
Sporting goods and services by COICOP consumption purpose	Mean consumption expenditure of private households	Increase		Slovenia
Recreational and sporting services	Annual average rate of change	Increase	Slovakia, Hungary	Slovakia, Hungary
Recreational and sporting services	Annual average index	Increase	Slovakia, Hungary, Czech Republic	Slovakia, Hungary, Czech Republic
Equipment for sport, camping and open-air recreation	Annual average index	Increase	Slovenia, Hungary	Slovakia
Manufacture of sports goods	Number of enterprises	Increase	Slovakia, Bulgaria	Czech Republic, Poland
Manufacture of sports goods	Turnover – million euro	Increase	Bulgaria, Romania	Czech Republic, Hungary

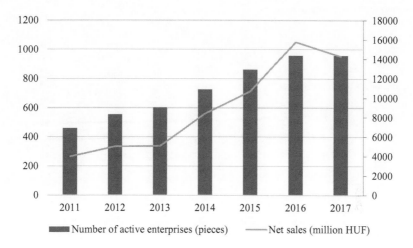

Figure 5.5 Number and financial performance of companies providing fitness services between 2011 and 2017.
Source: Edited by the authors based on KSH (2019).

Hungary since 2011. In 2017, there was a slight decline in revenue, but the number of companies remained at the same level.

Leisure sport organisations often operate in a non-profit form. Following the economic crisis that began in 2008, the number of sport-related foundations and non-profit organisations established with sport-related aims continued to rise after 2011 and, in 2017, exceeded 9,000. Between 2014 and 2017, the revenue of these organisations increased very significantly, tripling in three years, from 94.6 billion HUF to 290.8 billion HUF.

Figure 5.6 shows that between 2010 and 2018, the market for sportswear and sports equipment experienced a very strong growth. The sales revenue of the three top-selling companies (Decathlon, Hervis and Sports direct) almost tripled in the period under review.

The Hungarian market leader in organising leisure sport events, Budapest Sport Office (BSI), increased its net revenue by 76% between 2011 and 2018 (E-beszamolo, 2019), which indicates stepped-up purchasing power.

The three biggest running events in Budapest and in the country are *Vivicitta* in spring, the *Half Marathon* and the *Marathon* in fall. The number of foreign runners is increasing. In 2018, it was as high as 17% of all participants (Futanet, 2019). In addition, according to the data of the BSI (Futanet, 2019), it is a significant change in trends that the participation of women in the *Half Marathon* quintupled between 2008 and 2017.

Summarising the Hungarian results, it can be seen that after the period of economic crisis, the demand for leisure sport services and products in the private sector has developed significantly, mostly between 2013 and 2017. The question for the coming years is whether the leisure market could grow further, or has reached its limits, ending the rapid growth typical of emerging countries.

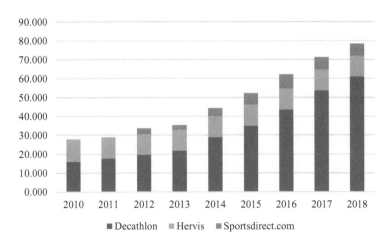

Figure 5.6 Net revenue increase (million HUF) of the three largest sport stores in Hungary.

Source: Edited by the authors based on E-beszamolo (2019).

Conclusion

The data presented in this chapter highlight a significant expansion of the service sector in the CEE region in the 2010s, including the leisure sport industry. We have focused on eight emerging-market countries in the region that have made significant strides in increasing both the value and the quality of recreational sport over the past few years. Leisure sport providers have flourished as consumers spend, more thanks to positive economic developments. Leisure sport creates value at both the micro- and macro-levels. Improvements in human capital, health conditions, quality of life, social capital and cohesion, productivity and GDP are value-creating factors that contribute to competitiveness.

However, it must be emphasised that not everyone has the aptitude or the money for leisure sport. This presents both an opportunity and a challenge for regional recreational sport companies. While international trends suggest that the CEE leisure sport sector can expect further growth, companies must concentrate on shaping public attitudes towards leisure sport. Since there has been a significant rise in expenditures on leisure sport in developed nations, we can assume that similar increases can be expected in CEE, even beyond 2023. But if these positive developments are to be realised, it is crucial for public attitudes to change. Specifically, CEE countries must 'overwrite' the old attitudes that persist from the era of socialism. As we have seen, this change is well under way. More and more business opportunities are opening up that will reinforce the development of sport.

An important lesson for governments is that the increase in demand for recreational goods, including sport services, is not primarily due to an increase in the number of athletes, but rather due to an increase in former athletes' sport expenditures. We are presently witnessing a net decrease in the number of people who are spending more on sporting goods and services. Eurobarometer data for the CEE region show that the number of people who never participate in any sport at all is on the rise. At the same time, we see growth in the number of sport providers as well as their revenues; sales at sports stores have also grown (although the pace seems to be slowing). This increase in leisure sport spending coupled with a decrease (or stagnation) in the frequency of recreational sport participation reflects a duality that has also been detected in earlier research. People in higher income brackets, city dwellers and people with higher levels of educational attainment are more likely to participate in sport than people in other sectors of society. A certain segment of the consumer class is able to exercise and spend more on leisure sports, while the 'masses' cannot. Trends vary in different geographic regions within CEE. Therefore, it is incumbent upon governments as well as the civil sector to promote recreational sport, stimulate the market and boost demand so that sporting goods and services will no longer be the 'luxury' of the few. Demand for leisure sport goods and services can remain relevant if governments, business and non-governmental groups focus on providing flexible opportunities that attract participants. This will ensure sustainable growth for the leisure sport sector and help achieve the highest possible rate of public participation.

As emerging-market economies continue to grow, demand for leisure sport products and services is likely to increase significantly. Data from the region and from Hungary indicate that the field of leisure sport events, equipment and services represent a major growth area for companies. This is something for which companies should be prepared in terms of capacity and know-how. However, government leaders must understand that the market cannot solve everything on its own. States should reach out to those who are 'lagging behind' in order to preserve the wealth and health of society.

In conclusion, the growth of the CEE leisure sport industry is bringing positive developments to society and the economy and vice versa. This chapter has sought to add to global knowledge of leisure sport development in CEE in hopes that it might serve as an example to other emerging-market regions and give useful inputs to investment decisions and governments. We believe our examination of regional data will help businesspeople, academics and the general public improve their understanding of leisure sport and the trends in different leisure sport markets.

References

Ács, P., Hécz, R., Paár, D. and Stocker, M. (2011). A fittség (m)értéke. A fizikai inaktivitás nemzetgazdasági terhei Magyarországon (The value (degree) of fitness. The national economic costs of physical inactivity in Hungary). *Közgazdasági Szemle*, 58(7–8), pp. 689–708.

Ács, P., Prémusz, V., Melczer, C.S., Bergier, J., Salonna, F., Junger, J. and Makai, A. (2018). Nemek közötti különbségek vizsgálata a fizikai aktivitás vonatkozásában a V4 országok egyetemista populációjának körében (Examining gender differences in physical activity among the student population in the V4 countries). *Magyar Sporttudományi Szemle*, 19(73), pp. 25–31.

Ács, P., Stocker, M., Füge, K., Paár, D., Oláh, A. and Kovács, A. (2016). Economic and public health benefits: The results of increased regular physical activity. *European Journal of Integrative Medicine*, 2, pp. 8–12.

Allied Market Research (2018). *Sports equipment and apparel market by product (equipment and apparel & shoes), sports (bike, outdoor, tennis, other racket sports, running, fitness, football/soccer, other team sports, winter sports, watersports, and others), and distribution channel (online and offline) - Global opportunity analysis and industry forecast, 2017–2023.* [online]. Available at: https://www.alliedmarketresearch.com/sports-equipment-and-apparel-market/ [Accessed 15 Jan. 2020].

András, K. (2003). *Üzleti elemek a sportban, a labdarúgás példáján (Business elements in sports, through example of football).* PhD. Budapest University of Economic Sciences and Public Administration.

András, K. (2006). A szabadidősport gazdaságtana (The business of leisure sport). *Budapest: BCE Vállalatgazdaságtan Intézet.* [online].Volume 75 Available at: http://edok.lib. uni-corvinus.hu/113/1/Andr%C3%A1s75.pdf [Accessed 10 Mar. 2020].

András, K., Havran, Z.S., Kajos, A., Kozma, M., Máté, T. and Szabó, Á. (2019). A sportgazdaságtani kutatások nemzetközi és hazai fejlődése [The historical development of sport business research in Hungary and beyond]. *Vezetéstudomány-Budapest Management Review*, 50(12), pp. 136–148.

Bácsné, B.É., Fenyves, V., Szabados, G.Y., Dajnoki, K., Müller, A. and Bács, Z. (2018). A sportágazat nemzetgazdasági jelentőségének vizsgálata beszámoló adatok alapján 2014-2016-os időszakban [Examination of the significance of the sport sector in the national economy on the basis of report data in the period 2014–2016]. *Jelenkori társadalmi és gazdasági folyamatok*, 13(3–4), pp. 93–103.

Brajša-Žganec, A., Merkaš, M. and Šverko, I. (2011). Quality of life and leisure activities: How do leisure activities contribute to subjective well-being? *Social Indicators Research an International and Interdisciplinary Journal for Quality-of-Life Measurement*, 102(1), pp. 81–91.

Budai, E. (1999). Sport(t)örvényben fuldokolva [Sport law interpretation]. *Új Folyam*, 8(3–4), pp. 20–33.

Cesport (n.a.). *Home fitness equipment market in Poland, Czech and Slovakia.* [online]. Available at: http://www.cesport.eu/en/Nd/i/more/Home+Fitness+Equipment+Market+in+Poland%2C+Czech+and+Slovakia/idn/4070 [Accessed 15 Jan. 2020].

Cieślikowski, K. and Kantyka, J. (2018). Fitness market in Poland and its determinants. *European Journal of Service Management*, 26(2), pp. 37–44.

Cornia, G.A. and Paniccia, R. (2000). The transition mortality crisis: Evidence, interpretation and policy responses. In: Cornia, G.A. and Paniccia, R., eds., *The mortality crisis in transitional economies*. New York: Oxford University Press, pp. 3–37.

E-beszamolo (2019). *Hungarian company register website.* [online]. Available at: https://e-beszamolo.im.gov.hu [Accessed 5 Dec. 2019].

Eurobarometer (2006). *Health and food.* [online]. Available at: http://www.planamasd.com/sites/default/files/recursos/eurobarometro-2005.pdf [Accessed 1 Sept. 2014].

Eurobarometer (2010). *Sport and physical activity.* [online]. Available at: http://ec.europa.eu/public_opinion/archives/ebs/ebs [Accessed 1 Sept. 2014].

Eurobarometer (2014). *Sport and physical activity*. [online]. Available at: http://ec.europa.eu/public_opinion/archives/ebs/ebs12_en.pdf [Accessed 1 Sept. 2014].

Eurobarometer (2018). *Sport and physical activity*. [online]. Available at: https://ec.europa.eu/sport/news/2018/new-eurobarometer-sport-and-physical-activity_en [Accessed 15 Jan. 2020].

Eurostat (2019). *Eurostat website – Sport database*. [online]. Available at: https://ec.europa.eu/eurostat/web/sport/data/database [Accessed 15 Jan. 2020].

Eurostat (2020). *Eurostat website*. [online]. Available at: https://ec.europa.eu/eurostat/databrowser/view/teiis700/default/table?lang=en/ [Accessed 15 Jan. 2020].

Földesi, Sz. Gy. (2008). Post-transformational trends in Hungarian sport (1995–2004). *Physical Culture and Sport Studies and Research*, 46, pp. 137–146.

Futanet (2019). *Budapest sport office website*. [online]. Available at: www.futanet.hu [Accessed 22 Jan. 2020].

Georgian, B. and Lorand, B. (2016). The influence of leisure sports activities on social health in adults. *Springerplus*, 5(1), p. 1647. [online]. Available at: https://www.ncbi.nlm.nih.gov/pmc/articles/PMC5033792/ DOI: 10.1186/s40064-016-3296-9, PMCID: PMC5033792.

Gősi, Zs. (2019). A szabadidősport néhány gazdasági hatása (Some economic effects of leisure sport). In: Z.S. Gősi, S.Z. Boros, B.J. Patakiné, eds., *Sokszínű rekreáció (Multicolour recreation)*. Budapest: Eötvös Lóránd Tudományegyetem Pedagógiai és Pszichologiai Kar, pp. 69–85. Available at: https://esi.ppk.elte.hu/media/42/df/72da1729016e69cf9df9c6240a6855e8781b8acf5e217e3171292b86b304/ESI_SokszinuRekreacio201905.pdf.

Gratton, C. and Taylor, P. (2000). *Economics of sport and recreation*. London: E and FN Spon.

Ignatov, G., Popeska, B. and Sivevska, D. (2015). Sports activities during leisure time of the students from Sofia University St. Kliment Ohridski, Bulgaria and Goce Delcev University in Stip, Macedonia. In: *The 7th International Scientific Conference in Alma Mater "Modern trends of physical education and sport"*. [online]. Sofia, Bulgaria. Available at: http://eprints.ugd.edu.mk/15224/ [Accessed 15 Jan. 2020].

Ilieva, D. (2016). Expert assessment of the status and development of the "sport for all" system in the Republic of Bulgaria. *Activities in Physical Education and Sport*, 6(2), pp. 221–227. [online]. Available at: http://fsprm.mk/wp-content/uploads/2017/01/Pages-from-APES_2_2016_AVGUST_web-17.pdf [Accessed 15 Jan. 2020].

Kearney (n.a.). *Romanian health and fitness market*. [online]. Available at: https://www.kearney.ro/article/?/a/romanian-health-and-fitness-market/ [Accessed 15 Jan. 2020].

KPMG (2019): *Global leisure perspectives*. [online]. Available at: https://home.kpmg/content/dam/kpmg/uk/pdf/2019/03/global-leisure-perspectives.PDF [Accessed 30 Jul. 2020].

KSH (2019). *Central Statistical Office official website*. [online]. Available at: http://statinfo.ksh.hu/Statinfo/haViewer.jsp/ [Accessed 15 Jan. 2020].

Laki, L. and Nyerges, M. (2004). A fiatalok sportolási szokásainak néhány társadalmi összefüggése [Some social contexts of young people's sport habits]. *Magyar Sporttudományi Szemle*, 2(3), pp. 5–15.

Lipovčan, L.K., Brkljačić,T., Brajsa-Žganec, A. and Franc, R. (2018). Leisure activities and the subjective well-being of older adults in Croatia. *GeroPsych*, 31, pp. 31–39.

Neulinger, Á. (2007). *Folyamatos megerősítést igénylő tanult fogyasztás – A társas környezet és a sportfogyasztás viszonya* [Learned consumption that require continuous reinforcement –

The relationship between social environment and sport consumption]. PhD. Budapest University of Economic Sciences and Public Administration.

Paár, D. (2013). *A magyar háztartások sportfogyasztásának gazdasági szempontú vizsgálata* [The examination of the economic aspects of Hungarian households' sports consumption]. PhD. University of West Hungary.

Parks, B.J., Quarterman, J. and Thibault, L. (2007). *Contemporary sport management.* Champaign: Human Kinetics.

Sekot, A. (2013). Physical activities as a part of leisure in Czech society. *Journal of Human Sport and Exercise*, 8(2), pp. 261–270. [online]. Available at: https://www.researchgate.net/publication/271319198_Physical_activities_as_a_part_of_leisure_in_Czech_society [Accessed 15 Jan. 2020].

Simonyi, Á. (2015). *Synthesis report: Social cohesion and social policies.* GRINCOH Working Paper Series, No. 5. [online]. Available at: http://www.grincoh.eu/media/syhtnesis_reports/grincoh_wp5_synthesis_report_simonyi.pdf/ [Accessed 15 Jan. 2020].

Sniadek, J. and Zajadacz, A. (2010). Senior citizens and their leisure activity: Understanding leisure behaviour of elderly people in Poland. *Studies in Physical Culture and Tourism*, 17(2), pp. 193–204. [online]. Available at: https://www.researchgate.net/publication/228515515_Senior_citizens_and_their_leisure_activity_understanding_leisure_behaviour_of_elderly_people_in_Poland/ [Accessed 15 Jan. 2020].

Statista (2020). Statista website. [online]. Available at: https://www.statista.com/outlook/259/102/sports-outdoor/europe [Accessed 22 Apr. 2020].

Szabó, Á. (2012). *A magyar szabadidősport működésének vizsgálata. Piacok, értékteremtés, feladatok a szabadidősportban* [An examination of the operation of Hungarian leisure sports system markets, value creation, and challenges in leisure sports]. PhD. Budapest Corvinus University, Available at: http://phd.lib.uni-corvinus.hu/662/2/Szabo_Agnes_den.pdf [Accessed 15 Jan. 2020].

Szabó, Á. (2014). Leisure sports' industry, leisure sports' markets in Hungary. *Pamukkale Journal of Sport Sciences*, 5(3), p. 1–22. [online]. Available at: https://dergipark.org.tr/en/pub/psbd/issue/20585/219353/ [Accessed 15 Jan. 2020].

The First News (2019). *Polish sports industry worth EUR 2.2 bln – report.* [online]. Available at: https://www.thefirstnews.com/article/polish-sports-industry-worth-eur-22-bln---report-7224 [Accessed 15 Jan. 2020].

Vörös, T. (2017). A sportolási hajlandóság növelésében rejlő lehetőségek Kelet-Közép-Európa társadalmi-gazdasági fejlődése tükrében [Social and economic development opportunities in East Central Europe provided by increasing physical activity]. *Tér és Társadalom*, 31(2) . [online]. Available at: http://real.mtak.hu/73564/1/2788-9212-1-PB.pdf/ [Accessed 15 Jan. 2020].

Vörös, T. (2019). *Sportberuházások társadalmi-gazdasági értékelése – a költség-haszon elemzésben rejlő lehetőségek* [Socio-economic evaluation of sports investments - The potential of cost-benefit analysis]. PhD. Széchenyi István Egyetem, Regionális- és Gazdaságtudományi Doktori Iskola.

Waśkowski, Z. (2017). The strategy of coopetition. Value-creating networks of partnership relations – The case of the sports market. In: *Management International Conference.* Monastier di Treviso (Venice), Italy. [online]. Available at: http://www.hippocampus.si/ISBN/978-961-7023-71-8/1.pdf/ [Accessed 15 Jan. 2020].

Chapter 6

Sport and development in India

Professional sport league systems

Vipul Lunawat

Introduction

India has a long history as a sporting nation, with various sports playing a role in society since ancient times. India, though a superpower in the sport of cricket, has also tasted success in hockey, badminton and tennis since the late 1920s. The trend of Indian sport development, however, remained flat, except for in a handful of sports, until 2008 when the Board of Control for Cricket in India (BCCI), the body governing cricket in India, launched the Indian Premier League (IPL) and when Abhinav Bindra won India's first individual gold medal in the men's 10 m Air Rifle event at the Beijing Summer Olympics. The landscape of Indian sports changed after that when corporations, government and even private investors started pumping money into the sport industry. Many other sports, including ka-baddi, wrestling, football, tennis, table tennis and volleyball, followed the IPL format to start professional leagues in India, opening doors to new sport development initiatives and thereby boosting the stagnant sport market in India.

This chapter essentially provides answers to the following questions: How did the term "sport development" take shape in India? What kinds of development formats and structures have been introduced? How has sport development been used as a catalyst to foster participation in various sports and how has it impacted the Indian economy? This chapter also tries to understand and predict how the industry will grow and identifies further challenges involved in sport development in India.

Development of sport in India

The crux of development of sport has always revolved around generating and increasing participation in sports through various media, one important medium being the organisation of sport events. Continuous growth in participation has been one of the primary aims of sport development, and, still, organisations don't always aim to grow their memberships. Many sports like tennis, squash, swimming and basketball are facility-dependent sports as opposed to sports like cycling, football and cricket, which can be played anytime and anywhere. Sport administrators and managers have always faced challenges to grow memberships in facility-dependent sports as growth depends on access to the time slots available in the facility and hence are restrained from growing beyond their current facility's capacity. Sport development officers often have to innovate ways to persuade sports clubs to increase participation by providing more competition opportunities, through events, or by developing new marketing or operational strategies to add more members.

According to Houlihan and Green, the term *sport development* has three orientations (Nicholson, Hoye and Houlihan, 2010): The first is the promotion of sport-for-all objectives; the second prioritises talent identification, 'nurturing' and athlete pathways and the third orientation relates to sport's links with other policy objectives such as health or community regeneration. This chapter principally focuses on the first two, and how India, a country with 1.3 billion people, has developed a sports ecosystem that led to increased participation in sport and to the success of Indian athletes in international sport.

Sport was viewed as a recreational and leisure activity around the time of India's independence in 1947. Though there were many international sports events organised in India, there were very few athletes who excelled in sport and received the fame and accolades they deserved. As a result, participation in sport was never taken seriously. India topped the world in field hockey and has some astonishing records to its name. The Indian team dominated the game from 1928 to 1956 and won six consecutive Olympics medals. India overall has won eight Olympic gold, one silver and two bronze (Indian Sports News, 2012). Though India experienced success in hockey, the sport did not attract much participation. India has always been a cricket-centric country, with most of the sporting activity and significant developments revolving around cricket – the biggest irony being that hockey is actually India's national sport.

Development through commercialisation of cricket in India

The concept of sport development was actually introduced when Control for Cricket in India (BCCI), the national governing body for cricket in India commercialised the sport through huge broadcasting revenues. Today, BCCI is one of the wealthiest sports organisations in the world. The Indian cricket team made a noteworthy achievement in winning the Cricket World Cup in 1983, against all odds, which is perhaps the greatest milestone in the history of Indian cricket. "The significance of that win is that it changed the course of Indian Cricket forever" (Sardana, 2014, p. 6). Due to this win, India reclaimed its sporting identity, which it had lost with its diminishing performance in field hockey. Cricket picked up popularity and importance after the win of the 1983 World Cup. It became a door-to-door ambition of boys to play the game of cricket; a classic example was the great cricketer Sachin Tendulkar, who has shared many times that he was inspired by this amazing victory (The Economic Times, 2011).

This accomplishment of the Kapil Dev-led team gave confidence to the BCCI administrators to set their aims to take on the traditional powerhouses of the game – England and Australia. Before that win, the BCCI bosses attended the International Cricket Council (ICC) meetings as mere timid participants (Sardana, 2014). The event kick-started a cricket revolution in India which led to a shift in power. The World Cup was taken out of England in 1987, and with it went control of the game of cricket. The 1983 win gave new dimension to the way cricket was perceived in India (Deccan Herald, 2013).

Multi-national companies and corporations got behind the Indian cricket team; the media started to give them much-deserved recognition. The nation's identity became known with the sport of cricket (Sardana, 2014, p. 7). Until 1995, cricket events and matches were broadcast on the government-run Doordarshan National television channel. The Cricket Association of Bengal (CAB) wanted to break the monopoly of the state-run Doordarshan television and hence sold the broadcasting rights for a five-nation championship, the Hero Cup, to Trans World International (TWI) and obtained a ruling in its favour from the court. The BCCI, taking a cue from this, went on to obtain an order in 1994 in its favour and was granted a five-year exclusive broadcast rights as part of a US$30 million contract to a non-government broadcaster, wherein the BCCI was the direct beneficiary. In February 1995, the Supreme Court of India ruled that broadcasting is not a state monopoly as it constitutes public property and should be for the promotion of the fundamental rights of free speech, which was difficult to achieve under a strict monopoly. While this paved the way for BCCI to maximise their revenues by selling broadcasting rights to private broadcasters, the Government of India ensured the continued presence of Indian cricket on free-to-air television, thus allowing continued penetration of international cricket into the Indian markets. All these developments led to growth in the financial standing of the BCCI, and the other professional associations of cricket started looking forward to playing the Asian teams in the hope of increasing their own revenue streams (Sardana, 2014, p. 8).

In 1996, the ICC decided to have a rolling post of Chairman, with each country having three years of tenure. Under this system, the responsibility fell on the then-President of BCCI, Jagmohan Dalmiya, to head the ICC for the next three years. He was a visionary who brought about positive structural changes by devising a schedule where each country was supposed to tour others at regular intervals and inducted many new countries as associate members with the promise that ICC funds would be spent in these countries where cricket was not yet widely played. With such drastic changes, control in the ICC became realistic, and domination of the founder members decreased while equality increased. When Dalmiya took over as the ICC President, it just had US$16,000 in its kitty, but when he demitted office three years later, the ICC treasury was bulging with US$15 million. Besides this, the international body had established lucrative revenue streams in the World Cup and the Champions Trophy events via various sponsorship and broadcasting revenues (The Sunday Tribune, 2004).

The business of making money in cricket through advertising, television rights, franchises, sponsorships and merchandising by organising One Day International (ODI) matches involving India, Pakistan and Sri Lanka became so irresistible that between 1984 and 2003, more than 200 ODI matches were played between these nations alone (Sardana, 2014, p. 9). Given the tense relations between India and Pakistan, the model of commercialisation of cricket was heavily dependent on the participation of the two countries in the tournaments of an event because the viewership of the events on television and related information communication technology systems was drawn from these countries, and their supporters spread through immigrants to other countries all over the world.

The rise of pro-league culture in India

Cricket has always been ahead of other sports in terms of popularity. Even hockey, for that matter, being the national sport of India, doesn't enjoy the stardom which cricket does. Cricket is a spectator-friendly sport, and the governing body of the sport has successfully capitalised on this. Other sports in India, however, have been neglected and never really had a strong governance. There was much need for proper direction, a structure which could be executed in order to develop the standard of other sports in India. The solution to this came from cricket.

The commercialisation of cricket in India paved the way for a solid development model for other sports, which can be explained with the launch of the IPL in 2008 by the BCCI. The BCCI set a benchmark for organising world-class sport events and adding glamour. Inspired by this league format, many other sports organised league-based events not only increasing their participation in terms of audience and people playing the sport but also profoundly impacting the social, economic, cultural and the political sport landscape of India. In this chapter, examples of a few top leagues will be discussed to understand how they have impacted the sport development structure in India. The following table (Table 6.1) shows the various professional sport leagues organised in India since the inception of the IPL in 2008.

The Indian Premier League (IPL) 2008

In 2007, the Essel group, which is owned by one of the prominent TV channels in India, Zee Television, introduced a new cricket format – one with a lower entry cost and more value for money to sponsors associated with the event. They announced the creation of a new cricket series, the Indian Cricket League (ICL). This league would be a six-team league, and each of the players would represent a geographical region or city in India, with sponsorship tie-ups, suitable branding and the necessary media hype for marketing the event. International cricketers would be invited to play, opening up the possibility of domestic players from cricket-playing nations to play alongside foreign players of other countries (Zee News, 2007). This league, however, was not a property of the BCCI, but of the Essel

Table 6.1 Sports leagues in India

Sr.no	League name	Sport	Year of establishment
1	The Indian Premier League (IPL)	Cricket	2008
2	The Indian Super League (ISL)	Football	2013
3	Premier Badminton League (PBL)	Badminton	2013
4	International Premier Tennis League (IPTL)	Tennis	2013
5	Hockey India League (HIL)	Hockey	2013
6	Golf Premier League (GPL)	Golf	2013
7	Pro Kabaddi League (PKL)	Kabaddi	2014
8	Pro Wrestling League (PWL)	Wrestling	2015
9	United Basketball Alliance (UBA)	Basketball	2015
10	Maha Handball Super League (MHSL)	Handball	2016
11	Premier Futsal League (PFL)	Futsal	2016
12	Super Boxing League (SBA)	Boxing	2017
13	Ultimate Table Tennis League (UTT)	Table Tennis	2017
14	Ultimate Kho Kho League (UKKL)	Kho Kho	2019
15	Pro Volleyball League (PVL)	Volleyball	2019

Group, which posed a threat to BCCI's governance. Faced with the threat of young cricketers joining the ICL, the BCCI involved the ICC and other international boards to get their players banned from participating in the ICL event. They also forced the state associations to disallow their grounds to be used by the ICL.

Based on the blueprint of the ICL, the BCCI subsequently came up with their own version of a cricket league, naming it the IPL in 2007 and subsequently launching it in 2008. As the IPL wished to include famous individuals to add glamour, the prospective investors were not the usual risk-taking venture capitalists but celebrities and business tycoons. A lucrative, detailed revenue sharing model and format among the promoters, the franchises and the players in the form of huge prize money was decided, assuring that every stake holder would be in a win position (Kohli, 2009). A fundamental idea to the IPL's business plan was to invite private enterprises to own a portion of the cricket business, which had, until then, been a closed club.

By developing a branch of Indian cricket that could be run in a purely commercial model, corporates in India were allowed even more access to Indian cricket teams. The sale of the IPL franchises was a turning point for the commercialisation of cricket in India. Limiting the number of franchisees in the tournament ensured that the demand outpaced supply, fostering a rise in value of the teams. At the initial auction for the franchise rights during the launch in 2008, the total base price for eight franchises was US$400 million, whereas the player auctions fetched US$723.59 million (Sardana, 2014, p. 14).

The IPL has become a lucrative source of revenue for the BCCI and has generated huge profits every year of its existence through a host of revenue streams created by broadcasting, sponsorship, ticketing revenues and others. It can boast of being among the wealthiest sports bodies in the world and made US$800 million (INR 5,300 crores) during the year 2011–2012, per its annual report. Its reserves for the year 2011–2012 stood at roughly three times the revenue generated by the ICC in the same period (Sardana, 2014, p. 18).

The IPL is the most-attended cricket league in the world, and in the year 2014 was ranked sixth in average attendance among all sports leagues around the world (Barret, 2016). In 2010, the IPL became the first sporting event in the world to be broadcast live on YouTube (Hoult, 2010). According to the BCCI, the 2015 IPL season contributed US$160 million (INR 11.5 billion) to the GDP of the Indian economy (The Hindu, 2015). The brand value of the IPL in 2019 was US$6.8 billion (INR 475 billion) (Duff and Phelps, 2019).

The IPL had a huge impact on the minds of the Indian youth and has inspired them to take up the sport of cricket. Cricket is undoubtedly the most played sport in India with ever-increasing participation. With the development of the IPL and access to huge funds generated through the cash-rich league, the BCCI has successfully developed a sustainable model to fuel more participation in cricket. Besides the dominance of the men's cricket team, the Indian women's cricket team has also become one of the top teams today, and the BCCI has been successful in attracting female athletes to join the sport. The grand success of the IPL inspired a series of different sporting leagues to be launched in India, furthering the sport development scenario in the country.

The IPL was the trendsetter in league culture in India and what followed was a plethora of fantastic sporting events. With the league culture in place, glamour and fame became associated with the sport through the involvement of top Bollywood celebrities as league owners and investors. Cricket began increasing viewership on national television. There was huge money involved, along with the allure of associated movie stars. The promise of a professional career and assurance of earning good money through these leagues have undoubtedly attracted youth to take up sports at different levels. The league structure was a great opportunity for talent scouting, and many domestic athletes got their big break by getting a chance to shine for their league teams. While participation in sports has always been a driving force when we speak of sport development, the rise of these leagues and the associated opportunity for a promising career surely attracted more participation in sport. It would be safe to say that the league culture was a catalyst to propel huge participation in Indian sport, not just on the field but in the stands as well.

The Indian Super League (ISL), 2013

Inspired by the model and success of the IPL, in October 2013, the Football Sports Development Limited (FSDL) partnered with IMG Reliance Industries and Star

Sports jointly launched the Indian Super League (ISL). The ISL was launched to grow and promote the sport of football in India, which is governed by the All India Football Federation (AIFF). The league's first season took place in 2014 with just eight teams. The first three seasons operated without official recognition from the Asian Football Confederation (AFC), the governing body for the sport in Asia (Bali, 2017). However, before the 2017–2018 season, the league got recognition from the AFC and added two more teams and extended its schedule to five months (Bali, 2017).

As the ISL was launched on the lines of the IPL, during the initial bidding for the eight ISL teams, there was already high interest from big corporates, IPL teams, Bollywood stars and other business groups (Rao, 2013). It was also declared that not only would the bidders need to comply with a financial requirement for a team but they would also need to promote 'grassroots' development plans for football within their area of the team's city (Business Standard, 2014). With this clause for the respective franchise owners, the AIFF had successfully placed a development strategy to attract more participation in football.

The Indian Badminton League (IBL), 2013

India first saw success in the sport of Badminton when Indian athlete Saina Nehwal won a bronze medal at the 2012 Olympic Games in London in the singles event. This achievement led her to all the media hype and attention she deserved, and sponsors lined up to sign her. What followed after this phenomenal achievement was an added participation and interest in badminton, with the hope of a promising career in the sport of badminton. In 2013, the Indian Badminton League (IBL), a team badminton league was launched, then later renamed the Premier Badminton League (PBL) in 2015 (Sports NDTV, 2015).

This league invited many top seeds, world champions and Olympic medallists to be a part of the league. Teams bid on professional players from around the world. According to the prominent Danish player Victor Axelsen, this was a crucial part of the athletes' annual income. Each franchise had a purse of US$280,000 (INR 2 crore), and the maximum a team could spend on a single player was US$110,000 (INR 77 lakh) in the 2020 auction. The league earns US$2.5 million (INR 20 crore) in franchise fees from the nine teams and another US$2.5 million (INR 20 crore) through gate revenue (Bhattacharyya, 2018).

Hockey India League (HIL), 2013

In 2012, a new hockey league called the World Series Hockey was launched by the Indian Hockey Federation and Numbus Sports, which was not sanctioned by the International Hockey Federation (FIH). In order to launch a hockey league sanctioned by the FIH, in 2013, Hockey India, the governing body for the sport in India, launched the Hockey India League (HIL). The first season of the league was held in 2013 with just five teams. Since its inception, the HIL proved to be a financially successful event for Hockey India which was struggling financially. In 2015, league earned good profits from sponsors and broadcasting revenues.

Five seasons of the league have been successfully completed. In the year 2019, the HIL was revamped with a five-a-side format which replaced the traditional 11-a-side format to make it more fast-paced and exciting for the viewers. This strategy was implemented to cut down on expenses and make the game more spectator-friendly.

Pro Kabaddi League (PKL) 2014

Kabaddi is a very popular contact sport in South Asia that first originated in ancient India and is played across India. Outside of India it's a popular sport in Iran, is the national game of Bangladesh and is also one of the national sports of Nepal. The governing body of kabaddi is the International Kabaddi Federation, which consists of over 30 national associations and governs the game and its rules across the world.

Taking inspiration from the cricketing IPL, the Pro Kabaddi League was launched in 2014 with Star Sports as the broadcasting partner in India. The Pro Kabaddi League also has a franchise-based model, similar to that of the IPL, and its first season was held in 2014 with eight teams, each of which paid fees of up to US$250,000 to join (Atkinson, 2014). There were doubts over whether the PKL would be successful, noting that there were many other sports leagues attempting to copy the IPL's business model and success and that, unlike cricket, there were relatively very few well-known players in kabaddi.

The inaugural season of the PKL witnessed around 435 million viewers, second to the 2014 IPL's 552 million, while the first season's final between the Jaipur Pink Panthers and U-Mumba gathered 86.4 million views (The Hindu, 2014). The league gathered more viewership almost every season. In the seventh season of the PKL (2019–2020), it registered a 9% growth in viewership with 1.2 billion impressions. The broadcaster, Star India likely earned between $26.4 million (INR 200 crore) and US$30 million (INR 230 crore) from Season 7. In terms of sponsorships, the title sponsor was Vivo, which signed its association with PKL for US$34,594,300 (INR 262 crore) for five years, while the league roped in many other official sponsors. Other sponsor brands in the PKL have contributed around US$12 million (INR 90 crore) in total to the central sponsorship revenues (Saini, 2019).

One of the critical lessons from the example of the PKL is that, even though kabaddi is a traditional Indian sport, it had negligible viewership prior to the organisation of the PKL. The league model the KPL adopted allowed the sport to become more successful. The PKL altered a few rules and added a few elements in the game to make the sport more exciting and audience-friendly. This league is a classic example of how a sport like kabaddi, which was traditionally played in small towns and tier-2 and tier-3 cities, could gather an audience from metro cities too. The organisers have successfully created a model which has improved participation in the sport, has built a strong fan base, gathered good economic momentum through sponsors and broadcasting revenues and has created a sustainable development model for the sport.

Apart from the above-mentioned leagues which were relatively more successful in terms of viewership and revenues, a few other leagues were also launched, banking on the success story of the IPL. Many national sport associations and federations designed franchise-based leagues for their respective sports, creating opportunities for athletes, coaches and all other stakeholders of their sports. This helped them to increase participation and viewership. The social, economic and cultural impact of these leagues has surely brought about a positive change in the Indian sports landscape.

Impact of leagues on sport development in India

The 15-odd sporting leagues in India, which began with the IPL in 2008, have had a positive impact on Indian sport. We can briefly categorise them in terms of economic, social, cultural, political and personal significance.

The organisation of these various leagues has brought about a significant economic change in India's sport development. Until a decade or so, contributions of the sport industry to the Indian economy were negligible. Today, the sport industry contributes to 0.1% share of India's GDP. Globally, the sport industry contributes around 0.5% of GDP. The cash flow through leagues have enabled the governing bodies of the respective sport to provide better facilities, infrastructure and programmes to the athletes (Exchange4media, 2018).

Socially, the leagues have boosted interest for viewing sports broadcasted on television and in-person. Even non-mainstream sports like kabaddi and wrestling have generated a good fan base due to the leagues. There are big social media communities which follow certain teams or players, which have further promoted these leagues. Many non-sporting social events associated with the league teams have been organised in order to support sport development and other social objectives.

The league teams in India, in any sport, are mostly differentiated by the names of the various cities or regions in India. India is a land of different cultures, which are reflected in their regional teams. All these teams have absorbed the regional cultures in their respective team promotions and the way they are perceived by the audience. The league teams have also played a vital role in establishing a sporting culture among the region they are associated with and promoting their sport.

In terms of personal significance too, the leagues have played a crucial role. The league format has provided many domestic players with a platform to showcase their talent and an opportunity to play for the country. The league format has allowed many players to grow and earn more money and fame. The format to play with elite players from the world has helped many athletes to improve their skills, and we can see many of these athletes winning international accolades for the country.

The political significance of the league format is worth considering too. The involvement of huge funds in the cash-rich leagues has attracted bright minds to govern the sport. These leagues would not have grown every year if they were not managed by responsible individuals. The involvement of professionals, and even former elite athletes, to govern the sport that accompanied the rise in leagues has surely added value to the sport development structure of India. For example, in 2017, India got its first Sports Minister, Col. Rajyavardhan Singh Rathore, who had previously won an Olympic medal in shooting (The Hindu, 2017). Also, recently, former Indian Cricket team captain Saurav Ganguly was selected as the 39th President of the prestigious BCCI (India Today, 2019).

When we talk about participation in sports as an important tool for nurturing sport development it is important to consider other factors that developed along with the different franchise-based sports leagues in India. The sporting ecosystem in India started developing with huge investments in infrastructure and attracted sport mega-events to the country.

The development of sport infrastructure through sport events

Infrastructure has always been a vital element for the development of sport and increased participation in sport as well as attracting audiences. India's world-class sport infrastructure for cricket has been in place for a long time, given the following and participation it has enjoyed. However, other sports were lagging behind. If it were not for its hosting of a few sport mega-events in other sport codes, sport development in India would still be focused on cricket.

The Indian Grand Prix and the Buddh International Circuit

The Indian Olympic Association (IOA) and Bernie Ecclestone, then Chief Executive of the Formula One Group, signed an agreement for India to host a Grand Prix event. Estimated to cost about US$400 million (INR 20 billion) to build, the Buddh International Formula One circuit, having an approximate length of 3.192 miles and spread over an area of 874 acres, was built in the Delhi NCR and Greater Noida (Racing Circuits, 2011). The circuit was officially inaugurated in 2011, and the first Indian Grand Prix was held at the Buddh International Circuit on 30 October 2011. Many Formula One enthusiasts who would otherwise not have travelled to India attended this event – one of the most attended motor sport events in India.

The circuit was then used to host smaller racing events and tournaments in the country, including events for super cars and bikes for track day. This circuit provided an opportunity to Indian motor sport enthusiasts to participate in and witness world-class action. Many MotoGP enthusiasts from across the country have since used the circuit. Due to the availability of such a facility, the motorsport industry has seen a considerable boost in the country over the last decade.

2008 Commonwealth Youth Games, Pune, India

The Commonwealth Youth Games were held in Pune, in 2008, in the state of Maharashtra, India. They were the third Commonwealth Youth Games, which are held every four years, and the first Commonwealth Youth Games to be held in Asia. More than 1,300 athletes and around 350 officials from 71 commonwealth countries participated in these games, in nine disciplines –Athletics, Badminton, Boxing, Shooting, Swimming, Table Tennis, Tennis, Weightlifting and Wrestling (Pune 2008, 2008).

The best part of these games was that all the venues for these sports were on one single campus with the athlete village in close proximity. Due to the huge infrastructure built for the games, Pune has become a hub for many national teams and top athletes, who continue to train in the top-class facility. Many national sport events, corporate events and huge marathons have been organised at the facility. This highlights how ongoing sport development gets a boost by organising big events and their positive impacts on sport participation.

2010 Commonwealth Games, Delhi, India

The IOA organised the 2010 Commonwealth Games which were officially known as the XIX Commonwealth Games and commonly known as Delhi 2010. It was one of the biggest international multi-sport events held in the capital of Delhi from 3 to 14 October 2010 where around 7,000 athletes from 71 countries competed for 826 medals, making it the largest Commonwealth Games to date (Delhi 2010, 2010).

The games paved the way for development of world-class infrastructure in Delhi for various other sport disciplines apart from cricket. It was a major boost to sport development in India for various sports. Today, these venues are instrumental in developing top athletes for the country and host many domestic sports events to generate even more participation.

The infrastructure developed for the organisation of these events not only gave athletes access to world-class sports facilities but also developed the overall standard of other infrastructure in cities like Delhi and Pune. New roads, flyover bridges and many aesthetic projects for the beautification of the city were undertaken for the events. The ruling political party took pride in organising these events, which led to the development of additional public infrastructure in these cities. These events also helped establish a sporting culture in these cities, and these cities continue to serve as the sporting hubs of the country with many national teams of various sports.

Apart from these hallmark events, India has successfully hosted many world-class events, including the U-17 FIFA World Cup in 2017, and many international tournaments in various other sports like shooting, athletics, boxing and hockey. Due to an increased use of social media and all of these events being broadcast on national television, many underrated sports in India have received the much-needed visibility they required to become popular. This has attracted new audiences and supported the league structures with billions of dollars pumped in the sporting economy through sponsorships, broadcasting revenues, ticketing and merchandising. Given the numbers we have seen in the various sport leagues in terms of investment and viewership, sport has surely been an ever-increasing contributor to the GDP of India. The sport industry in India has grown from US$1.3 billion to US$2.7 billion in just the last five years. However, sport still contributes 0.1% share of India's GDP, while globally, the industry is sized at around 0.5% of GDP. It has therefore yet to achieve its full potential in the Indian market (Exchange4media, 2018).

Government initiatives for sport development

If one would break down the components of sport development, it would be noteworthy to see how sport governance plays a vital role in boosting the sport ecosystem, with government initiatives supporting the increasing demand for sports participation and viewership.

In September 2014, with the aim to increase India's Olympic medal tally, at the 2016 (Rio) and 2020 (Tokyo) Olympics, the Ministry of Youth Affairs and Sports (MYAS) started the Target Olympics Podium Scheme (TOPS or TOP). The Target Olympic Podium Scheme is a programme of the Government of India to provide support to India's top athletes to realise their Olympic dream. A special committee (TOPS Elite Athletes' Identification Committee) has been formed to identify elite athletes who could win a medal at the Olympics. Under this program, the committee identifies athletes who are considered to be potential candidates for medals at the 2021 and 2024 Olympics and support them in their preparations for the mega-event. The idea of this programme is also to identify, nurture and fund athletes who are medal prospects for the Olympic Games in Los Angeles in 2028 (Ministry of Youth Affairs and Sports, 2019).

Khelo India Youth & University Games

In October 2018, the Ministry of Youth Affairs and Sports, Government of India, launched the Khelo India programme to develop and promote the sports culture in India at the grassroots level. With an aim to develop a strong framework for all sports played in the country and establish India as a sporting super power, this programme helps identify talent at the school level. Talented players identified in priority sports disciplines by the special selection committees are provided annual financial assistance of US$6,600 (INR 5 lakh) per annum for 8 years (Khelo India, 2018).

The Khelo India Youth Games were mostly organised for athletes under the age of 17. It was then identified that there was a lot of untapped talent in colleges and universities as well. With the success of Khelo India Games in identifying grassroots talent in various sports in children and youth, the MYAS launched the Khelo India University Games in February 2020 to identify talented athletes in universities.

The Khelo India programme has been a game changing move by the government of India to identify hidden talent in sport and to promote sport from the grassroots level. It has ignited interest amongst young athletes to participate in the games as the platform provided is of a world-class level with all top facilities.

National Sports University (NSU)

In order to promote sports and allied education and have a sustainable sport development structure, the Government of India, under the aegis of the Ministry of Youth Affairs and Sports, launched the National Sports University (NSU) in the city of Imphal in 2018. India's Prime Minister, Narendra Modi, laid the foundation stone for the university's proposed 325-acre campus on 16 March 2018. The University was established to promote sports education in the areas of sports sciences, sports technology, sports management and sports coaching in addition to functioning as the national training centre for select sports disciplines (Hindustan Times, 2018).

The role of corporate and private funding in sport development

Looking at the rising interest in sport, we can see the glamour created by the various sports leagues in India, with many corporations instrumental in connecting with the sport industry through sponsorships and corporate social responsibility (CSR) activities. Big corporations in India like Reliance, Tata, JSW Group and Mahindra have sponsored the sport ecosystem either through investing in franchises of league teams or by setting up world-class sports academies and starting foundations to support top athletes. The IPL is a perfect example of why these corporates invested in sports. Over 700 million fans came in to enjoy the IPL. Compare this to the 550 million people who voted in the 2014 Lok Sabha government elections, the biggest elections that India has even seen, and it's clear that more citizens spent their time enjoying this spectacle of sports than politics (Campaign India, 2018).

The corporates have successfully capitalised on the viewership of these leagues through sponsorship initiatives. In India, the sport sponsorship market saw a healthy growth of 17% in 2019 and is currently valued at over US 41.17 billion (INR 9,000 crore). In 2019, sports-related advertising revenue reached US$675 million (INR 5,232 crore) with a growth rate of 18%. Over 80% of all advertisement spends were on television at US$545 million (INR 4,272 crore) (Farooqui, 2020).

Through their CSR ventures, many corporates have also invested in high-performance sports academies and training centres to support budding athletes in various sport disciplines. The Jindal Steel Works Group founded the high-performance centre Inspire Institute of Sports (IIS) in 2018 to promote science- and technology-driven training programmes for promising athletes. The institute offers full scholarships to talented athletes scouted from across the country in athletics, boxing, judo, swimming and wrestling. IIS is a recognised centre by the government's Sports Authority of India as a Khelo India-accredited development centre for boxing and wrestling. The athletics and swimming facilities at IIS are approved by the International Association of Athletics Federation and the International Swimming Federation (FINA), respectively.

Other corporates like TATA and Reliance have also invested in setting up foundations for the promotion and development of sports. The TATA Sports Academy, built over 30 acres, has world-class sports facilities to nurture and develop athletes. The JRD Tata Sports Complex is the home of Jamshedpur FC, making the football club the only ISL franchisee team to have its own stadium (Tata Steel, 2020).

Reliance Foundation Youth Sports (RFYS) is an initiative driven by Reliance Foundation, a non-profit and CSR front of the Reliance Group, which focuses on providing a platform for youth sports in India, especially at the school and collegiate level. Currently, eight cities are part of the foundation's long-term goal which aims to establish a sports association, similar to the NCAA of the United States of America that controls and collaborates with schools and athletes. Its overall contribution towards CSR initiatives is close to US$1.8 billion (INR 12,000 crore) every year in the Indian sport industry (Exchange4media, 2018).

Many former athletes and sports enthusiasts have also come together to support the development of sport in India. By initiating not-for-profit foundations and initiatives like Olympic Gold Quest (OGQ), founded by Indian sporting legends Geet Sethi, the billiards world champion, and Prakash Padukone, former top-ranked badminton player, or the GO Sports Foundation, these organisations have tried to support top athletes in India to achieve Olympic medals and international glory by helping them get sponsorships or fund their training. At the London 2012 Summer Olympics, four out of the six Indian medallists were supported by OGQ.

Conclusion and future challenges for sport development in India

With a population of 1.3 billion, India has a lot of potential to be one of the sporting superpowers in the world. To have a strong sport development model is of vital importance to develop sustainable governance across all sports. It will be one of the most important challenges to identify sport talent from the grassroots level, nurture them and develop elite athletes. To develop elite athletes, it is important to design long-term athlete development structures and to provide the best infrastructure, equipment, nutrition, coaching and participation in top events for athletes. It is also important for the governing bodies of various sports to develop multiple revenue streams though events and sponsorships broadcasting rights and to increase participation to support the development of elite athletes. Every sport is different, and it is a challenge for the governing bodies of sports to identify how they can develop strong governing structures to add to the development of their sport.

Sports science and technology have changed the way sport is played and perceived. Whether technology on or off the field, it has impacted sport outcomes in a profound way and is essential to sporting success. An important challenge for sport development in India is to introduce and adapt to new technologies backed by sports science.

Sport is all about experiences. Training hard for a medal, winning a medal and watching someone win a medal in the stadium are all different experiences. We pay for the tickets to a game to experience the magical atmosphere in the stadium, while athletes participate for good experiences to better their skills. Successful events are those which give the best of the experiences to their audiences, sponsors, athletes and other stakeholders.

While many sport organisations have tried to replicate the success story of the IPL by developing similar league structures for their respective sports, only those who put more impetus and importance to the experiences they created have experienced success. Many sports leagues have updated or changed rules to make them more attractive and spectator-friendly.

It will be an interesting challenge for sports organisations to innovate and study how they can make their sport more spectator-friendly and engaging, attract sponsors, generate more participation and eventually create better athletes by designing sustainable experiential models. Monetary success, fame and other developments will surely follow once any sport organisation identifies these elements.

If we quickly summarise the road map of development of sport in India, the credit will definitely be given to cricket and how on BCCI capitalised on the spectator-friendly sport in its various formats, while not discounting the efforts by a few other sport organisations to take up the franchise-based league format of the IPL and grow their respective sports. Participation in sports and viewership has grown due to the lucrative career opportunities created by these leagues. The government and the private sector have done their parts to add value to the sport development scenario of the country. The sport development map of India will essentially include the cash generating sporting leagues, the infrastructure developed for mega sport facilities, government initiatives and the role of corporations and private personalities in supporting the sports ecosystem through their various initiatives. Although we can conclude there is much to be done, the last decade has seen an exponential rise in the growth of the Indian sporting ecosystem. With the current developments and trends, it is inevitable that India is on the right path to achieving success and becoming a sporting superpower in the years to come.

References

Atkinson, S. (2014). *Kabaddi gets the IPL treatment*. [online]. BBC News. Available at: https://www.bbc.com/news/business-28660432 [Accessed 20 Mar. 2020].

Bali, R. (2017). *Indian Football: ISL gets recognition from AFC and FIFA*. [online]. Goal. com. Available at: https://www.goal.com/en/news/indian-football-isl-gets-recognition-from-afc-and-fifa/gdvxrob0spvu1tei948rtj295 [Accessed 17 Feb. 2020].

Barret. C. (2016). *Big Bash League jumps into top 10 of most attended sports leagues in the world*. [online]. The Sunday Morning Herald Available at: https://www.smh.com.au/sport/cricket/big-bash-league-jumps-into-top-10-of-most-attended-sports-leagues-in-the-world-20160110-gm2w8z.html [Accessed 19 May 2020].

Bhattacharyya, A. (2018) *Premier Badminton League expects to break even in FY20*. [online]. Available at: https://brandequity.economictimes.indiatimes.com/news/media/premier-badminton-league-expects-to-boost-its-revenues/66874486 [Accessed 19 May 2020].

Business Standard, (2014). *Football league bids kick off with a roar*. [online]. Available at: https://www.business-standard.com/article/current-affairs/football-league-bids-kick-off-with-a-roar-114030600328_1.html [Accessed 7 Apr. 2020].

Campaign India, (2018). *Indian sports industry to touch $10 bn by 2025: Sanjay Gupta, Star Network*. [online]. Available at: https://www.campaignindia.in/article/indian-sports-industry-to-touch-10-bn-by-2025-sanjay-gupta-star-network/446205 [Accessed 19 May 2020].

Deccan Herald, (2013). *Our 1983 win gave new dimension to Indian cricket: Kapil*. [online]. Available at: https://www.deccanherald.com/sports/our-1983-win-gave-new-dimension-to-indian-cricket-kapil-331108.html [Accessed 13 March 2020].

Delhi 2010, (2010). *Delhi promised, Delhi delivered*. [online]. D2010.thecgf.com, Available at: http://d2010.thecgf.com/news/delhi_promised_delhi_delivered [Accessed 19 May 2020].

Duff and Phelps (2019). *Duff & Phelps Launches IPL Brand Valuation Report 2019: Varun Gupta, Santosh N.* [online] Available at: https://www.duffandphelps.com/insights/publications/valuation/ipl-brand-valuation-report-2019

Exchange4media, (2018). *Indian sports industry can become a $10 billion industry in next 5–7 years: Sanjay Gupta, MD Star India at the CII Scorecard forum, 2018*. [online]. Available at: https://www.exchange4media.com/media-tv-news/indian-sports-industry-can-become-a-$10-billion-industry-in-next-5-7-yearssanjay-guptamd-star-india-at-the-cii-scorecard-forum2018-91312.html [Accessed 17 May 2020].

Farooqui, M. (2020). *Indian sports sponsorship market in 2019 crossed Rs 9,000 cr-mark: GroupM ESP*. [online]. Moneycontrol.com. Available at: https://www.moneycontrol.com/news/trends/sports-trends/indian-sports-sponsorship-market-in-2019-crossed-rs-9000-cr-mark-groupm-esp-5027881.html [Accessed 21 May 2020].

Hindustan Times, (2018). *India's first national sports university to be set up in Manipur*. [online]. Available at: https://www.hindustantimes.com/education/india-s-first-national-sports-university-to-be-set-up-in-manipur/story-dSEKwFEs2sjGfAIJoGbBnO.html [Accessed 19 June 2020].

Houlihan, B. and Green, M. (2010). *Routledge handbook of sports development*. London: Routledge.

Hoult, N. (2010) *IPL to broadcast live on YouTube*. [online]. The Telegraph, Available at: https://www.telegraph.co.uk/sport/cricket/twenty20/ipl/7033597/IPL-to-broadcast-live-on-YouTube.html [Accessed 12 May 2020].

Indian Sports News, (2012). *1928–1956: Period which saw India dominate Hockey at world stage*. [online]. Available at: http://www.indiansportsnews.com/hot-picks/15810-india-hockey-at-olympics-glorious-past-to-struggling-past [Accessed 9 March 2020].

India Today, (2019). *Sourav Ganguly formally elected as the 39th president of BCCI*. [online]. Available at: https://www.indiatoday.in/sports/cricket/story/sourav-ganguly-takes-charge-officialy-as-39th-bcci-president-1612086-2019-10-23 [Accessed 29 May 2020].

Khelo India, (2018). *About Khelo India*. [online]. Available at: https://kheloindia.gov.in/about [Accessed 13 June 2020].

Kohli, R. (2009). *The launch of Indian Premier League.* [online]. Columbia. Available at: https://www0.gsb.columbia.edu/mygsb/faculty/research/pubfiles/5179/IPL.pdf [Accessed 02 March 2020].

Ministry of Youth Affairs And Sports, (2019). *Target Olympic Podium Scheme.* [online]. Sportsauthorityofindia.nic.in. Available at: https://sportsauthorityofindia.nic.in/index1.asp?ls_id=3812 [Accessed 22 June 2020].

Pune 2008, (2008). *About the games.* [online]. Available at: http://pune2008.thecgf.com/about-games/commonwealth-youth-games.php [Accessed 29 May 2020].

Racing Circuits, (2011). *Buddh International Circuit.* [online]. Available at: https://www.racingcircuits.info/asia/india/buddh-international-circuit/#.X28ijMLVKUk [Accessed 17 Apr. 2020].

Rao, K.S. (2013) *Indian Super League postponed by six months.* [online]. Times of India. Available at: https://timesofindia.indiatimes.com/sports/football/indian-super-league/top-stories/Indian-Super-League-postponed-by-six-months/articleshow/24780676.cms [Accessed 20 Feb. 2020].

Saini, S. (2019). *Pro Kabaddi League is scoring high on revenue, viewership & sponsors.* [online]. Exchange4media.com. Available at: https://www.exchange4media.com/media-tv-news/how-pro-kabaddi-league-has-emerged-as-a-favourite-among-viewers-brands-100881.html [Accessed 18 May 2020].

Sardana, M.M.K. (2014). *Shaping up sports economy in India through commercialization of cricket,* [pdf] New Delhi: Institute for Studies in Industrial Development. Available at: http://111.93.232.162/pdf/DN1401.pdf [Accessed 09 Feb. 2020].

Sports NDTV, (2015). *Badminton Association of India renames Indian Badminton League to Premier Badminton League.* [online]. Available at: https://sports.ndtv.com/badminton/badminton-association-of-india-renames-indian-badminton-league-to-premier-badminton-league-1489964 [Accessed 06 May 2020].

Tata Steel, (2020). *Sports is a way of life at Tata Steel.* [online]. Available at: https://www.tatasteel.com/corporate/our-organisation/sports/# [Accessed 17 June 2020].

The Economic Times, (2011). *1983 World Cup win changed course of Indian Cricket: Tendulkar.* [online]. Available at: https://economictimes.indiatimes.com/1983-world-cup-win-changed-course-of-indian-cricket-tendulkar/articleshow/7519663.cms?from=mdr [Accessed 11 Jan. 2020].

The Hindu, (2014). *Pro Kabaddi league viewership second only to IPL.* [online]. Available at: https://www.thehindu.com/sport/other-sports/pro-kabaddi-league-viewership-second-only-to-ipl/article6413148.ece [Accessed 21 May 2020].

The Hindu, (2015). *IPL 2015 contributed Rs. 11.5 bn to GDP: BCCI.* [online]. Available at: https://www.thehindu.com/sport/cricket/2015-indian-premier-league-ipl-contributed-rs115-billion-182-million-to-indias-gross-domestic-product-gdp-says-bcci/article7823334.ece [Accessed 22 Feb. 2020].

The Hindu, (2017). *Rajyavardhan Rathore appointed India's new sports minister.* [online]. Available at: https://www.thehindu.com/news/national/rajyavardhan-rathore-appointed-indias-new-sports-minister/article19615091.ece [Accessed 03 June 2020].

The Sunday Tribune, (2004). *Currency of power, the business of cricket, Abhijeet Chatterjee and MS Unnikrishnan, October, 24, 2004.* Available at: https://www.tribuneindia.com/2004/20041024/spectrum/main1.htm [Accessed 03 Mar. 2020].

Zee News, (2007). *Essel Group announces Indian Cricket League.* [online]. Available at: https://zeenews.india.com/sports/cricket/domestic-cricket-2012/essel-group-announces-indian-cricket-league_2116.html [Accessed 11 Mar. 2020].

Chapter 7

Sport and development in Indonesia

Sport policy in the Reformation era

Amung Ma'mun and Agus Mahendra

Introduction

This chapter discusses sport development in Indonesia, from the period of 1998 to the present. This period of history has been called the Reformation era and has witnessed five different presidents: B.J. Habibie (1998–1999), Abdurachman Wahid (1999–2000), Megawati Soekarno Putri (2000–2004), Susilo Bambang Yudoyono (SBY) (2004–2009 and 2009–2014) and Joko Widodo (2014–2019 and 2019 to date). However, the discussion of sport development, in general, will inevitably be connected with the preceding eras, *the old order era* (1945–1967) and *the new order era* (1967–1998). The scope of the discourse will cover the historical journey of sport development, the planning system and its implementation. This discourse reflects the development of the democratic political system in the country, which was allegedly based on the fourth amendment of the 1945 constitution.

At the beginning of the Reformation era (1998–1999 and 2000–2004), sport development was never a significant concern of the government, although the United Nations, in the same period, integrated sport into the Millennium Development Goal's (MDG's) for the 2000–2015 period. However, in 2005, Indonesian sport society was delighted when the new government launched the Law of the National Sports System (NSS). The ratification of this law, one that had been long awaited, was considered a victory by the community, for their efforts to develop the sport would have been legally reinforced by the formal policy. In essence, the Law of Sport put the emphasis on the government, both central and local, to plays the critical role in all efforts to develop the sport initiative in the country. With this emphasis, the sport community was convinced that the government would create a bigger budget for sport development efforts. The effort of the government to develop its sport initiative reached its peak at the moment Indonesia was entrusted to host the 2011 SEA Games and the XIV Asian Games 2018 in Jakarta and Palembang.

During the above period, the development of sports has always been connected with efforts to build the self-image of the country, both related to the national prestige earned when athletes obtain medals in international events and related to politics – crediting whoever was the leader in the moment the victory was accomplished.

The issue of Sport for Development and Peace (SDP) declared by the United Nations in the year of 2015–2030, under the umbrella of Sustainable Development Goals (SDGs), has never become an essential consideration in the view of the government. The practice of sport development in the Reformation era was mainly dominated by the frame of development of sport, aimed at fostering elite athletes in each biennial SEA Games, Asian Games and Olympic Games. From this perspective, it was not mentioned that the 2018 Asian Games hosted in Indonesia were considered a strategic moment to show to the Asian community that Indonesia has the ability to host sport mega-events.

Historical perspective of sport development in Indonesia

Indonesia is the largest archipelagic country in the world, with more than 17,504 islands and a population of 270,054,853 (BPS, 2018). Located in the South East region of Asia, most of the area of Indonesia was crossed by the equator and has been an independent country since 17 August 1945. Before its independence, Indonesia was a country that was occupied by the Dutch as a colony for about three and a half centuries and then by Japan for approximately four and a half years. Since its independence, there has been a process of replacing national leaders through general elections based on the 1945 Constitution.

During the time since independence, Indonesia has experienced the rise and fall of the Democracy of the Political System (DPS) but succeeded in electing its leaders (president and vice president), which political experts categorised as spanning three eras of national leadership orders, namely *the old order* (1945–1967) led by President Soekarno, *the new order* (1967–1998) led by President Soeharto and *the reform order* (1998–present) led by five presidents, as indicated previously. The sports policy that was implemented during these periods was reflecting the vision of each leader, so the style and the nuances of its leader also colouring much on how the government applied its sports development policies both in national and local government (Ma'mun, 2019b).

In *the Old Order* era, the development of sports in Indonesia was meaningfully utilised as an arena for international political diplomacy as part of the struggle of the nation to gain international recognition as a newly independent country. The International Olympic Committee's (IOC's) refusal of Indonesia to participate in the 1948 London Olympic Games was considered a very strategic moment for Indonesia, because it gave impetus to the birth of the 1948 National Sports Week (Games) in Solo, Central Java. The Games were more an arena for the country to declare its national pride and self-existence to the world, exhibiting that the country had become a free nation, independently existing and sovereign. It was also an event used to reinforce that all people were united, within regional identities.

It was in the same spirit that Indonesia also held the 4th Asian Games in Jakarta, in 1962. This mega event at that time was primarily used as an arena for international diplomacy in order to build new strength, followed by the hosting of the 1963 Games of the New Emerging Forces (GANEFO). This event was controversial because it was considered to be an adverse reaction to the sanctions set by the IOC, which, in turn, were a reaction to Indonesia's decision to break IOC rules by not inviting Israel and Taiwan to the Games as they were not bound by bilateral diplomatic relationships.

In fact, the 1963 GANEFO in Jakarta was initiated by Indonesia and supported by non-aligned countries as a cold war politics event, especially by those who attended the Asia Africa Conference in Bandung, Indonesia in 1955 (Trotier, 2017). Unfortunately, the 1963 GANEFO in Jakarta was the first and the last one (Lutan and Hong, 2005). However, on the other hand, the GANEFO fostered a love and a desire to participate in sport in the newly independent Indonesia people. It also encouraged a spirit of collectivism and confidence that the country would have the ability to fight together for national identity.

In *the New Order* era, the development of sport was continued by making improvements to the system and synchronizing international relations as the political strategy. In another stage, the new leader also believed that it was crucial to restore the relationship with the IOC for the sake of sport development. It was also critical to focus on bilateral relations with countries in Southeast Asia, by establishing the Association of Southeastern Asian Nations (ASEAN) organisation. It was then, on 8 August 1967, in Bangkok, that this regional organisation was founded by five original member countries: Indonesia, Malaysia, the Philippines, Singapore and Thailand (Cuyvers, Chen and Lombaerde, 2019). Ten years later, Indonesia participated for the first time, in the ASEAN multisport-event, known as the SEA Games of 1977.

Ever since, the focus of sport development in the country has shifted to efforts to expand sport as the mobilising means for the community to stay active, in line with the launch of UNESCO's charter on the importance of physical education and sports as human rights (UNESCO, 1978). As we have witnessed, it was this UNESCO charter that gave birth to the concept of *Sports for All* which was then translated as "*socializing sport and sporting society*" (Decree of the President of the Republic of Indonesia No. 17/1984 concerning Call for Sports at Work). To strengthen the previous decree, one year later, the President released the proceeding Decree No. 67/1985 on National Sports Day, to be celebrated on every 9 September, with the goal of developing a healthier Indonesia.

In *the Reformation* era, the development of sport was not employed adequately as the political vehicle to reconstruct something outside of the sport itself. The vision of the leader seemed to be more occupied with the attention on efforts to maintain the continuity of the national leadership dynamic pressure after President Soeharto resigned (1998). As a consequence, President B.J. Habibie (1998–1999) put his concentration more on the election process launched in 1999 and placed greater focus on improving the democratic political system. In addition, President Abdurachman Wahid (1999–2000), who was elected through a People's Consultative Assembly (PCA) session, made a drastic change by demolishing the existence of the Sport Ministry and put the function of sport development as part of the Ministry of Education at the level of Directorate General. Through his policy, the work of sport development as a government function was reduced to the smallest extent.

Since then, the policy and process of developing sport has continuously changed in line with the changes of the leadership policies along the decades. It was in the era of SBY that the sport affair was returned to the ministry level, with the creation of the Ministry of Youth and Sports (2004–2009 and 2009–2014) and continued in President Jokowi's era (2014–2019 and 2019–present).

There are two distinctive paradigms that can be identified and offered for these two country leaders to be chosen. They are the strong and dominant role of a government paradigm like China on one side; and the dominant role of the private sector or society like America on the other side. Indonesia seems to have chosen a position that prioritises the important role of the state and society together. Similarly, Indonesia is taking a middle ground in the implementation of sport development, where the role of the state or government and the community is equally important.

Sports systems and the structure of organised sport

Law No. 3/2005, concerning the NSS as the legal basis for organising sport development in Indonesia, essentially followed the Cooke (1997) sport development system model, better known as the House of Sport. This model was then further translated according to the historical outlook and basic comprehension of the country's leader to be modified and manifested in the country sport system. From this perspective, it is understandable that Cooke's model was easily accepted for its resemblance but broader and more comprehensive than the traditional pyramid model. This new model follows the underlying principles:

Stage 1 represents sport activities that form the foundation and are developed in the family and community, which can be described with five characteristics: simple, cheap, fun, massed, and beneficial. The emphasis was on how the public could fall in love with sport and participate regularly because sports contain so many benefits for health while being easy, cheap, fun and done with many other people. It is at this foundational level that people could understand what sport is, especially those related to human motion as a locus of sport, understand its benefits for quality of life, understand how to do it correctly, begin doing it regularly and, last but not least, enjoy it for the purpose of non-sport aspects, such as ethics and morals, social relations and psychological harmony.

Stage 2 represents sport activities developed in a formal educational environment, like school or clubs, in the name of sports education or physical education. This stage also includes sports and health subjects as well as school sports, such as extracurricular activities, student sports activities units, sports classes, and competitions. For this purpose, sports in an educational setting have been formed under the Ministry of National Education and Culture, namely the Indonesian Board of Sport (School) Students Development (BAPOPSI) and the Indonesian Board of Sports (University) Student Development (BAPOMI). The government representing the Ministry of National Education, by involving these two organisations (BAPOPSI and BAPOMI), regularly organise national sport competition activities in a biennial championship cycle.

Stage 3 represents sport activities in the recreational stream that grow and develop in the community as an effort to encourage community healthy active lifestyle, with facilitation and regulation from the government, such as the requirement that all government officials do sports or physical activities during a half day of office hours, sports for all activities in almost all public space available in the neighbourhood, healthy heart exercise, groups of active living for diabetics, healthy bicycle communities, and others. For these kinds of sports, the government encouraged the community to establish sport for all organisations (ICRSF: Indonesian Community and Recreation Sport Federation) and through the Ministry of Youth and Sports, this organisation was also financially subsidised.

Stage 4 represents sports activities for Elite athletes under the National Sports Federation (NSF). The NSF affiliates with the National Sport Committee (NSC) whose function is internal affairs, which in Indonesia, has been separated from the National Olympic Committee (NOC) whose function is more on international affairs. The difference between Indonesia's NSF and other countries is that it is structured at municipal, provincial and national levels.

In addition to the NSF that operates in each region, the National Sports Committee (NSC) has the same structure and essentially has the right to set policy in each region, especially on how each province can excel in terms of colleting medals in the National Games (held every four years). For that reason, the Provincial Sport Committees always strive to obtain more budget from provincial government. Likewise, the municipal sports committees require resources to prepare their elite athletes for the provincial games. The National Paralympic Committee (NPC) operates similarly in each region for the Paralympic games at each level.

Stage 5 represents superior sports that are developed and coordinated by prestigious sports associations in the country (and government) through the sports development centres in various regions and nationwide. To this date there are only two sports categorised as superior sports: badminton and weightlifting. This is only due to their achievement in the Olympic Games as they are the main source for medals gained. Badminton is considered unique since its organisational structure was fully occupied by famous former athletes and some high ranking outstanding military generals who devoted their time and budget to supporting the financial needs for the development processes. So far, badminton has become Indonesia's identity in world-class sports competition, in addition to its role in gaining national pride.

Stage 6 represents entertaining sports games that are integrated with community entertainment, such as soccer, basketball, futsal and volleyball. Those sports were facilitated by the private sector and supported by the government, along with the development of the sports industry containing high economic value.

Stage 7 represents the top sport in the form of high performance achievement in various multi-events and/or single events that elevates the nation's dignity. The top sports are represented by Badminton and Weight Lifting, two sports that regularly contribute the most gold medals in many Asian and Regional Championship events. The training and coaching system is directly carried out independently by NSF and coordinated by the Indonesia Gold Program (IGP) and the National Sports Development Centre (NSDC), among others. For this system to run, its financial expenses were provided fully by the government. Hence, all NSF executing those excellence programmes must be subject to government supervision. This coordination between IGP and NSDC was just like the triadic project among the ministry of youth and sport, NSC and all NSF.

In addition to the NSC, the Indonesian sport system also acknowledges the role of the NOC. As has been mandated by Law No. 3/2005 on NSS, the duties and functions of the NOC is more focused on international relationships, such as chairing and managing the Indonesian contingent to multi-sport event competition, attending the IOC and the Association of National Olympic Committees (ANOC) meetings, paving the way for bidding for and hosting the Regional Sport Organisation meetings and bidding for and hosting regional Games such as SEA Games and Asian Games. The success of this NOC effort was exemplified by the hosting and organising of the 2011 SEA Games and the 2018 Asian Games in Jakarta, Palembang.

To provide a clear picture regarding the Indonesian Sport System, we could take Cooke's model of the House of Sport as the analogy of the stages. This model was adopted in the period of SBY's leadership in 2010–2014 and was modified to cater to the specific needs of Indonesia characteristics. This model was called the National Sports Building Model (Strategic Plan of the Ministry of Youth and Sport, 2010–2014).

The framework of institutions related to sport development in Indonesia, both those formed by the government (governmental) and the community (nongovernmental) can be seen in Figure 7.1 below. From the figure, it can be seen that each institution is connected by arrow lines with different shapes. Each shape determines the relationship between the institutions, whether it means command or coordination.

Financial support for sport development

Overall, the financial support for the purpose of sport development in Indonesia is provided by the government in the form of grants or funds. Law Enactment number 25 of 2004 concerning the National Development Planning System (NDPS) outlines that every development sector including the sports sector is part of the national development system, both long term and medium term. In 2007, Law No. 17 regarding the National Long-Term Development Plan (NLTDP) considered sport as one sub-sector of the national development plan.

The budget obtained during the four years, from 2015 to 2018, is illustrated in Table 7.1 below. There was a significant increase in yearly budget in 2017 and 2018, for it coincided with the preparations for hosting the 2018 Asian Games.

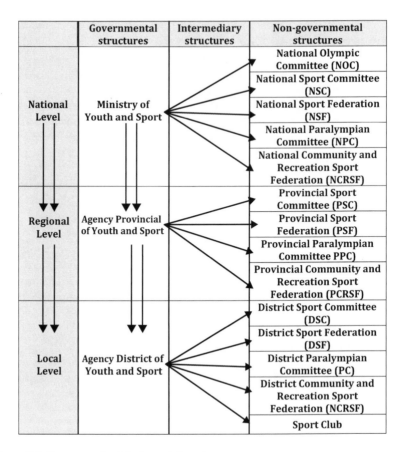

	Governmental structures	Intermediary structures	Non-governmental structures
National Level	**Ministry of Youth and Sport**		**National Olympic Committee (NOC)**
			National Sport Committee (NSC)
			National Sport Federation (NSF)
			National Paralympian Committee (NPC)
			National Community and Recreation Sport Federation (NCRSF)
Regional Level	**Agency Provincial of Youth and Sport**		**Provincial Sport Committee (PSC)**
			Provincial Sport Federation (PSF)
			Provincial Paralympian Committee PPC)
			Provincial Community and Recreation Sport Federation (PCRSF)
Local Level	**Agency District of Youth and Sport**		**District Sport Committee (DSC)**
			District Sport Federation (DSF)
			District Paralympian Committee (PC)
			District Community and Recreation Sport Federation (NCRSF)
			Sport Club

Figure 7.1 Framework of Indonesia's sport structure.

Policy on sports development in Indonesia

In line with the vision of the national leadership during the Reformation era, which was also influenced by the previous leadership era, sport development in Indonesia in general was built based on the theory of sport development developed by Cooke (1997), which placed the importance of the role of government and society together.

In article 17 of Law No. 3/2005 concerning NSS, the scope of sport consists of *educational sport*, *recreational sport* and *competitive sport*. Educational sport is all activities related to physical activities, physical education and sports competition organised in the milieu of schools (from Primary to Secondary High School), carried out as part of the educational process in obtaining knowledge, personality, skills, health and physical fitness (UU SKN, 2005). For this purpose, physical education and sport integrated into the educational curriculum at each level

Table 7.1 Budget allocation of the Ministry of Youth and Sports (2015–2018)

No	Budgeting field	2015	2016	2017	2018
1	Youth Sector	—	—	—	—
a	Youth Empowerment	—	—	135,000,000	211,381,000
b	Youth Development	—	—	319,000,000	186,600,000
2	Sports Sector	—	—	—	—
	Youth and Sport Empowerment	1,346,207,200	1,931,161,173	—	—
a	Civilization/Socialization	—	—	430,000,000	421,494,000
b	Achievement improvement for sport	1,361,972,200	1,071,344,173	1,962,000,000	3,917,000,000
3	Support/secretariat	256,929,276	262,372,968	292,000,000	300,009,000
4	Others	69,004,600	37,376,394	201,000,000	1,790,000,000
	Asian Games Organizing Committee	—	—	1,500,000,000	—
	Asian Games Athlete Development	—	—	140,000,000	735,006,000
	Amount	3,034,113,276	3,302,254,708	4,778,000,000	5,037,540,061
	Amount in US$	216,722.00	235,875.00	341,285.00	359,824.00
	Total State Budget	2,039,500,000	2,095,700,000	2,133,200,000	2,204,400,000
	Percentage (sport)	0,00129	0,001289	0,002046	0,00210

Source: Edited by the authors based on the data were derived from planning documents, accountability reports, newspapers and the Ministry of Youth and Sports and Ministry of Finance websites and State Revenue and Expenditure Budget.

should become a vehicle to develop both the students' potential and athletes' career paths. Physical education and sports ranging from primary education to secondary education are considered relatively adequate in teaching physical activity and sport culture of the society in navigating daily life throughout childhood and adulthood.

Recreational sports are sports that are carried out by people with a passion and ability to grow and develop in accordance with the conditions and cultural values of the local community for the purposes of improving health, fitness and excitement (UU SKN, 2005). In general, recreational sports are synonymous with filling leisure time. Over time, the position of sports has become increasingly crucial in utilising the leisure time of city dwellers (Depei, 1989). Physical activities and sports are the choice of the community, intended to maintain health while building social interaction and excitement so that people are encouraged to schedule physical activity and sports in their free time and daily activities.

Competitive sports are sports that foster and develop athletes in a planned, tiered and sustainable manner through systematic training sessions and regular competitions to achieve high performance with the support of sports science and technology (UU SKN, 2005). This achievement is based on the FTEM concept that has been developed in Australia, namely: Foundation, organised by educational institutions and the community that is fun, without coercion, and without competition; Talent, which focuses on further coaching that is more directed, both in the training system, the specificity of the type of sport, as well as the organisation, along with a model of collaboration with educational institutions to expand sports activities accompanied by tiered initial competition activities; Elite, is a coaching stage in addition to a more programmed training process, both in associations and at the training centre accompanied by a scheduled, tiered and sustainable participation in the local and national competition system; and Mastery, a group of athletes that are fostered in on-going training camps throughout the year and/or are fostered in an association, ready to defend the name of the country in the arena of international competition (Gulbin et al., 2013a). The FTEM rules are in line with the elite athlete development model through the concept of the Athlete Development Triangle (ADT) (Gulbin et al., 2013b).

The development of educational sports

Fostering and developing educational sports includes comprehensive organisation related to sports education. This involves the standardisation of its implementation, regarding its human resources, facilities and infrastructure in all lines and levels of education.

The role of the government is to incorporate sports activities of non-physical education and sports as part of intra-curricular in schools, extracurricular, sports activities units (school sports clubs), sports classes, student coaching and training centres, and sports schools. This programme requires a competition system that runs throughout the year. Unfortunately, the competition system is not integrated into the community, because it is infrequent for school sports clubs to partner with community sports clubs (club links). The competition system targeting all school levels only took place just as routine ceremonial celebrations of school events.

The development of recreational sports

Physical activities and sports for the community are directly focused on improving the quality of life of the community members. For that purpose, the community is encouraged to adopt an active lifestyle, and one of the strategies to drive the people to sport is by providing guidelines and information about physical activities. Community participation rates in sports are continuously driven through the promotion of sport and physical activities by the government and other sport organisations on any great day celebration or even exposed in many TV programmes. This was implemented in conjunction with the UNESCO declaration of the importance of physical education and sports (1978). Indonesia made a strategic and relevant 'motto' for promoting sports through Presidential Decree number 17/1984 and yearly celebration of National Sports Day on September 9. In the Reformation era, the motto "let us do sport" was also created and promoted as a movement to increase participation numbers within the community.

A particular challenge for Indonesia was how sport could become an integral part of the concept of "sport for development and peace" launched by the United Nations through the Sustainable Development Goals (SDGs) in 2015–2030 and the MDG's in 2000–2015. Sports for development and peace in the umbrella of SDGs offers a practical approach for sports programs to be conceptualised and organised as part of a holistic approach (Darnell and Dao, 2017). SDP is a rapidly developing field of activity in which sport is used as an intervention tool to pursue broader social goals, not just sports objectives (Giulianotti, Hognestad and Spaaij, 2016).

The development of competitive sports

Fostering and developing overall performance sports from the stage of talent development to the elite Olympic class athletes continue to be goals. However, since the development programme through educational sport has not been well organised and cannot support the development of elite sports, this arm of sport strategy hasn't seen much improvement, except in some provinces where training centres, student training and sports schools have been integrated successfully. In addition, the development of associations has not been widespread, and the annual competition system is weak. Only a few sports such as soccer, basketball, volleyball, futsal, and other sports that have their own competition calendar saw improvements in both the organisation and the performance gain for their athletes.

System of elite sports in preparation for multi-sport events

The preparation of elite athletes for multi-sport events such as SEA Games, Asian Games, Olympic Games and other single-sport events is generally executed by the NSF. Only with some exceptions is the preparation of elite athletes conducted by the National Training Centre of Sports (NTCS), under auspices of the Ministry of Youth and Sport as the government representatives. However, in that case, the involvement of sports personnel from the NSC, NOC or NSF will still exist. The preparation process of developing badminton athletes that adheres to the FTEM and ADT rules demonstrates the significant influence of this government involvement on badminton's progress. Badminton itself is the only sports federation in Indonesia that has its own system, both in expanding badminton as a cultural activity (foundation and talent) and in the development of the elite level.

Sports competition system and its challenges

The competition model being developed in Indonesia is oriented to the type of sport (single event) following FTEM and ADT rules and the government system (municipal, provincial and national). However, while the model may be simple, putting it into practice in Indonesia has not been easy, as the multi-sport event competition has been relatively developed for decades, even in the beginning of this nation. The competition model of Indonesia has been based regional and national competition. The National Sport Games (NSG) were held for the first time in 1951, and the regional sport games were also organised following afterward.

It should be wisely understood that, for Indonesia, the development of NSG had its root in the IOC's rejection of Indonesia's participation in the London Olympic Games in 1948. The NSG was an alternative created by the founding father of the country to develop and build the national identity of the new emerging country to catalyse unity in the spirit of independent Indonesia (Ma'mun, 2019a). However, in its further development, the implementation of the spirit of the NSG has been systematically ignored and the spirit of noble sport values unconsciously abandoned. Nowadays, NSG and regional sport games (RSG) (Lim and Aman, 2016) experience changes to the number of events to provide an advantage to the hosting province or city to become the winning team. In other words, the hosting province or city would arbitrarily add events in some sports, especially in the events they are strong at, only for the sake of drastically increasing their medals tally. In that situation many athletes migrate from one region to another region just to earn more money for the medals they collected.

From an academic perspective, these practices were considered unfair and not at all healthy for sport development itself. Efforts have been made to minimise these loopholes by standardising regulation regarding the participants' enrollment based on age limit and performance levels. Following lessons from other countries, academic studies with the involvement of the government and

Table 7.2 The comparison between numbers of matches in national games and other events

No.	Games	Province/country, year and number of events		
1	National Games	East Kalimantan 2008 **755**	Riau 2012 **650**	West Java 2016 **756**
2	SEA Games	Indonesia 2011 **554**	Myanmar 2013 **461**	Singapore 2015 **402**
3	Asian Games	PRC 2010 **477**	South Korea 2014 **436**	Indonesia 2018 **485**
4	Olympic Games	PRC 2008 **302**	England 2012 **302**	Brazil 2016 **306**

Source: Adapted from Ma'mun et al. (2018).

bureaucracy that outline the practice of applying appropriate and measurable regulations, must be a criterion that is used as a common reference (Tinaz, Turco, and Salisbury, 2014). The comparison of the numbers of events is summarised in Table 7.2 below, between NG, SEA Games, Asian Games, and Olympic Games in three periods.

While the competition management of the elite stream has not yet been refined in terms of its competition format (Harris and Houlihan, 2015), the same pattern has also been replicated by other forms of competition. To name a few, Indonesia has also developed competition for students, in the national, provincial and municipal levels. In this students' competition there are two streams of competition: first, the National/Provincial Student Sport Games, organized by the Ministry of Youth and Sport, and second, the National/Provincial Students Olympiad Games, organized by the Ministry of Education and Culture. In the university level, there has been a competition called the National University Students Sports Games, organised by the Ministry of Education and Culture under the auspices of the Directorate General for Higher Education. Those student competitions were organised on a regional or provincial basis.

Other than the above competition organised regularly on such an annual or biennial basis, Indonesia also has a competition for the members of civil services from different ministries of government offices and a competition organized for members of the educational services, including teachers and lectures. These are organised both for the national level and provincial level. The members of the military services were also provided with the same competition structure. All these competitions were financially born by the institution budget, which originated from the government's annual budget. All those situations will, of course, need a comprehensive evaluation whether all those competition are really needed and give benefit to people's health, for instance.

Conclusion

Sports development proliferating in a country, as happened in Indonesia, could never be separated from the local situation of the country, which also influences the policy priorities declared and implemented by its leaders. Thus, the national leadership of a country need to exercise its power and policy choices in various fields of development, including in the field of sports.

The sport development in Indonesia in the Reformation era, at an early stage, stagnated due to leadership transitions, which sometimes produced political turbulence. However, changes in leadership colour the policies chosen and adopted, as some leaders focus less on sports and more on political stability, while others find ways to expand sport development in conjunction with their political strategies. In that context, sport policy is more a reflection of how a leader comprehends the realm of his country being led, his vision for the future, and his manifestation of that vision.

For Indonesia, the legal basis for the implementation of sports development, Law No. 3/2005 on NSS, was successfully established by referring to the theory of Cooke (1997), known as the House of Sport, for which it was then adjusted to prioritize policies and experience of sports development from the previous era. This theory was adopted with slightly different emphasis by tasking the sports development system solely to developing the sport as it was implemented in other countries - that is, to obtain the highest performance. This fact has influenced the public's perspective that sport is synonymous with athletes, training, winning competition, collecting medals and awards. As a result, Indonesia is still far from the achieving the goals of the SDP strategy.

Sport development in its broadest scope, as outlined in Law no. 3/2005 on NSS, should be equally focused on educational, recreational and high-performance sports. Educational sports take place in schools and colleges, including physical education, sports and health as subjects, sports extracurricular activities and sport clubs in school as a talent development arena. Recreational sports, on the other hand, are more about developing public space, sports clubs in the community and festivals. High-performance sports are developed at sporting associations in the community, coordinated by the National Sports Federation and sports development centres in various regions nationwide.

Last but not least, the competition system needs to be perpetuated by encouraging more single-sport competition to be regularly and more frequently conducted in the NSF competition system. In other words, competitions needs to not rely on multi-sport events, which are scheduled every two and four years. At the same time, a competition system focusing on those sport industries gaining economic value also need to be regularly scheduled, as well as competitions that provide the broadest opportunities for young people relevant to the Sport Development Policy principle.

References

BPS, (2018). *Statistical Yearbook of Indonesia 2018*, Badan Pusat Statistik. Jakarta. ISSN: 0126-2912.

Cooke, G. (1997). Pathways to success: A new model for talent development. *Super Coach* (a publication of the National Coaching Foundation), 8(5), pp. 10–11.

Cuyvers, L., Chen, L. and Lombaerde, P. (2019). 50 years of regional integration in ASEAN. *Asia Pacific Business Review*, 25(5), pp. 609–618.

Darnell, S.C. and Dao, M. (2017). Considering sport for development and peace through the capabilities approach. *Third World Thematics: A TWQ Journal*, 2(1), pp. 23–36.

Depei, L. (1989). Sports and the leisure lives of Chinese City Dwellers. *Loisir et Société / Society and Leisure*, 12(2), pp. 325–340.

Giulianotti, R., Hognestad, H. and Spaaij, R. (2016). Sport for development and peace: Power, politics, and patronage. *Journal of Global Sport Management*, 1(3–4), pp. 129–141.

Gulbin, J.P., Croser, M.J., Morley, E.J. and Weissensteiner, J.R. (2013a). A closer look at the FTEM framework. Response to "more of the same? Comment on 'An integrated framework for the optimisation of sport and athlete development: A practitioner approach'". *Journal of Sports Sciences*, 31, pp. 1319–1331.

Gulbin, J., Weissensteiner, J.R., Oldenziel, K. and Gagné, F. (2013b). Patterns of performance development in elite athletes. *European Journal of Sport Science*, 13(6), pp. 605–614.

Harris, S. and Houlihan, B. (2015). Competition or coalition? Evaluating the attitudes of National Governing Bodies of Sport and Country Sports Partnerships towards School Sport Partnerships. *International Journal of Sport Policy and Politics*, 8(1), pp. 1–21.

Lim, P. H. and Aman, M. S. (2016). The history of the South East Asian Peninsular Games, 1959–1975. *International Journal of the History of Sport*, 33(5), pp. 545–568.

Lutan, R. and Hong, F. (2005). The politicisation of sport: GANEFO–A case study. *Sport in Society*, 8(3), pp. 425–439.

Ma'mun, A. (2018). *Pembangunan Olahraga Nasional*. Bandung: Lekkas.

Ma'mun, A. (2019a). Governmental roles in Indonesian sport policy: From past to present. *International Journal of the History of Sport*, 36(4–5), pp. 388–405–19.

Ma'mun, A. (2019b). *Kebijakan Olahraga Indonesia: Dulu, Sekarang dan Tantangan Masa Depan*. Bandung: Makalah Posisi Guru Besar.

Ma'mun, M., Abdullah, C.U., Slamet, S. and Khairunnisa R. (2018). The Indonesian national sports games: Expectations and reality. *Jurnal Pendidikan Jasmani dan Olahraga*, 3(1), pp. 122–128.

Tinaz, C., Turco D.M. and Salisbury, P. (2014). Sport policy in Turkey. *International Journal of Sport Policy and Politics*, 6(3), pp. 533–545.

Trotier, F. (2017). The legacy of the games of the new emerging forces and Indonesia's relationship with the International Olympic Committee. *The International Journal of the History of Sport*, 33(12), pp. 1–20.

UNESCO, (1978). *International charter of physical education and sport*. [online]. Available at: https://unesdoc.unesco.org/ark:/48223/pf0000216489 [Accessed 19 May 2020].

UU SKN, (2005). Undang Republik Indonesia. Nomor 3 Tahun 2005, Tetang Sistem Keolahragaan Nasional. Kemenpora: Jakarta.

Chapter 8

Sport and development in Mexico

NGOs and community-based organisations underpinned by neo-liberal logics using sport as educational tools

Vanessa García González

Introduction

Playing sport has been turned into a social practice used as a tool to generate positive outcomes that lay beyond the realm of leisure or pleasure among the most disadvantaged communities in the world. Different stakeholders, such as the United Nations (UN), the International Olympic Committee (IOC), national governments, major professional sport leagues, the academic community and civic society, have argued that the Sport for Development and Peace (SDP) movement has remobilised sport as a vehicle for broad, sustainable social development (Kidd, 2008) for populations that lack participation opportunities and face challenges caused by poverty, war, natural disasters or oppression (Coakley, 2011). Nowadays, as Giulianotti et al. (2019) have argued, SDP has become a distinctive and strongly institutionalised field of international development activity, with its networks of stakeholders that can be described through the concept of *Sportland*, which:

> ... is intended to encapsulate the metaphorical, separate world inhabited by SDP officials, volunteers, researchers, and consultants, with their own networks, discourses and customs, which are anchored in the convictions (or hopes), held with varying degrees of critical reflection or fervour, that sport can contribute towards development and peace ....
>
> (Giulianotti et al., 2019, p. 3)

Svensson and Woods (2017) argued that Latin America remains mostly under-represented in SDP research. Furthermore, in their systematic overview of SDP organisations around the world (n = 944), these authors identified that 99 (10.5%) of the organisations included in their study operated somewhere in Latin America. Still, only 84 of them were headquartered in the region. On the other hand, in an integrated literature review conducted by Schulenkorf, Sherry and Rowe (2016), the authors reported that the top five nations for academics undertaking sport-for-development research (viz. the United States, the United Kingdom,

Australia, Canada and South Africa) were also the top five research sites. Accord-ing to Svensson and Woods, "this lack of research on Latin America is concern-ing, since established SDP models and theories may not be suitable for the Latin American contexts" (2017, p. 42). In this sense, there is a gap in the literature regarding specific SDP practices and research in Latin America, Mexico included, which must be addressed. Findings presented in this chapter aim to contribute to bridging this gap.

There is a need to identify the scope and diversity of SDP initiatives actually operating in Mexico in an effort to pinpoint specific aspects, challenges and op-portunities the Sportland field is facing in the country, along with the specific locations and types of programmes delivered. Such a study can help us to un-derstand how sport is contributing to development in Mexico and to identify future directions for researchers, practitioners and policymakers. Accordingly, the purpose of this chapter was to reflect on a systematic analysis of SDP organisa-tions in Mexico in order to determine: where grassroots SDP organisations are located in Mexico, along with a time frame for SDP programmes operating in the country; the main thematic area of SDP initiatives; the type of sport used to deliver programming; target population and social issues addressed through SDP programming; publicly available information (i.e., results, evaluation and annual reports); and funding sources reported by organisations operating grassroots SDP programmes in Mexico.

After presenting a brief description of the background and methods used to conduct this study, findings are discussed in six sections. These include describ-ing Sportland practices and agents in Mexico, first as mainstream NGOs and community-based organisations underpinned by neo-liberal logics and then as agents operating within 'bubbles' of networks and resources. Target populations and social issues addressed by SDP programming in Mexico are described as ex-amples of *developmental interventionism* themes. Next, grounded on available data, it is argued that developmental interventions of Sportland agents in Mexico are mainly focused on using sport as an educational tool. Additionally, preferred sports to deliver SDP programming are presented. Finally, it is discussed how relying on the *Great Sports Myth* is a distinctive feature of Sportland practices in Mexico.

Social contrasts in Mexico

According to the World Bank Country Classification for the 2020 fiscal year, Mexico is an upper-middle-income economy (World Bank, 2020a) with a popula-tion of almost 120 million (INEGI, 2020b). It has a Human Development Index of 0.767 (PNUD, 2019) and a Gini Index of 45.4 (BM, 2020). Mexico is a country with great cultural diversity, a rich history and abundant natural resources. Fur-thermore, Mexico is a country of great contrasts and inequalities. Although it is the second largest economy in Latin America and the 11th largest economy in the world (World Bank, 2020b), there are 61.1 million people (48.8% of the total population) living on an income below the monetary poverty line; of these, 21 million do not have sufficient economic resources to afford basic food products (CONEVAL, 2018). Adding to these contrasts, according to Campos, Esquivel and Chávez (in Esquivel, 2015), the wealth share of the wealthiest 1% in Mexico accounted for 21% of the total income in the country. Moreover, *The Global Wealth Report 2019* noted that the share of the wealthiest 10% in Mexico concentrated 62.8% of the total wealth in the country (Credit Suisse, 2019).

Social and economic contrasts in Mexico can also be geographically linked. For instance, in 2018, 76.4% of the population in the state of Chiapas was poor, followed by Guerrero (66.5%) and Oaxaca (66.4%). These three states are located in southern Mexico, where they have abundant natural resources, wide ethnical diversity and a rich historical background. However, the state with the highest absolute number of poor people is located in the central region, namely the State of Mexico (7.5 million). In contrast, the northern states of Nuevo Leon (14.5%), Baja California Sur (18.1%) and Coahuila (22.5%) were the states with the lowest percentage of poor people (CONEVAL, 2018).

Additionally, it is worth mentioning that millions of Mexicans face social deprivations in multiple dimensions. For instance, as reported by the National Council for the Evaluation of Social Development Policy (CONEVAL) in 2018, as in all previously reported years (2008–2016), the area with the highest deprivation population-wise is access to social security (i.e., insurance against health or labour risks and old age pensions), as 71.7 million Mexicans lacked this support in that year. The next most widespread deprivations in Mexico were: lack of access to nutritious and quality food (25.5 million); lack of basic housing services (24.7 million); educational lag (21.1 million); lack of access to health services (20.2 million) and housing with an inadequate quality or insufficient space (13.8 million). It is worth noticing that the number of people suffering economic and social deprivations in Mexico and around the world is expected to increase due to the Covid-19 pandemic (Ahmed et al., 2020; Dorn, Cooney and Sabin, 2020).

The most vulnerable groups in Mexico are children, teenagers, youth, seniors (aged 65 years or older), those with a mental or physical disability and indigenous peoples (CONEVAL, 2018). These groups are systematically at a higher risk of living in conditions that threaten their dignity and limit their rights and freedoms, preventing the fulfilment of their basic needs and hampering their full social integration.

Regarding social rights in Mexico, access to physical culture and sport participation is stipulated as a fundamental right for all Mexicans in Article 4 of the Mexican Political Constitution. Additionally, this fundamental right is regulated by the General Law in Physical Culture and Sport (LGCFyD, Ley General de Cultura Física y Deportes), in which sport is defined as an organised and regulated physical activity that aims to preserve and improve physical and mental health as well as social, ethical and intellectual development, the former through the achievement of results in competitions (Cámara de Diputados, 2019). The LGCFyD distinguishes at least three types of sports: (a) social; (b) performance and (c) high performance. However, resources are allocated unevenly among these three sectors, with the high-performance sector receiving the highest percentage among the three.

Despite the government recognising sport participation as a fundamental right for all Mexicans, regardless of gender, age, ethnicity, economical status or religious beliefs, in 2019, less than half (42.1%) of the population 18 years and older played a sport in their spare time (according to data collected by INEGI through the Sports Practice and Physical Exercise Module: MOPRADEF, Módulo de Práctica Deportiva y Ejercicio Físico). This value is 1.9 points lower than the 44% reported by the same source in 2015 (INEGI, 2020a), indicating a worrying decline in sport participation. Pöllmann and Sánchez Graillet (2015) reported similar findings in 2015, based on data collected through a national survey. Their results showed only a third (34.3%) of the respondents declared playing a sport. Additionally, in a national study published in 2011, it was reported that only 40% of children and youth between the ages of 5 and 18 years old played a sport (Arellano Trejo and Tenorio Colón, 2011). The landscape depicted in this section shows the potential for a range of SDP organisations to deliver their programming in Mexico.

A systematic analysis of SDP organisations

In order to address the issues and knowledge gaps identified, the author undertook a systematic analysis of organisations involved in the operation of grassroots SDP practices in Mexico. Following the methods proposed by Svensson and Woods (2017), between November 2019 and January 2020, data was retrieved by reviewing the organisational lists of the *Beyond Sport Network*, the International Platform for Sport and Development and the streetfootballworld. Additionally, a manual search of Mexican 'social sport' organisations was also completed on the Internet, looking for entities referred to as allies by the organisations identified in the earlier stage. Specifically, the organisational network lists of the *Laureus Sport for Good Foundation, Fight For Peace* and *Coaches across Continents* were checked. For the purposes of this review, an organisation was included when its purpose was primarily focused on using grassroots sports for social change, meaning these organisations combined sports activities at the grassroots level with at least one non-sport activity (e.g., academic enrichment, career development, health awareness, peace-building, social inclusion and building sport facilities, among others) and showed evidence of a plus-sport or sport-plus intervention (Coalter, 2010). Data was collected from sources written in Spanish, English and Portuguese.

Mainstream NGOs and community-based organisations underpinned by neo-liberal logics

A total of 33 organisations met the inclusion criteria for this study. These organisations were either mainstream NGOs or community-based organisations (e.g., religious bodies, hobby and sports groups and youth movements) delivering SDP programming in partnership with business corporations and government agencies. Of these, 31 organisations were found to have a publicly available creation or arrival date in Mexico. The entities under examination were determined to have operated SDP programming somewhere in Mexico at some point between 1985 and December 2019. Most entities (87%, n = 27) were created or started delivering their grassroots SDP programmes in Mexico between 2007 and 2017. More specifically, close to 60% of the organisations (n = 18) started running SDP programming between 2012 and 2015. A total of three organisations were founded between 1985 and 1988. However, it is not clear if they had been using grassroots sports for social change since their inception or if they incorporated SDP programming later on. Among the entities in the study, the oldest organisation claiming in its organisational description to only deliver SDP programming surfaced in 1999.

The blooming of organisations operating grassroots SDP programmes in Mexico in the 2000s and 2010s concurs with the institutionalisation of the Sportland field globally (Darnell, Field and Kidd, 2019; Giulianotti et al., 2019). At the same time, this phenomenon converges with at least two developments in Mexico: (a) the late consolidation of sports institutionalisation in the country through the passing and constant reformulation of a law related to sports in the 2000s and 2010s, along with the strengthening of the National Commission of Physical Culture and Sport (CONADE, Comision Nacional de Cultura Física y Deporte) as the institution in charge of sport policy in the country and (b) an institutional shift towards the implementation of social policies based on evidence, linked to the passing of the General Law of Social Development (LGDS, Ley General de Desarrollo Social) in 2004, along with the creation of government institutions such as CONEVAL to measure, for the first time in the country, poverty from a multidimensional spectrum and to systematically evaluate social programmes implemented by the state.

These developments in Mexico are of relevance to the Sportland field in the country at different levels that require further analysis. However, at first glance, the sports-related laws that were passed opened up the possibility for the social and private sectors to participate in the Mexican Sport System, with granting tax incentives as one possibility. This is an example of "signature neo-liberal policies of deregulation, privatisation and the 'rolling back' of welfare services" (Giulianotti, 2011, p. 767), in this case, to let private corporations serve choice-making individual consumers of sports.

On the other hand, the recognition of social rights (e.g., access to food, health, education, social security or dignified housing), along with the availability of evidence showing millions of Mexicans experiencing not only economic disadvantages but also a variety of social depravations converged, amongst other things, with the involvement of a variety of actors, civic society included, to aid the Mexican government in tackling this wide range of social deprivations along with related issues, such as violence and insecurity. NGOs and community-based organisations delivering SDP programming in Mexico have illustrated these developments, as described by Hartmann and Kwauk: "... SDP programs represent low-cost, short-termed, neoliberal alternatives to the substantive delivery of youth, sport and educational services by the state" (in Giulianotti et al., 2019, p. 415).

In line with Giulianotti's ideal type of mainstream NGOs and community-based organisations (2011), it was found that the entities included in this study implemented sports-related interventions by themselves with support from outside institutions, most of them in the form of 'public-private partnerships'. The funding sources of SDP programming were identified for 32 of the 33 organisations in the study. Besides retrieving information from programme (n = 33) and organisational descriptions (n = 28), along with annual reports (n = 11) and mission statements (n = 22), additional information was extracted from organisational websites (n = 23) or network digital platforms (n = 10). Based on these, it was determined that the SDP organisations in the study obtained resources (e.g., financial, material and human) to operate through at least one of the following five main funding sources: voluntary donations through a web site, the Mexican government, international funding agencies, private companies and universities.

The majority of SDP organisations (84.4%, n = 27) asked for donations through a website. Additionally, a total of 44% of the SDP organisations (n = 14) reported receiving some sort of aid from the Mexican government (at the federal, state or municipal level). Furthermore, more than a third (34.4%) of the entities (n = 11) stated being supported by one or more international funding agencies. Likewise, more than a third (34.4%) of the SDP organisations (n = 11) identified being assisted by private companies (national or transnational). Moreover, 19% of the entities (n = 6) disclosed being the beneficiaries of a Mexican university; most of the universities mentioned were private institutions linked to the Catholic Church.

As it was outlined earlier, more than a third of the NGOs and community-based organisations delivering SDP programming included in this study were associated with national or transnational business corporations (e.g., Nike, Coca-Cola, Bayer, Ford, Mattel, Lego, LaLa and Bimbo), listing them as allies funding their SDP programming efforts under the label of corporate social responsibility (CSR). Further research is needed to inquire about the relations with donors, especially about the commitments towards and the involvement of those funding agencies (i.e., business corporations, international funding agencies, the Mexican government and universities). Overall, the nature of the power relations between SDP organisations and funding agencies requires further exploration. This is particularly so in the case of business corporations, considering that one of the biggest health concerns in Mexico is the obesity pandemic (seven out of every ten adult Mexicans is either overweight or obese: INEGI, 2019) and that companies from the processed food (e.g., Bimbo) and sweet beverages industry (e.g., Coca-Cola), as well as fast food chains (e.g., Carl's Jr.), are funding SDP programmes in Mexico.

Sportland agents operating within 'bubbles' of networks and resources

The geographical location of SDP programming was identified for 32 out of the 33 organisations in the study. Of these, 66% (n = 21) specified the city or locality in which they have delivered their grassroots programming. Of these, only two delivered programming in rural areas, the rest operated in urban settings, high-lighting the fact that 11 of them were capital cities. Close to 88% of the entities (n = 28) under examination were headquartered somewhere in Mexico. Of these, three operated SDP programmes in other countries as well. Four of the organisa-tions in the study (12.5%) were found to be headquartered abroad; two were based in the United States, one in Chile and another in the United Kingdom.

Furthermore, the majority of the organisations (n = 22) in the study were de-termined to have delivered programming in only one state. Of these, 20 entities were headquartered in the same state where they operated their SDP programmes; the remaining two were headquartered abroad. Additionally, it was found that ten organisations operated in multiple states. Of these, six were headquartered in Mexico City, one in Sinaloa, another in Tamaulipas and the remaining two in another country.

Overall, it was found that SDP programmes have operated in all 32 states (Table 8.1) in Mexico at some point during the period contemplated in this study (1985–December 2019). Half of the organisations (n = 16) have delivered grass-roots programming in Mexico City. In the states of Mexico, Jalisco and Morelos, seven different organisations have operated in each of them, followed by Baja Cal-ifornia and Oaxaca with six different organisations each, while in Chiapas, Chi-huahua, Durango, Guanajuato, Michoacan and San Luis Potosi, there have been five distinct organisations operating in each of them. As shown in Table 8.1, four dissimilar entities were found to have delivered SDP programming in 11 states, and in the remaining nine states, the same three organisations have operated at some point in each of them. It is worth mentioning that the three aforementioned entities have actually operated in all 32 states of Mexico. In addition, it was found that seven out of the 32 organisations have operated in multiple states spread all over the country. Figure 8.1 provides a visual overview of the location of the organisations that have operated SDP programmes in Mexico.

Table 8.1 Geographical location of SDP organisations in Mexico

States	No. of organisations
Mexico City	16
State of Mexico, Jalisco, Morelos	7
Baja California, Oaxaca	6
Chiapas, Chihuahua, Durango, Guanajuato, Michoacán, San Luis Potosí	5
Aguascalientes, Campeche, Guerrero, Hidalgo, Nuevo León, Puebla, Querétaro, Quintana Roo, Sinaloa, Sonora, Tamaulipas	4
Baja California Sur, Coahuila, Colima, Nayarit, Tabasco, Tlaxcala, Veracruz, Yucatán, Zacatecas	3

Note: The number of organisations does not add up to 31 because 10 of them operate in multiple states; of these, three operate in all the states of Mexico.

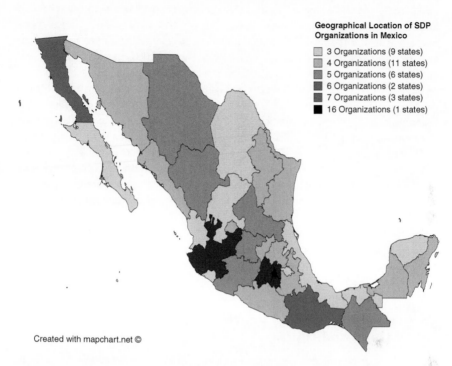

Geographical Location of SDP
Organizations in Mexico

☐ 3 Organizations (9 states)
☐ 4 Organizations (11 states)
▨ 5 Organizations (6 states)
▨ 6 Organizations (2 states)
▨ 7 Organizations (3 states)
■ 16 Organizations (1 states)

Created with mapchart.net ©

Figure 8.1 Geographical location of SDP organisations in Mexico.

These results related to the geographical location of SDP organisations indicate that Mexico City is overrepresented, as not only 16 out of the 33 entities under examination operated SDP programmes there but also 6 out of the 10 organisations operating in multiple states were headquartered there as well. Additionally, we have to consider that the organisations delivering SDP programming in the State of Mexico are located in municipalities surrounding Mexico City; in other words, they are situated in what is known as the Mexican Valley Metropolitan Zone (ZMVM, Zona Metropolitana del Valle de Mexico). This area is the capital of a heavily centralised country. According to the Organisation for Economic Co-operation and Development (OECD, 2015), the ZMVM is Mexico's economic, financial, political and cultural core. It is the OECD's third largest Metropolitan area, with more than 20 million people living there representing 17% of the total national population. Therefore, the concentration of SDP organisations operating and headquartered in this area may be related to the concentration of resources of various types in the ZMVM.

The Sportland notion introduced by Giulianotti, Colter, Collison and Darnell in 2019 may be of aid in understanding this concentration of SDP organisations in the ZMVM as well as in urban settings, particularly in capital cities across the country. These authors suggest that SDP "agencies, officials and experts work with familiar networks, partnerships, policies and practice, rather than being open to alternative agencies, new voices, and innovative or disruptive types of knowledge" (Whiteley et al. in Giulianotti et al., 2019, p. 413). This suggests that Sportland agents operating in Mexico may be reproducing practices found in Aidland by operating within exclusive 'spaces of aid' and working within the 'bubbles' of networks and resources structured within the ZMVM, and capital cities. In this sense, agents in the SDP sector in Mexico may be reproducing hegemonic practices from the Global North, although research is needed to further explore this hypothesis. In this regard, research inquiring about the profiles and backgrounds of agents delivering SDP programmes, particularly digging into their cultural and social capitals, may shed some light on Sportland practices in Mexico.

Contrary to the overrepresentation of the ZMVM, an underrepresentation of SDP organisations was identified in the states of Chiapas and Guerrero, which hold the highest percentage of the deprived population in the country (CONEVAL, 2018). Rural settings were also inadequately represented. Some of the challenges faced by the Sportland field in Mexico have to do with working outside the bubbles of resources and networks to implement programming in rural settings, particularly in those situated in the poorest regions in the country to reach the most deprived (economically and socially) populations.

Targeting children and youth living in vulnerable conditions

A total of 32 organisations were found to identify the target group receiving their SDP programming either in their mission statement or in their organisational and programme descriptions. Of these, close to a third (31.3%) of the SDP organisations (n = 10) were identified as mainly orienting their grassroots programming efforts to help children and youth. A total of 28.1% of the entities (n = 9) stated that children alone were their target population of choice. Similarly, another 28.1% of the organisations delivered their SDP programming to a predominantly youth population (n = 9). This was followed by entities aiming to aid communities with high violence rates (6.3%, n = 2), those fighting for the recognition of generic gender identities (3.1%, n = 1) and others seeking to help adults deprived of their liberty (3.1%, n = 1). It is worth mentioning that organisations targeting children, youth or both represent a total of 88% of the SDP entities in the study (n = 28).

Based on information retrieved from annual reports (n = 11) and organisational (n = 28) and programme descriptions (n = 33), 85% of the organisations (n = 28) in the study were found to use a combination of the following social issues to describe the communities of their target populations – and to justify the necessity of their grassroots SDP programming: domestic or organised crime violence (n = 14); vulnerability (n = 9); poverty, impoverishment, low income, or scare resources (n = 9); drug addiction (n = 7); marginalisation (n = 6); at risk (n = 6); crime, including delinquency (n = 5); alcohol abuse (n = 3); gangs (n = 3); homelessness (n = 3); socially disadvantaged position (n = 3); school desertion (n = 2); insecurity (n = 2); social exclusion (n = 2); immigrants on their way to the United States (n = 1), phobia (n = 1); remote places (n = 1) and social abandonment (n = 1).

A total of 18.2% of the organisations (n = 6) under examination stated that their SDP programming aimed to address one or more of the 17 Sustainable Development Goals (SDG) contemplated in the 2030 UN Agenda. Of these, five of the organisations identified operating SDP programmes to contribute to the achievement of SDG 5 – Gender Equality. This was followed by SDG 16 – Peace, Justice and Strong Institutions (n = 4); SDG 1 – No Poverty (n = 3); SDG 4 – Quality Education (n = 3); SDG 8 – Decent Work and Economic Growth (n = 3) and SDG 11 – Sustainable Cities and Communities (n = 2).

This evidence suggests that the identified NGOs and community-based organisations delivering SDP programming in Mexico advocate themes described by Giulianotti as 'developmental interventionist,' "such as the right to intervene when the personal safety of individuals is threatened, the value of sport as a tool of intervention and the critical role of building human capacity and public participation within underdeveloped settings" (2011, p. 769).

As a result of the identified organisations delivering SDP programming in Mexico predominantly targeting children and youth, other vulnerable groups are underrepresented. Therefore, an area of opportunity for the Sportland field in Mexico is to include programmes aimed at some of these other groups, such as indigenous peoples, those with a mental or physical disability and seniors in their SDP programming efforts. Additionally, further research is needed to identify what interventions work better to address these populations. Furthermore, the available evidence does not indicate whether or not organisations delivering SDP programming in Mexico are identifying the local needs to tailor programming to address those particular issues.

Sport used to deliver SDP programming

The sport or activity of preference to deliver SDP grassroots programming was specified in the organisational or programme descriptions of 28 out of the 33 organisations in the study. Of these, more than a third of the organisations (35.7%, n = 10) chose to use multiple sports, which were a combination of the sports, play and physical activities listed at the bottom of Table 8.2. A total of 32% of the entities (n = 9) used soccer to deliver their programming, followed by boxing (10.7%, n = 3) and martial arts (7.1%, n = 2). The remaining 14.3% of the entities (n = 4) declared as their activity of choice one of the following: basketball, chess, circus arts or rugby. It is worth mentioning that only one of the organisations in the sample listed adapted sports as one of the multiple activities used to deliver their programming. Similarly, only one of the organisations using multiple sports considered the inclusion of indigenous sports in their SDP programming.

In line with the findings reported elsewhere (Svensson and Woods, 2017), multiple sports and soccer were reported as the first two choices to deliver SDP programming. However, unlike Svensson and Wood's findings, they were followed by boxing and martial arts. It is worth mentioning that these last two sports were far down on the list of preferences reported among Mexicans, as only 1.2% of the

Table 8.2 Type of sports and physical activities

Type of sport	No. of organisations
Multiple sports[a]	10
Soccer	9
Boxing	3
Martial Arts	2
Basketball, Chess, Circus arts, Rugby	4
Not Specified	5

a Athletics, adapted sports, baseball, basketball, chess, cycling, dodgeball, gymnastics, handball, indigenous games, physical activity, soccer, swimming, ultimate frisbee, volleyball.

respondents of the National Survey of Culture, Reading Habits and Sport declared practising boxing, and none reported martial arts (Pöllmann and Sanches Graillet, 2015). We need to know more about the motivations behind choosing a particular sport to deliver a specific programme; that is, are sports being chosen because there is evidence that they work better to address particular social issues, because those are the sports supported by funding agencies, due to the personal beliefs or likes of SDP agents delivering programming, or are they based upon target population preferences? More research is needed to address these issues.

Using sport as educational tools

Programme descriptions were found for the 33 organisations in the study. Also, organisational descriptions were pinpointed for 28 (85%) of them, and a mission statement was publicly available for 22 of the entities under consideration (67%). Based on the coding of this information, more than half (54.5%) of the organisations (n = 18) were identified to primarily focus on Education (Figure 8.2). The next most common type of SDP areas were livelihoods and gender and peace (9.1%, n = 3 each), followed by health and infrastructure (6.1%, n = 2 each). It was found that the remaining organisations were mainly focused on social cohesion and disability (3.0%, n = 1 each).

Regarding the organisations with SDP programmes that have a primary focus on education, it was found that they combined sport activities at grassroots level with workshops or similar activities aimed at accomplishing at least one or a combination of the following aims: to achieve personal development through the acquisition of a variety of life skills (e.g., dialogue, reflection, conflict resolution, resilience, confidence and tolerance); to improve social skills to build up relationships at different levels (e.g., family and community); to use sports as catalysts to experience values such as teamwork, solidarity, respect, honesty, discipline, leadership; to empower target populations by helping them to see themselves as agents of change; to strengthen, from a human rights perspective, target populations' civic attitudes in the fulfilment of their rights; to provide tools to learn

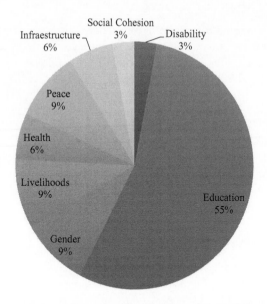

Figure 8.2 Primary thematic area of SDP organisations in Mexico.

how to deal with their own emotions; or to enrich participants' academic level by teaching them how to read, write or undertake mathematical logical reasoning.

Organisations concentrating their SDP efforts on livelihoods combined sports activities with the learning of a trade, in addition to workshops providing instruction on values, emotion management and personal development. The organisations categorised in this group were working either with populations deprived of their liberty, living on the streets or lacking opportunities to be formally trained for a trade. Hence, their intervention efforts were mainly aimed at economically empowering their beneficiaries and aiding them in their pathways to social reintegration.

The organisations with a gender focus in their SDP programmes combined grassroots sports activities with efforts to promote gender equality, as well as to empower girls, and young women. In some other cases, SDP programming aimed to promote strategies to tackle homophobic hate crime and phobia against the lesbian, gay, bisexual, transgender community. In particular, the organisations categorised in this SDP area provided workshops to develop one or a combination of the following: leadership skills, life skills or knowledge of human rights.

Overall, the discourse in the programme and organisational descriptions as well as in mission statements focused on experiencing and teaching values (e.g., teamwork, solidarity, respect, honesty and discipline) or on developing life skills through sports (e.g., dialogue, reflection, conflict resolution, resilience, confidence and tolerance). In this sense, sports were mainly conceived either as a tool or a bridge to educate, even in those whose primary SDP area of focus were livelihoods, gender, peace or health.

Relying on the great sports myth

In addition to reviewing mission statements, along with organisational and programme descriptions, annual reports were identified for 34.4% of the entities
(n = 11) in the study. Two-thirds of the SDP organisations in the study did not
have publicly available annual reports (n = 22). Based on this information, it was
found that more than half (54.5%) of the entities (n = 18) delivering grassroots
SDP programmes in Mexico reported results achieved (e.g., number of beneficiaries reached, number of workshops conducted, percentage of beneficiaries changing target attitudes and life skills learnt). In contrast, almost half (45.5%) of the
organisations (n = 15) did not have openly accessible outcomes related to their
SDP programming efforts. It was also found that only a quarter (24.2%) of the
SPD organisations (n = 8) under examination plainly displayed a financial report
on their respective digital platforms. Additionally, the majority (91%) of organisations (n = 30) did not have a publicly available evaluation report.

This suggests that idealistic beliefs permeate Sportland practices in Mexico
about sports (Svensson and Woods, 2017) or, more precisely, by what Coakley
(2015) described as the *lasting power of the Great Sport Myth* (GSM). As Coakley
(2015) explained, the GSM is anchored in the beliefs that sport holds an inherent
purity and goodness that can be transferred by a sort of osmosis process to those
who practice or consume sport and that sport practices inevitably lead to individual and community development.

In general, there was a lack of evidence to support the results they reported,
when in fact they did so, as almost half of the organisations in the study did
not have openly accessible outcomes related to their SDP programming efforts
(e.g., only three organisations had a publicly available evaluation report). Further
research is needed to help us understand the link between sports with reported
outcomes. In particular, we need to further our knowledge about what particular
outcomes (e.g., values, life skills and personal development) are due to which particular sport participation or to which particular content implemented in workshops. As Whitley et al. (2019) concluded in their systematic review of sport for
development interventions, "there is a need for more rigorous, systematic research
and evaluation efforts that are openly shared and assessed" (p. 191).

Conclusion

There was a boom of NGO's and community-based organisations delivering SDP
programming in Mexico between 2007 and 2017 featuring properties of 'developmental interventionism'. It was found that most of them have been delivering
SDP programming in partnership with business corporations (national and transnational), the Mexican government, international funding agencies and national
universities. SDP programmes have been operated in the 32 states in Mexico.
However, Mexico City was overrepresented. Notably, it was observed that there is
a concentration of SDP organisations in the ZMVM as well as in urban settings,

mainly in capital cities across the country. These findings suggest that Sportland agents operating in Mexico may be working within the 'bubbles' of networks and resources structured within the ZMVM and capital cities.

Additionally, it was found that organisations targeting children, youth or both represent a total of 88% of the SDP entities in the study. In this sense, some of the challenges of the Sportland field in Mexico are to implement programming in rural settings, particularly in those situated in the poorest regions in the country, and to include other vulnerable groups (e.g., indigenous peoples, those with a mental or physical disability and seniors) in their SDP programming efforts. Findings suggest that multiple sports, soccer, boxing and martial arts were the sports of preference to deliver SDP grassroots programming. In this regard, further research is needed to inquire about motivations behind choosing a particular sport to deliver SDP programming.

The findings indicated that education is the primary focus of more than half of the organisations operating SDP programmes in Mexico, followed by livelihoods, gender and peace. Up until now, grassroots sports activities have been combined with workshops or similar endeavours to teach values or life skills, and with less frequency to impart skills to strengthen target populations' civic attitudes in the fulfilment of their rights, or to provide tools to help them to see themselves as agents of change. In this sense, sports were mainly conceived either as a tool or a bridge to educate. In general, there was a lack of evidence provided by the organisations under analysis to support the results they reported, when in fact they did so. The findings suggest that Sportland practices in Mexico are permeated by idealistic beliefs about sports, relying on the *lasting power of the Great Sport Myth*. Further research is needed to help us understand the link between sports practices with reported or intended outcomes.

It represents a challenge to compare findings reported in this chapter with Sportland practices in other low and middle income countries, particularly with SDP programming in Latin America, as Parnell and colleagues explained, "there is a gap in the literature describing and evaluating programmes that have proven successful in Latin America and the Caribbean" (Parnell et al., 2018, p. 3). This argument is consistent with the findings from an integrated literature review on Sport for Development, which showed that only 3% of research was conducted in South and Central America, and only 1% of researchers were located in the continent (Schulenkorf, Sherry and Rowe, 2016). In another literature review examining publications about Sport for Development in Google Scholar between 1998 and 2012, it was reported that only 4% of research was published in Spanish (Van Eekeren, Ter Horst and Fictorie, 2013). Additionally, findings by Cronin (2011) showed that only 1.89% of Sport for Development (SfD) reports focused on South American countries.

Despite the former, findings in this chapter are consistent with those reported by Jaitman and Scartascini (2017) who, after analysing 18 SfD initiatives implemented in 18 Latin American countries that were sponsored by the Inter-American Development Bank (IDB), found that those initiatives "used sports to reach and retain young people in programmes with broader objectives including employability, skills for life, education, health and well-being, violence prevention, and social and gender inclusion". (p. 58) They also concluded that there was a lack of evidence, finding few systematic and rigorous evaluations; therefore, they recommended "improving data collection, starting with small projects and designing projects so they can be evaluated" (p. 59).

Findings are also consistent with Sportland practices globally. For instance, the burgeoning of NGOs and community-based organisations delivering SDP programming in Mexico concurs not only with the institutionalisation of the Sportland field globally but also with Sportland practices such as neoliberal logics underpinning organisations in the form of 'public-private' partnerships to deliver SDP programming (Giulianotti, 2011; Giulianotti et al., 2019); primary focus on education (Schulenkorf, Sherry and Rowe, 2016; Svensson and Woods, 2017); targeting children and youth mostly (Coakley, 2011; Kidd and Donnelly, 2007); the use of multiple sports, and soccer as the preferred sports to deliver programming (Schulenkorf, Sherry and Rowe, 2016; Svensson and Woods, 2017); working within 'bubbles' of networks and resources (Giulianotti et al., 2019); and a majority of organisations headquartered in the country (Svensson and Woods, 2017).

Overall, this chapter has helped to identify research gaps such as the scarcity of knowledge about how the agenda behind SDP programming is built and the role played by donors in the planning, delivering, evaluation and dissemination of results of SDP programmes. In particular, the nature of power relations between SDP organisations and funding agencies requires further scrutiny. There is also a need to identify what sport-based interventions work better to address vulnerable groups in Mexico not only children and youth but also deprived populations in rural settings, indigenous peoples, those with a mental or physical disability, and even seniors. Additionally, we should explore motivations behind choosing a particular sport to deliver a specific programme. In general, further research is granted to help us identify and understand the mechanisms linking sports with reported outcomes. Specifically, we need to further our knowledge about what particular outcomes (e.g., values, life skills and personal development) are due to which particular sport participation or to which particular content implemented in workshops. The former research gaps must be addressed in an effort to forge a grounded understanding of how sport is related to development in Mexico.

This systematic review provides a starting point in a field where literature is scarce. Additionally, this chapter has provided an overview of the Sportland field in Mexico, which furnishes a foundation to build upon and further our understanding and knowledge about Sportland practices in the country.

Acknowledgements

The author would like to thank the editors for their constructive comments on an earlier version of this chapter.

References

Ahmed, F., Ahmed, N., Pissarides, C. and Stiglitz, J. (2020). Why inequality could spread COVID-19. *The Lancet Public Health*, 5(5), p. e240.

Arellano Trejo, E. and Tenorio Colón, K.N. (2011). Los adolescents hoy en día. *Reporte CESPOP*, Centro de Estudios Sociales y de Opinión Pública, 50, pp. 4–18.

BM, Datos.bancomundial.org. (2020). *Índice De Gini - Mexico | Data*. [online]. Available at: https://datos.bancomundial.org/indicador/SI.POV.GINI?locations=MX&name_desc=true [Accessed 11 June 2020].

Cámara de Diputados del H. Congreso de la Unión, (2019). Ley General de Cultura Física y Deporte. Disponible en: www.diputados.gob.mx › pdf ›.

Coakley, J. (2011). Youth sports: What counts as "positive development?". *Journal of Sport and Social Issues*, 35(3), pp. 306–324.

Coakley, J. (2015). Assessing the sociology of sport: On cultural sensibilities and the great sport myth. *International Review for the Sociology of Sport*, 50(4–5), pp. 402–406.

Coalter, F. (2010). Sport-for-development: Going beyond the boundary? *Sport in Society*, 13(9), 1374–1391.

CONADE. (2020). *QUIÉNES SOMOS*. [online]. Available at: http://historico.conade.gob.mx/portal/?id=1959 [Accessed 11 Jun. 2020].

CONEVAL, Consejo Nacional de Evaluación de la Política de Desarrollo Social, (2018). *Informe de Evaluación de la política de Desarrollo Social 2018*. México: CONEVAL, p. 233.

Credit Suisse Research Institute, (2020). *Global wealth report 2019*. (Research Report). Available at: https://www.credit-suisse.com/about-us/en/reports-research/global-wealth-report.html [Accessed 11 Jun. 2020].

Cronin, O. (2011). *Comic relief review: Mapping the research on the impact of sport and development interventions*. Manchester: Orla Cronin Research.

Darnell, S. Field, R. and Kidd, B. (2019). *The history and politics of sport-for-development. Activists, ideologues and reformers. Global culture and sport series*. London: Palgrave Macmillan.

Dorn, A., Cooney, R. and Sabin, M. (2020). COVID-19 exacerbating inequalities in the US. *The Lancet*, 395(10232), pp. 1243–1244.

Esquivel Hernández, G. (2015). Desigualdad Extrema en *México. Concentración del Poder Económico y Político*. México: OXFAM, p. 42.

Giulianotti, R. (2011). The sport, development and peace sector: A model of four social policy domains. *Journal of Social Policy*, 40(4), pp. 757–776.

Giulianotti, R., Coalter, F., Collison, H. and Darnell, S. (2019). Rethinking sportland: A new research agenda for the sport for development and peace sector. *Journal of Sport and Social Issues*, 43(6), pp. 411–437.

INEGI, (2019) Encuesta Nacional de Salud y Nutrición 2018. ENSANUT. Presentación de resultados. INEGI, INSP.

INEGI, (2020a). *Módulo De Práctica Deportiva Y Ejercicio Físico (MOPRADEF)*. [online]. Inegi.org.mx. Available at: https://www.inegi.org.mx/programas/mopradef/ [Accessed 11 Jun. 2020].

INEGI, (2020b). *México En Cifras*. [online]. Available at: https://www.inegi.org.mx/app/areasgeograficas/?ag=00 [Accessed 11 June 2020].

Jaitman, L. and Scartascini, C. (2017). *Sports for development monograph*. [ebook] Inter-American Development Bank, p. 96. Available at: https://publications.iadb.org/en/sports-development [Accessed 7 Aug. 2020].

Kidd, B. (2008). A new social movement: Sport for development and peace. *Sport in Society*, 11(4), pp. 370–380.

Kidd, B. and Donnelly, P. (2007). *Literature reviews on sport for development and peace.* Toronto: International Working Group on Sport for Development and Peace.

OECD, (2015). *OECD territorial reviews: Valle de México, Mexico.* Paris: OECD Publishing. La Available at: http://dx.doi.org/10.1787/9789264245174-en. [Accessed 11 Jun. 2020].

Parnell, D., Cardenas, A., Widdop, P., Cardoso-Castro, P. and Lang, S. (2018). Sport for development and peace in Latin America and the Caribbean. *Journal of Sport for Development*, 6(10), pp. 1–5. [online]. Available at: http://www.jsfd.org [Accessed 7 Aug. 2020].

PNUD, (2019). *Panorama General Informe sobre Desarrollo Humano 2019. Más allá del ingreso, Más allá de los promedios, más allá del presente: Desigualdades del desarrollo humano en el siglo XXI.* New York: PNUD, p. 31.

Pöllmann, A. and Sanches Graillet, O. (2015). *Los Mexicanos vistos por si mismos. Los Grandes Temas Nacionales. Cultura, Lectura y Deporte. Percepciones, Prácticas, aprendizaje y capital intercultural.* Mexico: UNAM, p. 210.

Schulenkorf, N., Sherry, E. and Rowe, K. (2016). Sport for development: An integrated literature review. *Journal of Sport Management*, 30(1), pp. 22–39.

Svensson, Per G. and Woods, H. (2017). A systematic overview of sport for development and peace organisations. *Journal of Sport for Development*, 5(9), pp. 36–48.

Van Eekeren, F., Ter Horst, K., Fictorie, D. (2013). *Sport for development: The potential value and next steps review of policy, programs and academic research 1998–2013.* Arnhem: Foundation LM Publishers.

Whitley, M.A., Massey, W.V., Camiré M., Blom, L.C., Chawansky M., Forde, S., Mish Boutet, M., Borbee, A. and Darnell, S.C. (2019). A systematic review of sport for development interventions across six global cities. *Sport Management Review*, 22, pp. 181–193.

World Bank, (2020a). *World Bank country and lending groups – World Bank Data Help Desk.* [online]. Available at: https://datahelpdesk.worldbank.org/knowledgebase/articles/906519-world-bank-country-and-lending-groups [Accessed 11 Jun. 2020].

World Bank, (2020b). *Mexico overview.* [online]. Available at: https://www.worldbank.org/en/country/mexico/overview [Accessed 11 Jun. 2020].

Chapter 9

Sport and development in Poland

National strategies and their implementation

Michał Marcin Kobierecki

Introduction

Poland is a post-communist country which has been undergoing political transition since 1989. Following the settlements of World War II, Poland fell within the Soviet sphere of influence, resulting in the seizure of power by the communists. This meant the resignation of Poland's participation in the European Recovery Program (the Marshall Plan) offered by the United States to rebuild European economies. Communist reforms were meant to set Poland on the track of industrialisation. Still, as a result of nationalisation and a centrally planned economy, the reforms also led to underdevelopment in many areas.

The year 1989 was a turning point in Poland's modern history. The first non-communist government since 1945 was formed by Tadeusz Mazowiecki, and soon Poland initiated economic reforms meant to move the country into a free-market economy. In 1990, oppositional hero and Nobel Peace Prize laureate Lech Wałęsa was elected President.

These developments initiated the long period of reforms and transformation of Poland, which resulted in OECD accession in 1996, joining NATO in 1999 and becoming a European Union Member State in 2004. During the past 15 years of EU membership, Poland has experienced a development leap. The impact of political transformation is most evident in the change in GDP per capita. In 1990 it amounted to 1,731.21 USD. After joining the EU in 2004, it increased to 6,681.179 USD, while at the end of 2018, it was estimated to be 15,420.911 USD (World Bank, 2019). This economic progress was also accompanied by changes in other general human development factors. According to the UN's Human Development Index, in 2017, Poland reached the level of 0.865 and ranked 33rd worldwide, after experiencing a growth trend since 1990 (UNDP, 2019). Thus, Poland is on its way to becoming a developed country, and according to some indexes, it already is (Radu, 2018). Its recent transformation and continued development make it a great subject for the study of the role of sport development in the functioning of an emerging state. Polish sport can be considered to be one of the tools of social transformation and a means of fostering the development of the country.

Polish sport during the transition

Economic and political transition left a mark on Polish sport both in terms of elite sport and sport for all. The country developed a high level of sporting achievement during the Communist period, as evidenced by its top ten rankings on the Olympic Games medal tables (see Table 9.1). Such performance is connected to the political function that sport was attached to in communist Poland. Initially, the physical culture was first and foremost meant to be a means of preparing to work and defend the country (Godlewski, 2007). Mass participation in sport was promoted, for example, through *Spartakiads* – mass sports events organised in all countries of the Communist block (Pędraszewska-Sołtys, 2015). However, beginning in the 1950s, Polish sports authorities attempted to maximise achievements in elite sport performances, following the example of the Soviet Union (Godlewski, 2007).

Political and economic transition in Poland meant a totally new situation for Polish sport both in the context of sport for all and elite sport. If the latter is considered, there was a marked decrease in the level of Polish achievements in international competitions in the 1990s, although its roots can already be seen in the 1980s, for example, in the boycott of the Los Angeles Olympics (Polish Olympic Committee, 1990). However, the economic difficulties that Poland experienced in the 1980s and that continued during the economic reforms of the 1990s significantly contributed to the decline of Polish sport. Even today, it is widely agreed that the level of financial resources allocated to Polish sport is unsatisfactory. Other obstacles often include faulty legal regulations (Polish Olympic Committee, n.d.). In general, the Polish elite sport system, according to Żyśko (2013), can be assessed as strongly interventionist, centralised, bureaucratic, formalised and unstable.

The new reality of the post-Communist transition meant not only worse results for Polish elite athletes in international competitions (although, as indicated in Table 9.1, the 1990s marked a slight improvement). An unfavourable change could also be observed in the level of participation in sport, although it has been increasing more recently. In 2008, 37.5% of Poles participated in sports and recreational activities. In 2012, this level reached 45.9% (Central Statistical Office, 2013) and in 2016 remained at an almost similar level (Central Statistical Office, 2017). A low level of participation in sport in Poland was also observed in Eurobarometer research, according to which 5% of Poles exercise or play sport regularly, 23% with some regularity and 15% seldom, which is worse than the EU average (Special Eurobarometer 472 Report, 2017). Apart from financial reasons, this problem is also correlated with the Polish transition. As a result of the commercialisation of sport and the collapse of many sports organisations, associations and clubs (Lenartowicz, Dziubiński and Jankowski, 2017), the opportunities for organised physical activity have decreased.

Insufficient sports infrastructure was a problem that hit both elite and mass sport. Supposedly, it was one of the weakest points of the Polish sport system at the time and presumably one of the reasons for other problems. In 1996, there

Table 9.1 The number of Olympic medals won by Polish athletes at each
respective Olympic Games

Olympic Games	Year	Gold medals	Silver medals	Bronze medals	Unofficial medal table rank
London	1948	0	0	1	36
Helsinki	1952	1	2	1	20
Melbourne	1956	1	4	4	17
Rome	1960	4	6	11	9
Tokyo	1964	7	6	10	7
Mexico	1968	5	2	11	11
Munich	1972	7	5	9	7
Montreal	1976	7	6	13	6
Moscow	1980	3	14	15	10
Seoul	1988	2	5	9	20
Barcelona	1992	3	6	10	19
Atlanta	1996	7	5	5	11
Sydney	2000	6	5	3	14
Athens	2004	3	2	5	23
Beijing	2008	3	6	1	20
London	2012	2	2	6	30
Rio de Janeiro	2016	2	3	6	33

Source: Edited by the author based on Miller (2008), ESPN (2011, 2012), BBC (2016).

were fewer than 20,000 sport facilities in the whole country, which means approximately one facility for 2,000 people, with team sport pitches, gymnasia, multisport pitches and tennis courts being the most numerous. In 1992, the Physical Fitness Development Fund, financed from the national lottery, was established to improve the sporting infrastructure for both sport for all facilities and strategic projects for elite sport (Żyśko, 2008). These three interconnected problems of Polish sport in the post-transition period – economic difficulties, low participation and poor infrastructure – constituted a framework for state initiatives in sport development.

Development for sport in Poland

According to Astle, Leberman and Watson (2019), *development for sport* is the provision of quality systems, infrastructure and events within countries to enhance elite sport to achieve international success. In general, it includes investments in elite sport and hosting major international sport events. Increasing the level of elite sport and hosting sport events often become the subject of government policy to accomplish several political objectives, such as international prestige, diplomatic recognition, ideological competition and domestic political benefits such as the 'feel good factor' or economic impacts (Houlihan and Green, 2008). For example, hosting a sport event may make the foreign public more aware of the virtues of the country as a tourist destination, while Olympic medals may make people happy and proud of the nation. Accordingly, governments decide to spend public money on sport-related initiatives to achieve other objectives in the long run. It is regarded as a relatively cheap and potentially effective means of achieving such goals. There are few countries that do not engage in sport development. Of course, different governments attach priority to various aspects or sub-categories of sport development. For example, there are certain countries which host large-scale sport events very frequently, such as South Korea or China, and some that do not even bid for them despite being capable of staging them.

Development for sport is one of the most crucial sub-categories of sport development within Polish sport policy, although others are also pursued. Generally, sport in Poland is supposed to play several social roles, in principle to increase the level of health and fitness of society and to develop social capital. Government activities include developing infrastructure and organisational structure, training staff and financing development of the elite sport (Ministry of Sport and Tourism, 2019a). This implies that Polish sport development is strongly centred on the sub-categories of *development of sport* and *development through sport* as well, both being strongly correlated. This chapter is dedicated to the issue of *development for sport*, but it should be stressed that other forms of sport development are also employed in Poland.

Strategic goals

More active state engagement in sport development in post-Communist Poland can be connected to key strategic documents adopted since the beginning of the 21st century. In 2003, the Ministry of National Education and Sport prepared, and the Council of Ministers adopted, the Strategy of Development of Sport, which outlined the next nine years of sport policy. Two social objectives of sport included the development and promotion of various forms of sport and promotion of the state in the international arena. The state assumed that the creation of the law would tackle aberrations and contribute to the safety of events, subsidising central links of the system, educating experts, training talented youth, organising Olympic preparations and building facilities of particular significance for sport. However, it was soon clear that its implementation was ineffective due to faulty monitoring and the partially obsolete nature of some of the tasks.

Accordingly, in 2007, the Ministry of Sport (in Poland, the exact names and responsibilities of ministries vary based on the particular governments, and their competencies might be widened or narrowed) created the Strategy of Development of Sport until 2015. The main strategic goal was to create an "active and fit society" (Ministry of Sport, 2007, p. 3). Three priorities were identified: popularisation of sport for all, increasing the level of sport achievements and the development of sport and recreation infrastructure. Each of the priorities was supplemented with several areas of activity and tasks.

From the perspective of this study and its focus on development for sport, tasks within the areas of qualified sport (second priority) and sports infrastructure (third priority) are of the highest importance. In the first case, these included identification of principles and factors necessary to provide continuity of sports training, improvement of the system of sport training for talented youth, modification of the system of youth sport competition, formulation of the strategy for development of Olympic sport and phased programmes of Olympic preparations (also for the Paralympic Games) and a programme of hosting major sport events in Poland. As for the sport infrastructure, the strategy was primarily focused on the sport-for-all facilities, but it also included the continuation of a programme of investments, with particular significance placed on the construction of the National Sports Centre – supposedly, a modern sports complex located in Warsaw, although in the end only a multi-sport national stadium was built – one of the venues for UEFA EURO 2012.

With regard to the indicators measuring the implementation of the strategy (between 2005 and 2015), the expectations included the increase of the percentage of society declaring systematic physical activity from 7% to 13%, the increase of the number of medals in the world and European championships from 621 to 670 or the improvement of Poland's position in the Olympic medal table from 20 (in 2004) to 15 (in 2012). The revised strategy was not far from the previous version. What can be observed is the focus on both sport-for-all and elite sport, while the third priority of infrastructure was intended to serve the first two targets.

Currently, Polish sport is being developed under the Sport Development Programme 2020. It was designed to respond to the ongoing problems of Polish sport, namely insufficient participation in sport, ineffective sports organisations, weak sports infrastructure and unsatisfactory performance of competitive athletes. It includes a vision similar to previous strategies of an active and healthy society, and its primary goal is to create a habit of undertaking sports activity in order to enjoy a healthy life for a longer time, contributing to higher satisfaction and lower social costs that accompany unhealthy lifestyles. Accordingly, the state is supposed to create conditions for the development of sport and the promotion of the physical activity.

This main objective is composed of two components: activities concerning the creation of conditions (e.g., infrastructure, opportunities and organisational structure) and promotion of a healthy and active lifestyle. The detailed goals associated with the main objective include creating conditions and opportunities for common participation in physical activity for every stage of life; using sport to build social capital; improving the organisational and legal conditions of the development of sport, including increasing the availability of trained staff; and using the potential of competitive sport to popularise physical activity and to promote Poland internationally.

As did the previous strategy, the Sport Development Programme 2020 promotes several priorities connected with four specific goals:

1   Forming the habit of undertaking physical activity and increasing the physical fitness of children and youth; promoting and facilitating the integration of adult physical activity with studying and professional and private life;

supporting activities towards social integration of older people through physical activity and creating public space that encourages physical activity.

2   Supporting social activity in the field of sport; countering negative occurrences in sport and promotion of positive values shaped through sport and promoting social inclusion through sport.

3   Improving the organisational system and rules of financing sport; providing a legal environment to facilitate the development of sport; disseminating the rules of good governance in sport; adopting rules for effective cooperation between the Ministry of Sport and Tourism and Polish sport associations; increasing the availability of highly qualified personnel in sport and pursuing a sports policy based on facts.

4   Strengthening the role of Polish sports associations as entities comprehensively responsible for the development and popularisation of specific sports; providing optimal conditions for the development of sport with the highest potential to popularise physical activity and promote Poland on the international arena and garnering support for the organisation of international sport events in Poland.

The implementation of the strategy was supposed to be measured based on a much higher number of indicators than previously, including the average length of life, percentage of people undertaking physical activity, number of sports facilities of various kinds and the efficiency of Polish athletes in international events (Council of Ministers, 2015). What can be observed is a shift towards the role of sport to improve the health and fitness of the society. Elite sport is still present, but its development does not aim simply to improve its competitiveness but to achieve other goals – to popularise physical activity and to promote the country internationally.

Although the programme was adopted in 2015, it was updated in 2019 as a result of specific changes in the direction of the state's policy and the adoption of the Strategy towards Sustainable Development for 2020 (which looks ahead to 2030) by the Council of Ministers and the evaluation of the implementation of the programme from 2015. It was also observed that some of the activities undertaken by the Ministry of Sport and Tourism were not reflected in the original version of the Sport Development Programme 2020, while some that were included were not intended to be realised (Ministry of Sport and Tourism, 2019a).

We should therefore underline that sport development initiatives and undertakings pursued in Poland recently were not always stemming from the strategic documents and that the Polish sport authorities have been aware of it. However, the changes were not particularly profound. The new initiatives included the engagement of the Minister of Sport and Tourism in the realisation of the National Health Programme 2016–2020, which corresponds with the priority to form a habit of physical activity in children and youth and the adoption of the Code of Good Governance for Polish Sports Associations in 2017.

Implementation of sport development

The practical functioning of Polish sport and its development is easier to under-stand based on the actual activities rather than theoretical strategies. We can divide them into those connected to hosting UEFA EURO 2012 and others. In the first case, staging the tournament was to serve several social, political and economic objectives itself, but apart from this, there were several development programmes pursued in conjunction with the tournament.

UEFA EURO 2012 and its legacy in Polish sport development

Recent Polish sport development is strongly connected to the European men's football championships UEFA EURO 2012, co-hosted with Ukraine. Generally, Poland does not belong with countries that have a rich history of hosting sport mega-events. This has begun to change more recently, and Poland has attracted a growing number of major sport events. These include hosting prestigious events in sports such as volleyball (Men's World Championships in 2014; several Men's and Women's European Championships since 2009), basketball (Men's and Wom-en's European Championships, in 2009 and 2011, respectively) and track and field (World Indoor Championships in 2014). However, the UEFA EURO 2012 is by far the most crucial sport event Poland has ever hosted and the most important in the context of its impact on sport development.

UEFA EURO 2012 is regarded as the first sport mega-event to be hosted in post-Communist Eastern Europe (Cope, 2015). From the perspective of Poland, staging the event had several goals. Most importantly, the rhetoric of Polish decision-makers implied that EURO 2012 was an essential part of the programme to modernise Poland, which was undertaken primarily through projects financed by the EU. New investments included motorways, railway stations, airports and new stadia (Cope, 2015). Hosting the event was also supposed to shape the desira-ble image of Poland by enhancing its visibility. As Dembek and Włoch (2014) ob-served, UEFA EURO 2012 succeeded in improving the image of Poland, mostly as a result of the direct experience of opinion leaders – journalists who wrote about Poland from the perspective of long-existing stereotypes and were pleasantly sur-prised by the reality about Poland.

After the event, the Ministry of Sport and Tourism (2012a) announced the 'Polish effect' of the UEFA EURO 2012, which was supposed to be higher than the famous 'Barcelona effect'. It included faster infrastructure modernisation, an increase in the productivity of the economy, a strengthening of the image of Po-land, a larger-than-expected increase in foreign tourism and the establishment of a major social capital. Of course, it is difficult to compare the legacies of the UEFA EURO 2012 and the Barcelona Olympics simply because of the different scales and the time when they were each held. Still, it is difficult not to notice the changes Poland underwent in conjunction with the tournament.

If the size of tourism is considered, according to Eurostat (n.d.) in 2011, arrivals in Polish tourist accommodation establishments amounted to 4,409,550. In the year of UEFA EURO 2012, it increased to 4,979,294 and kept increasing in the years that followed, reaching 7,082,231 in 2018. This meant an increase between 2011 and 2018 of almost 61%. At the same time, tourism in the EU-27 grew by 42%. It is, of course, difficult to precisely measure whether this was the effect of hosting the football tournament or instead of the more general development of Poland fuelled by European funds. Still, there is no reason to question the positive impact of the UEFA EURO 2012. It was particularly important as an incentive for the government to finalise the infrastructural investments on time, although not all the goals were reached.

UEFA EURO 2012 was an incentive to increase the efforts around the development of infrastructure in Poland. Accordingly, four new stadiums were constructed, although not all of the objectives were achieved by the time of the tournament. For example, parts of the planned road network were not completed on time. However, from the perspective of sport development, co-hosting of the mega-event was not only about showcasing the country and its people, boosting tourism and improving infrastructure.

Some of the sport development objectives may be derived from the remarks of Polish Prime Minister Donald Tusk, a sports enthusiast himself, in 2007. In his three-hour speech, Tusk referred to hosting UEFA EURO 2012 as one of the government's priorities. According to Tusk, hosting the tournament was supposed to be a critical element of the strategy of promoting Poland. At the same time, he claimed that he considered the tournament to be a chance to increase participation in sport among children and youth. Tusk also referred to supporting competitive sport to reverse the declining trend of Polish athletes in international competition, particularly in the Olympic Games (Tusk, 2007). These goals were generally connected to the strategic documents mentioned earlier, but Tusk's speech reveals how much UEFA EURO 2012 reflected this strategy: The tournament was not mentioned in those documents as they were created before Poland and Ukraine were selected as the hosts.

Interestingly, very little space was dedicated to hosting sport events in the already-mentioned Strategy of Development of Sport until 2015, which was in force at the time of the EURO 2012. It included a programme of hosting major sport events in Poland. However, it only enumerated procedures of conduct for sports federations in bidding for them (Ministry of Sport, 2007). This obvious contradiction is connected to the fact that few people in Poland believed in the success of the bid (Woźniak, 2015). As the Polish Prime Minister at the time of submitting the bid, Marek Belka, later recalled, Poland's slim chances of winning the bid were one of the arguments he used to persuade the Minister of Finance to provide government guarantees for the event (Polskie Radio, 2012). Considering such an attitude, it is hardly surprising that UEFA EURO 2012 was not part of broader sport development strategies. Still, the Polish government attempted to use this unexpected opportunity to reach various goals.

Even though hosting UEFA EURO 2012 was not anticipated, it became a catalyst for multiple sport development aims of the national sports strategy. Accordingly, several sport development programmes were pursued in conjunction with UEFA EURO 2012. My *Pitch – Orlik 2012* was the flagship programme implemented by the government. It operated between 2008 and 2012. Its main goal was to catch up with the level of sport infrastructure dedicated to children and youth and to provide society free access to modern sport facilities. Within five years of the programme being pursued, 2,604 complexes of sport pitches had been constructed. Based on its success, a sister programme called *Biały Orlik* [White Orlik] was established to finance the construction of seasonal and permanent ice rinks (Ministry of Sport and Tourism, 2015). The results of this initiative have, therefore, extended the initial goal that Donald Tusk (2007) spoke about in his speech.

The programmes run in conjunction with EURO 2012 were also pursued under the umbrella of the *Programme of Social Responsibility*. These included Respect Your Health (Street Football World), Respect Inclusion (CAFE), Respect Diversity (FARE) and Respect Fan Culture – Embassies of Fans. Respect Your Health's goal was health education through *Orlik* pitches and included training for coordinators and promoters, organising tournaments, workshops and promotional campaigns. Respect Inclusion focused on providing access to the tournament for disabled people. Respect Diversity countered racism in football, while Respect Fan Culture created an information service with the needs of fans in mind (Ministry of Sport and Tourism, 2012b).

These programmes were intended to increase the level of participation in sport and improve the level of sport for all infrastructure. In both cases, there has been an improvement. As mentioned earlier in the text, the level of participation in sport has been rising recently, although probably not as quickly as expected. The real legacy, however, concerns the infrastructure. For example, within the My Pitch – Orlik 2012 programme, between 2008 and 2012, 2,604 outdoor football pitches (and pitches for other sports) were built (Ministry of Sport and Tourism, 2015). They are available to the general public, but schools also use them for PE classes. Of course, such investments would/could have been possible without hosting UEFA EURO 2012. Still, it appears that staging the tournament was a strong incentive for the decision-makers to increase efforts in developing sports infrastructure.

Current programmes

Apart from the programmes run in conjunction with preparations for UEFA EURO 2012, the government pursued regular programmes of sport development. These can be divided into five categories which basically constitute the frame of Polish sport development to date: competitive sport, youth sport, sport-for-all, disabled sport and infrastructure (Ministry of Sport and Tourism, 2019b).

Within the last four years, there were several new initiatives performed by the Ministry of Sport and Tourism, managed by one of the highest-rated Ministers in the Polish government, Witold Bańka (Żukowski and Szczepłek, 2019), recently appointed as the head of World Anti-Doping Agency. Governmental Programme "KLUB" [Club] appears to be one of the flagship initiatives. Accordingly, small- and medium-sized sport clubs receive funding for purchasing equipment and organising sport camps or salaries for coaches. The formerly cancelled School Sports Club Program was re-established recently, financing additional sport classes in schools. Alongside the National Base of Talents and Programme "SKAUT", which has the goal of searching for sports-gifted youth, these programmes are supposed to constitute the base of the so-called *consistent training pyramid* (see Figure 9.1). Voivodeship teams (*kadry wojewódzkie*) are supposed to form its second stage, with financing for representations of two age groups restored and one older age group added.

As for the higher level of sports, Programme Team100 was established to support young, talented athletes under the age of 23 who are members of national teams and compete in individual Olympic sports. Older athletes are supposed to be backed by state-owned companies that sign individual agreements with them. There was also an attempt to further incentivise coaches through Programme First Coach, which provides financial prizes to the first coaches of the Olympic medallists. Ministry's activities also include support for disabled athletes, who, for example, can benefit from programmes such as Team100, development of sports infrastructure and anti-doping policy (Ministry of Sport and Tourism, 2019c).

Regarding elite sport in Poland, we should also refer to the prizes for Polish athletes. In general, those who achieve a high international level are entitled to receive scholarships. Their training, healthcare, physical rehabilitation and the help of psychologists are financed by sport associations that receive funds from the Ministry of Sport and Tourism. Such status of competitive athletes is sometimes called a *hybrid*. Poland belongs to the countries which also reward Olympic achievements. Olympic medallists receive financial prizes from the Polish

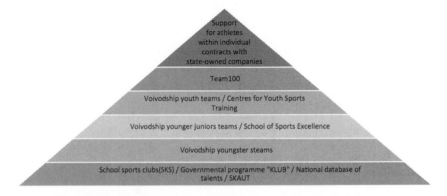

Figure 9.1 Consistent training pyramid.
Source: Edited by the author based on the Ministry of Sport and Tourism (2019c).

Olympic Committee. They are different during particular Games and depend on the class of the medal and whether it is an individual or a team sport but are, in general, rather high. For example, during the Winter Olympics in Vancouver, an individual gold medallist from Poland was entitled to receive 250,000 PLN (approximately 65,000 EUR) (Godlewski, 2012).

More interestingly, the Polish government pays Olympic medallists a monthly allowance. The allowance was introduced in response to situations when some former sports champions encountered financial problems after retiring from sport. Based on the Act on Sport, Polish athletes who have won a medal at the Olympic Games, Friendship 1984 Games, Paralympics (or their equivalents before 1992) or Deaflympics (or their equivalents before 2001) and who are older than 40, receive a monthly payment. In 2019, these athletes received a total of 2,683.72 PLN (approximately 630 EUR) monthly (Ministry of Sport and Tourism, 2019d). Poland appears to be an exception in this area compared to other countries. While today, this sum might be regarded as modest, at the time of its introduction, it was close to the average salary. Such allowances might be particularly important to athletes in niche sports who might find it hard to earn enough for their retirement throughout their sport careers.

Regarding sport infrastructure, there are several programmes financed by the Ministry of Sport and Tourism through the Fund for Development of Physical Culture. They include specific programmes such as Programme Sports Poland, Programme of Strategic Investments, Programme of Regional Investments and School Programme (Ministry of Sport and Tourism). Their detailed objectives are different, including support of construction of publicly available sport for all facilities, development of elite sports facilities and financial support for the modernisation of the existing facilities. It should be noted that many of these initiatives are a continuation of earlier activities. For example, the Fund for Development of Physical Culture receives a lot of its funds from the National Lottery *Totalizator Sportowy*. The lottery was established during the communist period in 1956 with the goal to collect money for the renovation and construction of sports facilities. *Totalizator Sportowy* also supports other sports-related enterprises; for instance, it is one of the leading partners of the Polish Olympic Committee (Totalizator Sportowy, n.d.).

There were also new initiatives concerning the problem of doping in sport. New legislature, the Act on Countering Doping in Sport, was adopted on 21 April 2017. It defined doping in sport and established the Polish Anti-doping Agency POLADA. Governmental activities also referred to the issue of governance of sport. The amendment of the Act on Sport in 2017 was an attempt to improve the organisational operation of Polish sports organisations through, for example, countering cronyism and increasing the Minister's control (Ministry of Sport and Tourism, 2019c).

Additionally, the Code of Good Governance for Polish Sports Associations was adopted by the Ministry of Sport and Tourism. It includes over 180 recommendations, and associations' compliance with them is the precondition for receiving additional funding (Ministry of Sport and Tourism, 2017, 2019c). These undertakings basically aimed to increase the regulation of Polish sport and counter many of the negative aspects, particularly concerning sport associations. These problems have been exemplified by various scandals in Polish elite sport, such as accusations of corruption and match-fixing. The recent legislature was simply an attempt to improve the situation, although it is too early to assess its effectiveness.

Conclusion

Sport may play many developmental roles in different societies. Most importantly, from the perspective of this chapter, it may allow the achievement of specific objectives of the government, ranging from increasing the health and fitness of society to fostering social inclusion and boosting the international prestige of the country. Governments pursue sport policies hoping to reach specific objectives – social, political and economic. As for Poland, the governmental engagement in principle is dedicated to four pillars: sport for all, youth sport, elite sport and sport infrastructure. However, since sport infrastructure in principle is supposed to serve both elite sport and sport for all, while youth sport can be considered as the base for both elite and mass sport, then, we may assume that the social roles of sport in Poland are intended to be reached through these two dimensions.

The social role of sport including its contribution to the broader development of the country might be derived from the strategies and umbrella programmes of the development of sport that have been adopted by the Ministry of Sport (or its equivalents) or by the Council of Ministers in the 21st century. Relevant documents were adopted in 2003, 2007 and 2015 (updated in 2019). They all have certain differences, but also similarities. One of the common elements is the reference to the promotion of physical activity, which appears to be considered as the key priority and assumes the development of elite sport and sport infrastructure. As for elite sport, it is supposed to serve such goals as the mentioned popularisation of sport and the promotion of the country internationally. Still, many of the initiatives are dedicated exclusively to elite sport, including the training of youth, selection of talents, facilitating the transition from youth to adult sport and support for elite athletes.

The declared and implemented goals according to the sports programmes run by the state in recent years reveal a close bond with the transformation and development of the post-communist Poland. Sport, in principle, is supposed to serve society. As has been emphasised in the most recent programmes, it is supposed to build social capital. Elite sport, on the other hand, is supposed to contribute to this social capital and to promote Poland internationally.

This is particularly important when considering the changes that Poland underwent in recent decades. One of the goals is to showcase the country's new face internationally, and sport is supposed to be a medium for this. This goal was clearly visible when Poland co-hosted European football championships EURO 2012, one of the most critical projects pursued by the country in recent years. The tournament posed a central point for many development projects concerning infrastructure and, according to certain studies, strengthened the Polish image among visitors and football fans. In this context, sport is not only to use the progress that has been achieved to improve the quality of life in Poland but also to contribute to further development, such as the promotion of the state in the international arena, which further increases its international competitiveness.

Considering the development of sport in Poland, it should be noted that the policy of the country remained rather stable and consistent throughout the years reviewed, despite alterations of the governments formed by different parties, which in recent years became strongly adversarial. Still, strategically, the sport policy was not subject to significant alterations.

It should be observed, though, that the actual sport policy pursued by the Polish government has not always reflected the strategic programmes. This was most clearly visible in the context of co-hosting UEFA EURO 2012. It became the main priority of Polish sport policy for several years before the tournament, and many sport development programmes were designed to accompany the tournament, such as My Pitch – Orlik 2012. Still, staging sport events has never been a strategic goal in reaching development objectives, although it has been included in strategic documents.

Pursuing a sport policy not entirely in accordance with the strategic programmes is something the Ministry of Sport is aware of. For example, the recent update of the Sport Development Programme was the result of contradictions between what was supposed to be done and what was actually done. The strategic programmes themselves appear to have been developed evolutionarily. Consecutive programmes have been becoming more specific and detailed assessment measures have been added, but the general priorities of sport development have not been subject to more profound changes, despite alternation of governments during the analysed period.

The assessment of Polish sports policy in recent years cannot be unambiguous. If the performance of Polish athletes at the Olympic Games is considered, it has not improved (see Table 9.1) despite the projects that have been introduced. The level of mass participation in sport has improved, but it still appears to be lower than expected, particularly when compared to other EU Member states. On the other hand, the hosting of the EURO 2012 should be regarded as a success. In general, Polish sport policy has been undergoing an evolution in recent decades, which at least partly reflected the transformation of the whole country. It has not always been successful, but it should be noted that, unlike some other areas, since 2003, sport policy appears to be pursued in a more or less planned, coordinated and stable way, as evidenced by the strategies and programmes adopted by the government despite the fact that the plans have not always been realised.

References

Astle, A., Leberman, S. and Watson, G. (2019). *Sport development in action: Plan, programme and practice*. Abingdon: Routledge.

BBC, (2016). Medal table. [online]. Available at: https://www.bbc.com/sport/olympics/rio-2016/medals/countries [Accessed 29 Oct. 2019].

Central Statistical Office, (2013). *Uczestnictwo Polaków w Sporcie i Rekreacji Ruchowej w 2012 r* [Poles' participation in sports and physical recreation in 2012]. Warszawa: GUS.

Central Statistical Office, (2017). *Participation in sports and physical recreation in 2016*. Warsaw: GUS.

Cope, B. (2015). Euro 2012 in Poland: Recalibrations of statehood in Eastern Europe. *European Urban and Regional Studies*, 22(2), pp. 161–175.

Council of Ministers, (2015). *Program Rozwoju Sportu do roku 2020: Załącznik do uchwały nr 150 Rady Ministrów z dnia 31 sierpnia 2015 r.* (poz. 989) [Sport development programme 2020: Attachment to the Decree of the Council of Ministers No 150 of 31 Aug. 2015]. Monitor Polski: Warszawa.

Dembek, A. and Włoch, R. (2014). The impact of a sports mega-event on the international image of a country: The case of Poland Hosting UEFA Euro 2012. *Perspectives. Review of International Affairs*, 1, pp. 33–47.

ESPN, (2011). Beijing 2008 - Medal table. [online]. Available at: http://en.espn.co.uk/olympic-sports/sport/story/143119.html [Accessed 29 Oct. 2019].

ESPN, (2012). Summer Olympics - Medal tracker. [online]. Available at: https://www.espn.com/olympics/summer/2012/medals [Accessed 29 Oct. 2019].

Eurostat (n.d.). *Arrivals of residents/non-residents at tourist accommodation establishments: Foreign country*. [online]. Available at: https://ec.europa.eu/eurostat/tgm/table.do?tab=table&init=1&language=en&pcode=tin00174&plugin=1 [Accessed 8 Apr. 2020].

Godlewski, P. (2007). PKOl w służbie PRL [PKOl in service of the PRL]. In: J. Chełmecki, ed., *Społeczno-Edukacyjne Oblicza Współczesnego Olimpizmu: Wychowanie Patriotyczne przez Sport* [Social-educational faces of contemporary Olympism: Patriotic upbringing through sport]. Warszawa: AWF Warszawa, pp. 159–170.

Godlewski, P. (2012). Sportowiec w realiach organizacyjnych i ekonomicznych polskiego sportu wyczynowego [Athlete in organizational and economic reality of Polish competitive sport]. *Zeszyty Naukowe Uniwersytetu Szczecińskiego*, 725, pp. 75–90.

Houlihan, B. and Green, M. (2008). Comparative elite sport development. In: B. Houlihan and M. Green, eds., *Comparative elite sport development: Systems, structures and public policy*. Amsterdam: Elsevier, pp. 1–25.

Lenartowicz, M., Dziubiński, Z. and Jankowski, K. (2017). Aktywni Polacy: Dwie Dekady Uczestnictwa w Sporcie i Rekreacji Ruchowej: Próba Wyjaśnienia Zmian [Active poles: Two decades of participation in sport and physical recreation: An attempt to explain the changes]. *Kultura i Społeczeństwo*, 2, pp. 117–132.

Miller, D. (2008). *Historia igrzysk olimpijskich i MKOl: Od Aten do Pekinu 1894-2008* [History of the Olympic Games and the IOC: From Athens to Beijing 1894–2008]. Poznań: Dom Wydawniczy Rebis.

Ministry of National Education and Sport, (2003). *Strategia rozwoju sportu w Polsce do roku 2012* [Strategy of sports development in Poland until 2012]. Warszawa.

Ministry of Sport, (2007). *Strategia Rozwoju Sportu w Polsce do roku 2015* [Strategy of sports development in Poland until 2015]. Warszawa.

Ministry of Sport and Tourism, (2012a). *The Polish effect - The success of Euro 2012 beyond expectations.* [online]. Available at: https://www.msit.gov.pl/en/news/7357,The-Polish-effect-the-success-of-Euro-2012-beyond-expectations.html [Accessed 16 Dec. 2019].

Ministry of Sport and Tourism, (2012b). *Sprawozdanie z realizacji przedsięwzięć EURO 2012 oraz wykonanych działań dotyczących realizacji przygotowań Polski do finałowego turnieju Mistrzostw Europy w Piłce Nożnej UEFA EURO 2012 (marzec 2011 – styczeń 2012 r.)* [Report of the realization of the EURO 2012 undertaking and the activities concerning the preparation of Poland to the finals of the European Football Championships UEFA EURO 2012 (March 2011–January 2012)]. Warszawa.

Ministry of Sport and Tourism, (2015). *Informacja Ministra Sportu i Turystyki na temat realizacji programów "Moje Boisko - Orlik 2012" i "Biały Orlik" w latach 2008-2012* [Information of the Minister of Sport and Tourism on the realisation of the programmes "My Pitch – Orlik 2012" and "Biały Orlik" between 2008-2012]. Warszawa.

Ministry of Sport and Tourism, (2017). *Kodeks Dobrego Zarządzania dla Polskich Związków Sportowych* [Code of good governance for Polish Sports Associations]. Warszawa.

Ministry of Sport and Tourism, (2019a). *Program Rozwoju Sportu do roku 2020: Aktualizacja* [Sport Development Programme 2020: Updated]. Warszawa.

Ministry of Sport and Tourism, (2019b). *Biluletyn Informacji Publicznej* [Public information bulletin]. [online]. Available at: https://bip.msit.gov.pl/bip/finansowanie-zadan/sport-powszechny/2019-rok/2574,Lista-podmiotow-dofinansowanych-w-ramach-naboru-na-realizacje-w-2019-r-Programu-.html [Accessed 19 Dec. 2019].

Ministry of Sport and Tourism, (2019c). 4 lata [4 Years]. Warszawa.

Ministry of Sport and Tourism, (2019d). *Wysokości świadczenia w 2019 roku* [Height of the allowance for 2019]. [online]. Available at: https://www.msit.gov.pl/pl/sport/swiadczenia-pieniezne/8496,Wysokosci-swiadczenia-w-2019-roku.html [Accessed 30 Dec. 2019].

Ministry of Sport and Tourism, (n.d.). *Fundusz Rozwoju Kultury Fizycznej* [Fund for development of physical culture]. [online]. Available at: https://www.msit.gov.pl/pl/infrastruktura/fundusz-rozwoju-kultury/3596,Fundusz-Rozwoju-Kultury-Fizycznej.html [Accessed 20 Dec. 2019].

Pędraszewska-Sołtys, B. (2015). Współzawodnictwo sportowe w ruchu spartakiadowym w Polsce na przełomie lat sześćdziesiątych i siedemdziesiątych XX wieku [Sports competition in Spartakiad movement in Poland in the late 1960s and early 1970s]. *Prace Naukowe Akademii im. Jana Długosza w Częstochowie*, XIV(2), pp. 123–134.

Polish Olympic Committee, (1990). *Na olimpijskim szlaku 1988: Calgary, Seul* [On the Olympic Path 1988: Calgary, Seoul]. Warszawa: Polish Olympic Committee.

Polish Olympic Committee, (n.d.). The current situation of Polish sport. [online]. Available at: https://www.olimpijski.pl/en/299,the-current-situation-of-polish-sport.html. [Accessed 29 Oct. 2019].

Polskie Radio, (2012). Rozmowa z prof. Markiem Belką. [online]. Available at https://www.polskieradio.pl/7/259/Artykul/628967 [Accessed 14 Apr. 2020].

Radu, S. (2018). Poland graduates to developed status. *U.S. News* [online]. Available at: https://www.usnews.com/news/best-countries/articles/2018-10-02/poland-reclassified-as-a-developed-economy-by-the-ftse [Accessed 02 Jan. 2020].

Special Eurobarometer 472 Report, (2017) *Sport and physical activity.* [online]. Available at: https://ec.europa.eu/commfrontoffice/publicopinion/index.cfm/ResultDoc/download/DocumentKy/82432 [Accessed 02 Jan. 2020].

Totalizator Sportowy, (n.d.). *Wsparcie sportu* [Support for sport]. [online]. Available at: https://www.totalizator.pl/zaangazowanie/wsparcie-sportu [Accessed 30 Dec. 2019].

Tusk, D. (2007). Expose in front of the Parliament of the Republic of Poland. [online]. Available at: https://tvn24.pl/raporty/expose-donalda-tuska,87 [Accessed 18 Dec. 2019].

UNDP, (2019). *Poland: Human development indicators.* [online]. Available at http://hdr.undp.org/en/countries/profiles/POL [Accessed 23 Oct. 2019].

World Bank, (2019). *GDP per capita (current US$) – Poland.* [online]. Available at: https://data.worldbank.org/indicator/NY.GDP.PCAP.CD?locations=PL, GDP per capita (current US$) – Poland, 2019 [Accessed 8 Apr. 2020].

Woźniak, W. (2015). Euro 2012 i Kraków 2022: Polskie elity polityczne wobec wielkich imprez sportowych [Euro 2012 and Kraków 2012: Polish political elites towards large sport events]. *Przegląd Socjologii Jakościowej*, XI(2), pp. 60–83.

Żukowski, M. and Szczepłek, S. (2019). Witold Bańka: Związki sportowe funkcjonują czasem jak niektóre partie polityczne. *Rzeczpospolita*. [online]. Available at: https://www.rp.pl/Wywiady-i-rozmowy/309159954-Witold-Banka-Zwiazki-sportowe-funkcjonuja-czasem-jak-niektore-partie-polityczne.html [Accessed 17 Dec. 2019].

Żyśko, J. (2008). Poland. In: B. Houlihan and M. Green, eds., *Comparative elite sport development: Systems, structures and public policy.* Amsterdam: Elsevier, pp. 166–193.

Żyśko, J. (2013). Poland. In: K. Hallmann and K. Petry, eds., *Comparative sport development: Systems, participation and public policy.* New York: Springer, pp. 135–148.

Chapter 10

Sport and development in Qatar

International and regional dynamics of sport mega-events

Mahfoud Amara and Wadih Ishac

Introduction and background

Qatar, in the last decade or so, has been heavily investing in sport as a means of branding and positioning the country as a modern monarchy-state and of tackling health problems related to physical inactivity, particularly among the youth. Furthermore, the country is investing in sport to strengthen the national elite sport system and performance in the region, in Asia, and internationally, targeting some sports, such as track and field, swimming, squash, beach volley, 3 × 3 basketball, handball and, of course, football. The strategy has been to develop homegrown elite athletes, thanks to significant investments in sport infrastructure, including the Aspire Academy as well as the naturalisation of top athletes in some sports where Qatar has not yet had the capacity to compete and where it has struggled to gain a competitive advantage.

Another goal is to use sport as a strategy to diversify the country's source of revenue both through direct investment in sport (e.g., the takeover of PSG in France and the transformation of BeINSport into an international sport TV network) and in hosting international sport events. The most important of these events is the 2022 FIFA World Cup and its associated and ongoing mega urban regeneration projects (e.g., roads, railway system, airport, retail and tourism) across the country.

These are three very different aims for using *sport and development/sport for development* to achieve different types of development goals. Starting with the 2006 Asian Games, Qatar first engaged with the sport and development agenda to diversify the country's revenue, to reduce dependency on the petroleum sector and to prepare the country for hosting international sport events. In recent years, there has been more emphasis on the *sport for development* agenda, with a genuine effort to develop a local sporting culture and to make a difference in Qatari society and abroad.

Recent actions have aimed to alter the negative portrayal of the country in foreign media on issues pertaining, for instance, to the working and living conditions of construction workers. Since winning the bid to host the 2022 FIFA World Cup, Qatar has been under the spotlight, having to respond to criticism regarding the working condition of workers involved in the construction of football stadiums and other regulations related to the *Kafala* system – a system of sponsorship that binds workers to their employer (Owen, 2014). As a result, a number of labour reforms have been implemented in relation to the *Kafala* system, the contracts and mobility of construction workers, including their health and safety, and the introduction of minimum wage policy. To this end, the International Labour Organization (ILO) opened its office in Doha, and the Supreme Committee (SC) for Delivery and Legacy in charge of the planning and implementation of the 2022 FIFA World Cup Projects signed a Memorandum of Understanding with Building and Wood Workers' International (BWI) to learn from the organisation's expertise on workers' welfare programmes.

Having described the general context of sport and development in Qatar, the aim of this chapter is to examine how the discourse on sport for development has been framed in Qatar, particularly around the FIFA World Cup. In addition, how it is perceived and scrutinised externally – as a genuine effort to make a difference through sport or merely as a PR strategy.

The development agenda in the Midde East and North Africa (MENA) region

Sport has been mobilised in the assertion of nationalism, national unity beyond class and ethnic divides as well as around Pan Arab and Pan Islamic ideologies. Sport has been more recently organised as a means for integrating the new world system characterised by the end of the bi-polar system, replaced by the American hegemony, the liberation of the financial movement and multiplication of multinationals. As a consequence, the declining discourse on Pan-Arab solidarity and secular states' development ideologies, such as *Baathism* in Syria and Iraq or *Nasserism* in Egypt, has been replaced by the dominant discourse of economic (neo) liberalism (*infitah*) and regional economic cooperation, excluding (or at least delaying), however, principles of democratisation, individual emancipation and citizenship rights. This explains, according to El Kenz (2009), the perpetration of 'history' and 'tradition' as sources of 'authenticity' in the legitimisation of party-states and monarchy-states rules (in fusion with the religious institution and business interests) in the region. Moreover, accepting the values of free movement of capital and products has not involved either the free movement of people between Arab borders or between the Arab region and other regions. This is exasperated today by internal conflicts in Syria, Yemen, Iraq and Libya. The zone of conflicts is becoming a terrain of proxy wars between different Arab countries and external allies including Iran, Turkey, the United States and Russia as well as France and Great Britain.

El Kenz (2009) goes as far as to claim that the Arab world today is witnessing the end of a historical cycle for its state-driven development, which started with the Egyptian revolution led by "the free officers" in 1952 and ended with the American occupation of Iraq:

> In the Arab region, countries around which polarised experiences of development and "positive neutrality" [in the bipolar world system] such as Egypt,

Syria, Algeria and Iraq, have ended up falling through wars, either by an occupation for the latter, or as a result of strong economic and political pressures on governments and "civil societies", for the other countries. With the fall of the Soviet Union and the war in Afghanistan finishes the first cycle of Arab post-colonial history and its developmentalist ideology. The new cycle opens on different perspectives. The Pacified Arab world can and should welcome neo-liberal experience of capitalism already underway in the Occident, and in a number of Asian countries, as well in the Gulf countries and in Mexico.

(p. 5, translated from French)

The development of countries in the GCC was strongly associated with the discovery of oil. The period between the 1970s and the early 2000s can be considered as the era where the majority of economic and demographic growth took place in the GCC region (Al-Saidi, Zeidan and Hammad, 2019). Revenue from oil and gas has had a tremendous impact on the development, urban regeneration and economic growth of these countries. In reference to development models and modernisation approaches in the GCC, Al-Zo'by (2019, p. 565) suggested that "the GCC countries sought to embrace socio-economic transformation associated with development models that aimed to integrate culture, cultural organizations, and culture industry within their national development vision".

Under the framework of "nation-state building", the modernisation model in the region involved investment in the modernisation of infrastructures and development of human capital. The model still depends on the influx of foreign labour to meet the demands of rapid development in different sectors. It is also dependant on finding the right balance between integrating global (economic, financial and cultural) influences while maintaining and protecting local traditions. As explained by Kamla and Roberts (2010, p. 456), the aim was to enjoy the fruits of modernity (in its material sense), and at the same time maintain their [GCC countries] particular cultural identity. This is evident, for example, in the dress code for men and women, the continuing popularity of traditional sports and attachment to extended family codes.

The so-called "Gulf Cooperation Council" (GCC) model of development, with tighter economic, political and military coordination, has been challenged recently by political turmoil, which has affected the essence and future existence of the GCC. This is following the decision by Saudi Arabia, the UAE and Bahrain to impose a blockade on another member of the council, Qatar. This diplomatic tension resulted mainly from their disagreement over Iran, Turkey and military conflicts in Syria, Libya and Yemen, among others. The fall in oil pricing in the international market and political instability in the region has pushed countries in the GCC to accelerate their economic and political reforms in all domains, including the sport sector. Several reforms were implemented in Qatar to improve the health and safety conditions of workers in construction as well as in other sectors such as transportation, tourism and retail.

In sport, some reforms were implemented to secure decent salaries for professional players as well as access to education and job security post-retirement (Amara and Al-Emadi, 2018). A number of elite athletes are integrated during their sport career and post-retirement into the police and military to guarantee a full-time job and a more stable source of revenue, particularly for minor sports.

Sport, and football in particular, is being used to position Qatar as an active actor in development and aid programmes framed around UN Sustainable Development Goals and the Qatar Vision 2030. It is also being used to consolidate Qatar's international relations strategy and position in the moral debate around solidarity and conflict resolution, in response to both negative portrayal in foreign media and geopolitics in the region, characterised by the diplomatic tensions between Qatar and three Gulf neighbours, Bahrain, Saudi Arabia and the UAE.

The sport for development agenda

Sport is globally recognised and increasingly utilised as a vehicle to achieve development outcomes in areas such as health, social cohesion and gender equality/equity and disability inclusion. The United Nations has used sport for development programmes for decades. In 2003, the UN released a document entitled "Sport for Development: Toward achieving the Millennium Development Goals" in which the sport sector is recognised as presenting a natural partnership for the United Nations.

> By its very nature, sport is about participation. It is about inclusion and citizenship. Sport brings individuals and communities together, highlighting commonalities and bridging cultural or ethnic divides. Sport provides a forum to learn skills such as discipline, confidence and leadership and it teaches core principles such as tolerance, cooperation and respect. Sport teaches the value of effort and how to manage victory, as well as defeat. When these positive aspects of sport are emphasized, sport becomes a powerful vehicle through which the United Nations can work towards achieving its goal.
>
> (United Nations Inter-Agency Task Force on Sport for Development, & Peace, 2003, p. V)

The discourse on the sport for development agenda has been criticised in academic circles as lacking evidence-based results from the field and as a real medium of change in tackling global poverty, health problems and conflict resolution. Furthermore, the promoters of sport for development, government and non-government actors alike, despite their good intentions, are so immersed in the so-called "sport evangelism", which defines sport as a domain with an inherent capacity for a positive outcome (Coalter, 2010a, b), that they fail to recognise the divisive nature of sport. Sport can fuel ethnic and national sentiments as well as temptations for corruption and doping.

The sport for development agenda is also criticised for reinforcing neo-colonial stigma about the "south" (former colonies) and increasing dependency of developing countries for aid programmes coming from developed countries. Actors from the "north", including governmental and non-governmental organisations as well as private companies (such as corporate sport brands), are usually intervening with ready-made solutions without a full understanding of the socio-cultural fabric of these societies. These actors contribute to promoting neo-liberal (commercial) values of sport to serve the international sport system rather than long-term sustainable solutions for the receivers of these programmes.

Another challenge in sport for development occurs on a conceptual level. According to Coalter (2010a), only some aspects of sport-for-development organisations can contribute to certain types of social capital:

> The danger of decontextualized, overly romanticized, communitarian generalizations about the 'power' of sport-for-development. It seems that it is not simple sports participation that can hope to achieve most desired outcomes, but sports plus; it is not 'sport' that achieves many of these outcomes, but sporting organizations; it is not sport that produces and sustains social capital, enters partnerships and mobilizes sporting and non-sporting resources, but certain types of social organization.
>
> (Coalter, 2010a, p. 14)

Football for development in Qatar

The high visibility of Qatar in the domain of sport has put the country under more international scrutiny, with suspicion of the agenda behind its investment in sport, usually portrayed with questions of politics and identity. Qatar is presented in some foreign media as a country with no rooted sporting culture and not culturally open to international norms and values around sport, including on issues of gender equality and sexuality.

To counter this negative publicity and to show its willingness to be an agent for change in the international sport system, Qatar has invested in the ethical and moral issues surrounding sport. This includes the 2010 launch of the International Centre of Sport Security and Integrity (ICSSI) to promote and protect the integrity and security of sport. The other remit of ICSSI, via its "Save the Dream" initiative, focuses on the protection and education of children and young people through sport. Among its projects, the "Sport for Peace" project targets internally displaced populations in the region of Darfur (Sudan), and the "It's in your hands to protect" joint campaign (launched with UNICEF during the 2014 FIFA World Cup) encourages people to report violence against children during major sporting events.

The other organisation active in the sport for development agenda is Qataris Generation Amazing (GA). It is a branch of the SC for the Delivery and Legacy, the body responsible for the delivery of the required infrastructure, planning and operations of the 2022 FIFA World Cup. The subsequent section aims to explore the discourse around the SC and how its different initiatives are framed around sport (football) for development.

Generation Amazing: football for development initiatives

Generation Amazing (GA) was established with a focus on profiting from the power of football to implement different strategies that help to generate a positive social impact and sustainable social development inside Qatar and internationally (Q Life, 2018). Targeting national communities living in Qatar, labour migrants in particular and their extended families abroad and in refugee camps, GA implemented its community projects in Jordan, Nepal, Pakistan, Lebanon, India and the Philippines, as illustrated in Tables 10.1 and 10.2.

Inspired by the United Nations Sustainable Development Goals, GA's narrative has been constructed around themes such as equality, education for all, health and well-being. This year, GA started its Football for development (F4D) programmes reaching out to 500,000 participants (Gulf Times, 2020c). Hassan Althuwadi, the Secretary-General of the SC for Delivery and Legacy, mentioned that:

> Generation Amazing utilizes the power of football to help under-privileged people develop their leadership, communication, and organizational skills. It has been a great success. Our goal is to reach a million people by 2022.
>
> (Gulf Times, 2018, n.p.)

GA works with several local and international stakeholders with experience in the sport for development agenda as well as celebrities and international football clubs. To deliver F4D sessions in South America, GA teamed up with the United Nations Office on Drugs and with the Brazilian football team Flamengo FC, a finalist of the FIFA Club World Cup Qatar 2019, to deliver a football for development session to impoverished youth in Rio de Janeiro. In India, together with local partners, the Oscar Foundation and Slum Soccer, it inaugurated new community football pitches. Likewise, in the Middle East, GA is collaborating with the Jordan Hashemite Charity and Organisation for Arab and Islamic Relief, using its programmes to target Syrian refugees (Gulf Times, 2020c). GA collaborated with the Community Organized Relief Effort (CORE) charity to contribute to the rebuilding efforts of Haiti as a result of the 2010 earthquake. This partnership was to benefit more than 375 children from three Port-au-Prince schools within the CORE network located in the area of Delmas (Binu, 2020).

In the domain of education and training, GA collaborated with the University Campus of Football Business (UCFB) to share knowledge and ideas for students and promote research topics addressing social issues (The Peninsula, 2020). GA Programs Director, Mr Nasser Al Khori explained:

Table 10.1 GA initiatives and programmes in football for development

Community sport project

GA football for development programme 500,000+ beneficiaries in nine
   countries – since its launch in 2009
Football pitches: GA has built 27 community football pitches in Syria,
   Lebanon, Jordan, Pakistan, Nepal, India, Philippines, Qatar and Oman
Partnership with Leeds United and Sheffield FC for football development
   programmes. The programme will be supporting communities in both
   cities for the coming four years. Using football to help people learn a
   variety of life skills is the foundation of what GA does globally
Partnership with KAS Eupen (owned by Aspire in Qatar) and AS Roma
   (sponsored by Qatar Airways) to develop essential life skills in Belgium,
   Italy and Qatar
GA teamed up with the United Nations Office on Drugs and Crime
   and Flamengo FC to deliver a football for development session to
   impoverished youth in Rio de Janeiro on the sidelines of the 2019 Copa
   America in Brazil

Source: Edited by the authors based on *Gulf Times* (2020c).

Table 10.2 Supreme committee for delivery and legacy programmes

Legacy programmes

Challenge 22	Helping to push innovation in the field of assistive technology, and how this is changing the way people experience sport in Qatar and around the world. Ages: 16–18. Subjects: Design and Technology, Science, Citizenship and Business.
Ambassador Programme	Harnessing the power of football to create positive social change in Qatar, across the region and around the globe. Including FIFA World Cup winners Xavi Hernandez and Cafu. Our other ambassadors are Samuel Eo'o, Tim Cahill, Ali al Habsi, Mobarak Mostafa, Ibrahim Khalfan, Adel Khamis, Ahmed Khalil, Khalid Salman, Mohamed Aboutrika, Younis Mahmoud, Bader Al-Motawaa, Wael Gomaa and Mohamed Saadon Al-Kuwari.
Tamreen	Tamreen uses excitement around the FIFA World Cup Qatar 2022 to inspire young people to learn. These resources have been created with the Ministry of Education & Higher education, so they are aligned with the Qatar National Curriculum. It explores Qatar's FIFA World Cup™ journey – from the historic bid to become hosts, all the way through the legacy that the tournament will create. Films, games, quizzes and more, all aligned to the national curriculum, provide the basis for flexible and fun plans.

Source: Edited by the authors based on See You In 2022 (2020a).

> We look forward to embarking on a dynamic partnership which will see an exchange of knowledge and expertise around the topics of legacy, football for development and education in the build-up to and beyond 2022.
>
> (Ibid, n.p.)

Internally, GA was launched in partnership with the Ministry of Education and Higher Education Schools Sport Programme and with the participation of around 50 schools in Qatar. For children aged between 8 and 12 years, the programme focused on teaching school kids life skills, teamwork, communication and respect through football (*Gulf Times*, 2020c). The aim as promoted by GA Director is:

> Delivering these important learning initiatives through football for the next generation. When we teach values like inclusion, tolerance, respect, and communication, these create an inclusive generation.
>
> (ibid, n.p.)

As part of this programme, 50 physical education instructors and 45 coaches affiliated with the Qatar Football Association were trained in the implementation of these different values using football as a tool.

Having received much criticism for the condition of construction workers involved in mega-projects around the 2022 FIFA World Cup, GA provides specific programmes to workers following the "train the trainer/peer education", focusing on teaching them new skills, boosting their self-worth and self-awareness (See You In 2022, 2020b). In 2017, GA held a series of workshops for workers in the Al Khor region of Qatar. These workshops, given by an art teacher, focused on the idea of recycled art. Attendees created baskets, tissue boxes and decoration frames (Qatar is Booming, 2017).

The Workers' Cup tournament

Through a collaboration between Qatar Stars League and SC, GA started the Workers' Cup tournament in Qatar. This tournament, which started in 2013 and is held every year, brings together unskilled workers from different sectors to compete (Workers' Cup, 2020). Involving supporters to cheer their teams based on ethnic belonging or affiliation to the same company, the tournament focuses on encouraging peaceful relations between workers while increasing physical activities to decrease health problems. The Workers' Cup provides these workers opportunities to participate directly in football tournaments and to be active, and the fans earn the opportunity to cheer for their favourite team. Moreover, the fans enjoy a social gathering around football as a way to escape the daily routine of their work (ibid). When it first started, the tournament had 16 teams, though this number doubled in 2017, where 370 matches were played. In its sixth edition, the Workers' Cup offered the opportunity for 640 players competing in 32 teams to participate and engage in football games (Qatar 2022, 2018). High-profile visitors attended some of the games, including the head of FIFA, Gianni Infantino, as part of his visit to monitor Qatar's progress in the building of different stadiums to host World Cup matches.

Hassan Rabih Al Kuwair, the acting Director of Marketing and Communication at QSL, stated that:

> The annual tournament aims to promote a culture of sport and healthy lifestyles in the community of migrant workers' engaged in various projects across the State of Qatar, especially those related to the infrastructure of the 2022 FIFA World Cup.

> (ibid, n.p.)

The eighth edition of the tournament kicked off on 28 February 2020, with 20 teams participating. This event was slightly different from the previous tournaments since it was held on one of the training sites of the 2022 FIFA World Cup (Workers Cup, 2020a).

Football for development: between local and global

Qatar is to be the first Arab and Muslim country to host the FIFA World Cup. Since winning the bid, Qatar received much criticism about its readiness to host this sport mega-event. References to its relatively recent history on the modern sport and international football stages as well as in relation to its dominant Islamic culture have been made (*The Guardian*, 2019). Qatar Islamic culture has been portrayed as a challenge and a liability rather than an opportunity to promote and to celebrate diversity in football culture. Hence, Qatar's effort has been to concentrate on meeting FIFA's requirements around infrastructure and logistics for hosting World Cup matches and an estimated 1.5 million visitors during the event, including airport, transportation and accommodation (*The Peninsula*, 2018). Qatar has had to continue its effort to maintain supplies for its construction endeavour despite the blockade by neighbouring countries. Other issues included addressing FIFA hesitation as whether or not to extend the number of qualifying teams to 48, countering UEFA's temptation to expand its power, increasing FIFA's revenues and offering more opportunities for more national football federations to experience the World Cup.

Another significant effort has been to stop criticism and negative media portrayal targeting Qatar. Rather than going for a defensive position, Qatar has taken a proactive stance in positioning the country internationally in ethical and legacy debates around sport in general, and football in particular, thereby using football for development programmes as one of its public relation arms, while offering projects that can make a difference inside and outside Qatar. In adopting similar models and learning from the experience and projects of other host nations of sport mega-events, the priority has been given to targeting construction workers in offering them the opportunity to enjoy football practice and competition, beyond the routine of their work shift and, additionally, to implement football as a means to promote education and welfare among this community.

The other target of Qatar's sport for development strategy has been families and extended communities of workers in their country of origin, including the building of schools and football pitches. In addition, this strategy aims to develop a network for the implementation of football for development and community projects in the training of PE teachers and coaches and to use football to promote social inclusion and the prevention of crimes. It also builds upon the capacity of Qatar's networking in the international football industry through sponsorship (e.g., Qatar Airways), direct investment in football (e.g., PSG in France and KAS Eupen in Belgium) and the influx of professional players from Europe, Africa and Latin America to the Qatar Professional League. These players are potential ambassadors to endorse different projects in football for development, in Qatar and abroad. Football manager Xavi Hernandez was named a global ambassador for the 2022 World Cup local organising committee, associating his image with GA football for development projects and other corporate social responsibility (CSR) programmes of the SC. His first visit as part of the programme was a GA site in Mumbai to mark the construction of a new community pitch (See You In 2022, 2020a).

Last and not the least, targeting school kids in Qatar and using football as toolkits for the promotion of different educational values for both citizens and residents have been goals of the sport for development strategy, offering youngsters in Qatar a platform to showcase their innovative ideas around football. In terms of measuring real impact, there are few attempts to network with international research centres, with the exception of the University Campus of Football Business (UCFB) efforts to measure the impact of the FIFA World Cup Qatar 2022 legacy programme. The four-year partnership signed between the two parties will see UCFB and its students monitor the impact of football for development initiatives to address social issues. In addition, both sides will explore ways to develop educational pathways and opportunities for GA participants and beneficiaries (*Gulf Times*, 2020a). The article did not offer more details about the method and framework applied to monitor the impact and the desired change. One needs to recognise the importance of various target communities engaging in different football for development schemes, and the limitation of what sport can offer and do if this engagement is not followed with concrete measures. Another limitation of these research reports conducted from outside Qatar is that they can miss some of the local context and daily experience of participants of these programmes.

Conclusion

One could argue that the communication strategy adopted by the SC and GA is mainly outward-facing, promoting Qatar's sport development and legacy programmes to an international audience, and less towards the domestic audience, with the exception of the Challenge 2022 programme. In other words, Qatar engages with (existing) international networks of charities, NGOs, international football clubs and football celebrities as well as international research institutes, capitalising on Qatar's network in international football through direct investment and sponsorship.

The international communication strategy emphasises in particular Qatar's endeavour in contributing to international aid, conflict resolution and peace building. One of the main targets of its programmes are refugees camps and displaced populations that result from ongoing armed conflict in the Middle East region.

Acknowledging the seriousness of negative publicity around the working conditions of construction workers, the Workers' Cup offers an opportunity for the workers to change from the routine of the work shift and camps. For some of the players from Africa, it may be a chance to access the football industry with the hope of being scouted to sign a professional contract (Glendenning, 2017).

The real impact of these projects in changing the condition of these targeted communities and sustainability beyond the 2022 FIFA World Cup is yet to be seen, particularly following the dissolving of the SC before the event, which was the main body supervising and funding this football for development initiatives. Already, Qatar is preparing for after the 2022 FIFA World Cup, and bidding to host the 2030 Asian Games, in competition this time with Saudi Arabia, and the 2032 Olympic Games.

The 2022 FIFA World Cup has been an opportunity to build the foundation of sport for development in Qatar, with regards to planning, training and implementation. Furthermore, it positions Qatar in the international network of sport for development through collaborations with different NGOs and International sport clubs/brands, and with sport personalities to act as ambassadors of different projects. However, more needs to be done to communicate these initiatives nationally and to develop programmes that target national communities, including citizens and residents.

The 2022 FIFA World Cup has been promoted as being for the whole MENA region, hence the priority pre- and post-event should be for other countries in the region to learn from the experience of Qatar and, more importantly, to integrate sport for development and community sport as pillars of their national sport development strategies. One of the lessons to take from the Covid-19 pandemic is that we need to rethink the international sport system and promote more solidarity and cooperation between commercial and community sports.

References

Amara, M. and Al-Emadi, A. (2018). Business and governance of football in Qatar. In: S. Chadwick, D. Parnell, P. Widdop and C. Anagnostopoulos, *Routledge handbook of football business and management*, 1st ed. London: Routledge, pp. 539–547.

Al-Saidi, M., Zeidan, E. and Hammad, S. (2019). Participation modes and diplomacy of Gulf Cooperation Council (GCC) countries towards the global sustainability agenda. *Development in Practice*, 29(5), pp. 545–558.

Al-Zo'by, M. (2019). Culture and the politics of sustainable development in the GCC: Identity between heritage and globalisation. *Journal Development in Practice*, 29(5), pp. 559–569.

Binu, C. (2020). *Generation Amazing to deliver its football program in Haiti.* [online]. IloveQatar. Available at: https://www.iloveqatar.net/news/sports/generation-amazing-to-deliver-its-football-program-in-haiti [Accessed 17 Mar. 2020].

Coalter, F. (2010a). Sport-for-development: Going beyond the boundary? *Sport in Society*, 13(9), pp. 1374–1391.

Coalter, F. (2010b). The politics of sport-for-development. Limited focus programmes and broad gauge problems? *International Review for the Sociology of Sport*, 45, pp. 295–314.

El Kenz, A. (2009). *Le Cycle Arabe.* [online]. Al Watan Newspaper, Algeria. Available at: https://www.djazairess.com/fr/elwatan/126766 [accessed 5 May 2009].

Glendenning, B. (2017). *Wannabe footballers toiling for Qatar 2022 are required viewing.* [online]. *The Guardian.* Available at: https://www.theguardian.com/football/2017/oct/08/immigrant-workers-wannabe-players-qatar-2022-required-viewing-world-cup?CMP=Share_iOSApp_Other. [Accessed 23 Mar. 2020].

Gulf Times, (2018). *Generation Amazing reaches 250,000 beneficiaries globally.* [online]. Available at: https://www.gulf-times.com/story/609117/Generation-Amazing-reaches-250-000-beneficiaries-g [Accessed 14 Mar. 2020].

Gulf Times, (2020a). Generation Amazing and UCFB to monitor impact of Qatar 2022 legacy programme. [online]. Available at: https://www.gulf-times.com/story/655281/Generation-Amazing-and-UCFB-to-monitor-impact-of-Q [Accessed 1 May 2020].

Gulf Times, (2020b). *Generation Amazing to extend its outreach.* [online]. Available at: https://www.gulf-times.com/story/652678/Generation-Amazing-to-extend-its-outreach [Accessed 14 Mar. 2020].

Gulf Times, (2020c). Qatar 2022 in numbers. [online]. Available at: https://www.gulf-times.com/story/656878/Qatar-2022-in-numbers [Accessed 22 Mar. 2020].

Kamla R. and Roberts C. (2010). The global and the local: Arabian Gulf States and imagery in annual reports. *Accounting, Auditing & Accountability Journal*, 23(4), pp. 449–481.

Owen, G. (2014). *Death toll among Qatar's 2022 World Cup workers revealed.* [online]. *The Guardian.* Available at: https://www.theguardian.com/world/2014/dec/23/qatar-nepal-workers-world-cup-2022-death-toll-doha [Accessed 24 Mar. 2020].

Qatar 2022, (2018). *Qatar football family welcomes another Workers' Cup.* [online]. Available at: https://www.qatar2022.qa/en/news/qatar-football-family-welcomes-another-workers-cup [Accessed 23 Mar. 2020].

Qatar is Booming, (2017). *Generation Amazing teaches workers about recycled art.* [online]. Available at: https://www.qatarisbooming.com/article/generation-amazing-teaches-workers-about-recycled-art [Accessed 20 Mar. 2020].

Q life, (December 2018). *Generation Amazing: Getting the ball rolling on social change.* [online]. Available at: https://qlife.com/generation-amazing/ [Accessed 14 Mar. 2020].

See You In 2022, (2020a). *Inclusive generation.* [online]. Available at: https://www.qatar2022.qa/en/opportunities/generation-amazing/inclusive-generation [Accessed 8 May 2020].

See You In 2022, (2020b). *Xavi visits India to mark start of new Generation Amazing project.* [online]. Available at: https://www.qatar2022.qa/en/news/xavi-visits-india-generation-amazing [Accessed 17 Mar. 2020].

The Guardian, (2019). *How the 2022 World Cup is emerging from the desert of Qatar.* [online]. Available at: https://www.theguardian.com/football/2019/dec/22/world-cup-qatar-2022 [Accessed 22 Aug. 2020].

The Peninsula, (2018). *Qatar expects 1.5 million visitors as 2022 countdown begins.* [online]. Available at: https://thepeninsulaqatar.com/article/21/11/2018/Qatar-expects-1.5-million-visitors-as-2022-countdown-begins [Accessed 25 Mar. 2020].

The Peninsula, (2020). *Generation Amazing, UCFB to monitor impact of Qatar 2022 legacy* [online]. Available at: https://www.thepeninsulaqatar.com/article/07/02/2020/Generation-Amazing,-UCFB-to-monitor-impact-of-Qatar-2022-legacy [Accessed 17 Mar. 2020].

United Nations Inter-Agency Task Force on Sport for Development, & Peace, (2003). *Sport for development and peace: Towards achieving the millennium development goals.* New York: United Nations Publications.

Workers Cup, (2020). *2020 Workers' Cup all set to kick off.* [online]. Available at: https://www.workerscup.com/2020-workers-cup-all-set-to-kick-off/. [Accessed 22 March 2020].

Workers Cup, (2020). *Background & history.* [online]. Available at: https://www.workerscup.com/background-history/ [Accessed 22 Mar. 2020].

Chapter 11

Sport and development in South Africa

Sport in a changing society and economy

Kamilla Swart and Roberto Martín-González

Introduction

South Africa is a country with a rich, albeit contested, sporting history. It is also known for being a "sport-mad" nation. The development of sport in South Africa is an illustrative case of how sport is a microcosm of the broader socio-economic and political factors that have contributed to shaping South African society. It is therefore not surprising that *apartheid* – the policy that ruled relations in South Africa until 1993, segregating the population between the white minority and the non-white majority and sanctioning political, economic and social discrimination against non-whites (Apartheid, n.d.) – has played a central role in the development of sport in South Africa. This chapter provides a historical context for the development of sport in South Africa with a particular focus on sport in an apartheid society and the transition to post-apartheid sport in a democratic era. The governance of sport in South Africa is also presented. Furthermore, it highlights unique challenges currently facing the industry, such as transformation, women in sport and the use of sport in positioning South Africa as a globally competitive tourism and investment destination. The chapter further addresses other contemporary challenges and trends such as sustainability. Finally, precursory observations of how the global coronavirus pandemic affected major sport events in South Africa conclude the chapter.

Apartheid and the development of sport in South Africa

The development of sport in South Africa has been impacted deeply by the legacy of apartheid which legalised racial segregation from 1948 to 1994. During this period, sport boycotts and protests against South Africa's apartheid policies were commonplace, effectively isolating South Africa from international sport. Of significance was the emergence of the non-racial sports movement. In 1963, the South African Non-Racial Olympic Committee (SANROC) was instituted. By 1970, South Africa was officially expelled from the International Olympic Committee (IOC) due to failure to change its discriminatory sports policies; this ban remained in effect until 1992 (Kidd, 1998; Nauright, 1997). The Olympic boycott is considered to be one of the longest boycotts against the apartheid regime (Ibrahim, 1991). Many other international sport federations followed suit and banned South Africa from other major sport events (Swart, 2018). With cricket and rugby also joining the boycotts, South Africa was severely affected, as these sports were traditionally very popular amongst white South Africans and at which they excelled (Black and Nauright, 1998). The sport boycotts were aimed at defying the status quo (Nongogo, 2011), and by the 1980s global solidarity against the South African government peaked (Clark and Worger, 2011). During this period South Africa was renowned as a "pariah" state and was sanctioned by the international community, further pressuring the South African government to reform.

Internally, the non-racial sport movement was spearheaded by the South African Council of Sport (SACOS), which supported the principle of "No normal sport in an abnormal society". In other words, it was not acceptable to play on the same field as part of a multi-racial sport and then go home to segregated areas thereafter. Thus, SACOS did not want to negotiate with white sport organisations prior to the end of apartheid (Nauright, 1997). By the early 1990s the National Sport Congress (NSC) emerged as more prominent (Nauright, 1997): It was associated with the broader Mass Democratic Movement and linked to the African National Congress led by Nelson Mandela (Swart, 2018). Mandela's release from prison in 1990 symbolised the demise of apartheid, and by 1991, significant apartheid legislation was repealed. With negotiations taking place to form a new government, the NSC focused negotiations with their White counterparts on the sport structures that would be required post-apartheid (Murray and Merrett, 2004).

South Africa's reinstatement to the Olympic Movement was initiated with a visit by the IOC Commission to South Africa in 1991 (Nauright, 1997); South Africa was invited to participate in the 1992 Olympic Games in Barcelona (Swart and Bob, 2004). Wren (1991) noted that participation at the Games was dependent on completion of the process of unification in sport. South Africa went from a divided sporting nation and international isolation to sporting unification and competing fully in international competitions in a very brief period (Nauright, 2010).

The NSC hosted a national sport conference, "Vision for Sport", in 1993. This conference set out the framework for unifying sport structures and addressing equitable sport programmes. Under the new structure, the NCS organised sport under the direction of the then Department of Sport and Recreation (DSR) (Nauright, 1997). The NSC, DSR and NOCSA were represented on a National Sports Forum (Nauright, 1997). The conference also served as the basis for the drafting of the first White Paper on Sport and Recreation, "Getting the Nation to Play", which was tabled in 1996, two years after the establishment of the DSR. This White Paper was the first official policy on sport and recreation post-apartheid. This policy and subsequent updates as well as the structures of sport governance are presented in the next section to underscore the strategic role and significance of sport in South Africa.

Sport governance in South Africa

"Getting the nation to play" outlined government's policy on sport and recreation, which was focused on redressing legacies of apartheid by ensuring equitable access to sport and recreation (South African Government, n.d.). Additionally, sport was seen as a vehicle for promoting international success, and thus, sport development and high-performance sport were also key. In 2001, this White Paper was updated; partly due to South Africa's poor performance at the 2000 Olympic Games but also geared towards improving the sporting system (Swart, 2018).

In 2003, the sport structure in South Africa was rationalised. Seven independent sport institutions (DSR, the South African Sports Commission, NOCSA, Disability Sport South Africa, South African Commonwealth Games Association, South African Students Sports Union and the United Schools Sports Association) were merged into two macro-institutions (Maralack, Keim and de Coning, 2013). These two macro-institutions were DSR, which became known as Sport and Recreation South Africa (SRSA) and the South African Sports Confederation and Olympic Committee (SASCOC). SASCOC is responsible for all high-performance sport in South Africa, including preparation at multi-sport events such as the Olympic Games and Commonwealth Games, amongst others (SASCOC, 2013). SASCOC (2013) is also the controlling body for all affiliated national sport federations (NSFs) and their associated provincial counterparts. The NSFs operate according to the policies of their respective international federations and within the framework of the White Paper and accompanying legislation (Swart, 2018).

As South Africa has three tiers of government (national, provincial and local), each province has its own provincial sport and recreation department with regional sport and recreation policies, while on local level municipalities are responsible for delivering sport (Maralack, Keim and de Coning, 2013). The national sport system in South Africa represents a cooperative governance approach, with SRSA and SASCOC and its related regional and local structures representing the government and non-governmental structures (Maralack, Keim and de Coning, 2013; Swart, 2018). While all these organisations are formally connected, there has been a lack of coordination that subsequent policy documents have attempted to address.

Given the potentially significant economic and social benefits of sport to South African society, SRSA (2009) developed the "Case for Sport". It highlighted the economic and social value of sport to South African society (SRSA, 2009). As the 2007 White Paper did not adequately reflect the new dispensation, especially in relation to the new macro-structures and the related strategic documentation, a third White Paper was tabled in 2011 and finalised in 2012, "An active and winning nation", once again focusing on increasing participation in sport and recreation and simultaneously focusing on achieving sporting success (SRSA, 2013).

To broaden the base for sport and recreation in South Africa, the 2011 White Paper (SRSA, 2013) identified recreation, school sport and participation promotion campaigns as strategic focus areas. To enhance international sporting success, this White Paper highlighted several strategic areas, including talent identification and development, and athletes and coaches support programmes. Numerous enablers were also identified, such as financial resources, facilities, education and training (SRSA, 2013). Transversal issues that are considered critical building blocks for the South African sport system include transformation, priority sports and an ethical environment. Furthermore, sport as a tool to achieve national development objectives was also acknowledged and is encapsulated in the vision, "building an active and winning nation that equitably improves the lives of all South Africans" (SRSA, 2012, p. I). Three other specific strategic areas – sport tourism, sport for peace and development, and sport and the environment – were also identified.

Together with the 2011 White Paper, a National Sport and Recreation Plan (NSRP) was developed for the first time and is intended to achieve the vision as described by utilising an integrated, coordinated and performance-based approach to sport and recreation delivery and addressing the lack of coordination across previous structures as highlighted previously. The NSRP serves as an implementation plan of the policy framework for sport and recreation in South Africa. The NSRP underscores the importance of ensuring that in all activities, prominence is accorded to priority groups as identified by government: "the youth, the aged, women, rural communities and people with disabilities" (SRSA, 2012, p. 11).

As presented above and summarised by Maralack (2014), South African sport policy is demarcated by three stages. Post-apartheid, the first stage between 1994 and 2000, comprised policy initiation and development (Maralack, Keim and de Coning, 2013). Mass participation programmes and social and community development were significant components of early policy initiatives in order to increase sport participation by those who were disadvantaged during apartheid (Maralack, 2014).

Between 2000 and 2005, there was a noticeable change, with greater attention paid to high performance and elite sport. Given the lack of tackling social and economic inequalities in sport, the third policy shift came with the development of the NSRP and acknowledged the importance of both grassroots sport development and elite sport and the implementation of policy. Thus, it is evident that just as sport played a significant role in supporting the apartheid agenda, it has been used as a strategic instrument and a means of social reconciliation during the post-apartheid period.

However, one of the most critical challenges confronting the development of sport in South Africa is the alignment of policies with the NSRP (Maralack, 2014). It is important to note that this shortcoming seems to have been acknowledged with introduction of the National Sport and Recreation Bill in 2020 (SRSA, 2020). The focus of the bill was to (SRSA, 2020):

- Clarify the roles of SRSA and the associated organisations such as SASCOC and the national federations
- Establish a Sport Arbitration Tribunal

- Regulate sport agents
- Provide a framework for coaching development
- Ensure effective management of sport and creation regarding transformation and accessibility by the community.

It is evident that transformation is still a major issue for South African sport development and will be discussed further next, amongst other contemporary challenges and trends.

Contemporary challenges and trends

Transformation

The 1995 Rugby World Cup stands out as a significant moment in the history of South African sport (Swart, 2018). Swart (2018) explained that the event was considered symbolic of the transformation that was taking place in the aftermath of apartheid. The springbok jersey, a symbol of the apartheid state, was donned by Nelson Mandela on the day of the finals and represented the transition to a new South Africa, "the Rainbow Nation" (Van der Merwe, 2007). Much was anticipated in relation to transforming sport in South Africa. While the country witnessed the appointment of the first black South African Rugby captain, Siya Kolisi, in its 127-year history in 2018 (CNN, 2018), who went on to lift the Webb Ellis Trophy at the 2019 Rugby World Cup in Japan, after nearly three decades of democracy, transformation still remains a challenge. It is however important to point out that this challenge is evident across all sectors of South African business and society as apartheid created a society based on inequality and dispossession (Clarke and Bassett, 2016).

Within sport, transformation entails expanding access and opportunities to all South Africans. In the early years after the end of apartheid, a quota system was introduced in sport to redress historical inequities; however, due to the stigmatisation of some players due to this system (Swart, 2018), a broader approach was adopted. The essence of the NSRP is the adoption of a Transformation Charter and a Transformation Performance Scorecard. The Charter's objective was the establishment of an "accessible, equitable, sustainable and competitive sport system" (SRSA, 2019, p. 6). Figure 11.1 illustrates the multi-dimensional strategic framework that was adopted to effect change on and off the field.

The framework is unique and presents a more coordinated, integrated and holistic approach in addressing the challenges given all the sport stakeholders – the different spheres of government including community-based coordination – discussed in the governance section. It further underscores the magnitude of the transformation challenge. *Preferential procurement* refers to the securing of business contracts and the generation of income for marginalised sectors, whereas *employment equity* refers to redressing those groups who were disadvantaged in employment during apartheid, thus underscoring transformation beyond playing the field.

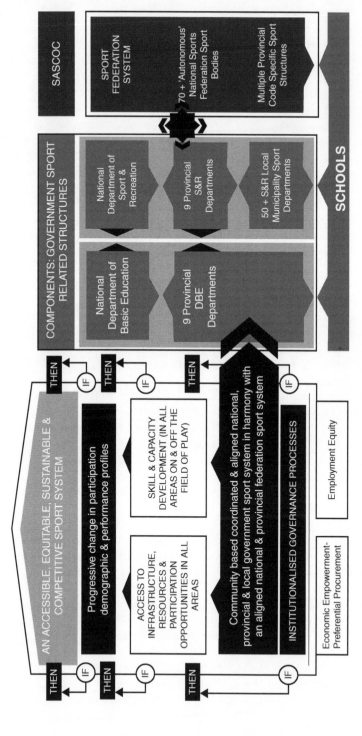

Figure 11.1 Multi-dimensional transformation strategic framework.
Source: Edited by the authors based on SRSA (2019).

The Transformation Performance Scorecard includes several measures that were identified in the Charter as important drivers of transformation (SRSA, 2019). Two types of formats were included, with both serving as milestones towards transformation: *one-size-fits all* and *self-set*. The *one-size-fit-all* views all federations equally and is not subjected to penalties, whereas the *self-set* format permits federations to forward project their targets in particular categories (SRSA, 2019). SRSA adds that the latter format includes penalties for non-achievement of at least 50% of these targets.

In 2012, the Minister of Sport appointed an independent transformation commission, the Eminent Persons Group on Transformation in Sport (EPG) to ensure the veracity of the results and accelerate change (SRSA, 2019). The results enable individual federations to enhance their effectiveness of transformation measures, simultaneously allowing comparative analysis across federations. It is disconcerting to note that the first report on transformation was only published in 2012, 18 years after the demise of apartheid (SRSA, 2019), further underscoring the deep-rooted challenge of transformation in South African sport.

The 2018/2019 report underscores three main elements influencing the pace and extent of transformation: the dysfunctional state of school sport, the changes in population demographics impacting the sustainability of sport structures dominated by whites and the increasing divide between those who can afford to play sport and those who cannot (SRSA, 2019). The following section presents highlights from the 2018/2019 audit.

In terms of the one-size-fits-all targets in relation to the generic Black Charter targets (including Black African, Coloured and Indian as per the historical racial classification in South Africa), more than half of the federations achieved the pre-set targets for presidents, CEO's, senior team managers and women board members. However, less than half of the federations achieved the one-size-fits-all, pre-set generic Black Charter targets for board members, senior male national team members, female umpire/referees and senior female representative teams, amongst other targets. Moreover, 42% of federations achieved the 50% *Preferential Procurement* and 32% the *Employment Equity* targets (SRSA, 2019).

SRSA highlighted that the results further revealed that lack of accessibility to sport for black Africans with the consequent risk of long-term sustainability for many sports. When reviewing the overall 2017 and 2018 targets as illustrated in Table 11.1, it is evident that 50% of the federations have achieved 50% or more of all their self-set targets while the other 50% did not. The most notable improvement was that of softball, while football and tennis experienced the highest drop in target achievements (SRSA, 2019).

SRSA (2019) further cautioned that transformation may need to be pursued more aggressively by federations that have been slow to transform. Other threats to sustainability included the ineffective development pathways towards high-performance sport and problematic school sport strategies (SRSA, 2019). The department remains optimistic regarding transformation noting that since 2011,

Table 11.1 Self-set barometer targets achieved in 2017 and 2018

Code	% of barometer self-set charter targets achieved -2017	% of barometer self-set charter targets achieved -2018	% points difference 2017 and 2018
Gymnastics	75	72	−3
Table Tennis	76	71	−5
Cricket	74	70	−4
Baseball	50	65	15
Softball	35	65	29
Football	73	59	−14
Rugby	60	59	−1
Netball	54	56	3
Tennis	65	53	−12
Volleyball	33	47	14
Athletics	31	44	13
Rowing	**LATE SUBM.**	43	**LATE SUBM.**
Swimming	39	39	0
Hockey	37	37	0
Jukskei	39	35	−4
Basketball	26	34	9
Amateur Boxing	12	26	14
Bowls	**LATE SUBM.**	13	**LATE SUBM.**
Chess	27	NO DATA	

Less than 50% of self-set barometer targets achieved.
More than 50% of self-set barometer targets achieved.
Source: Edited by the authors based on SRSA (2019).

sport in South Africa has become more representative with greater accessible sport structures despite the challenges highlighted. Attention is now turned specifically to women in sport in South Africa.

Women in sport

Just as transformation in South African sport in general remains a challenge, so too does gender. The former Minister of Sport and Recreation, Xasa (2018), reported that the Commission of Gender Equity has mandated SRSA to address gender equity by creating awareness to promote sport for girls, support women in sport and introduce measures to address gender parity across sports. Moreover, systems need to be created to guarantee accessibility to sport for all women and girls. She further highlighted some of the achievements to date by some sports due to interventions by SRSA:

• Brutal Fruit sponsors the Netball League; a major semi-professional league for women with 300 players. Some of these players now play in professional leagues overseas.

- SRSA provides support to the South African Hockey Association, where male and female players are paid the same. Women's hockey has also seen a boost with the establishment of the Investec Hockey Academy (Investec, n.d.).
- Attention has also been given to creating opportunities for women in South Africa's three most popular sports: cricket, football and rugby. Cricket South Africa (CSA) funds several programmes, including women coach development and the development of girls and women cricket. CSA has also started to contract female cricket players. SRSA earmarked additional funding for the establishment of the Women's Football League in 2018. Rugby received funding to host a rugby competition for girls and a women's inter-provincial competition.
- Some positive steps have also been taken in increasing participation by girls in school sport championships and in youth camps, which include leadership and life skills programmes.

However, Xasa (2018) also cautioned that the gender divide is still huge. She underscored that only 2 out of 20 sports audited have women presidents, viz. gymnastics and netball. She also referenced the lack of women representation in sporting structures, as highlighted in the transformation section earlier. Xasa (2018) emphasised the importance of transforming women in sport at the decision-making levels. Finally, she mentioned that a Women in Sport policy is in the process of being crafted and should address recognition for companies that sponsor women in sport, lobbying for regulation regarding women sport coverage as well as enforcing directives in relation to annual transformation audit findings. Women in sport is explored further in the sustainability section of this chapter.

Sport as a tool for tourism development

Sport tourism is considered one of the fastest growing niche sectors in the tourism industry (UNWTO, n.d.). Langkilde (2016) reports that according to the United Nations World Tourism Organisation (UNWTO), it contributed $600 billion to the global travel and tourism economy in 2014. It comes as no surprise that South Africa recognised the value of sport tourism with the successful hosting of the 1995 Rugby World Cup and soon became a regular player on the global mega-event circuit. While it failed at its attempt to host the 2004 Olympic Games, it went on to host the 2003 Cricket World Cup and the 2010 FIFA World Cup.

Other significant international events that South Africa have hosted include the 2009 Indian Premier League and the 2009 British and Irish Lions Tour. South Africa also benefits from the hosting of annual events such as the Comrades Marathon, the Cape Town Cycle Tour, the Two Oceans Marathon, and the Cape Epic, to name a few. These major, homegrown events continue to attract international interest, thus further enhancing the South Africa's sport event portfolio.

While the hosting of major international sport events and sport mega-events in South Africa has been primarily driven by economic reasons, the value of the events in relation to intangible benefits such as profiling South Africa as a tourism destination, nation-building and addressing broader transformation agendas has also been recognised. More recently, the significance of these events in relation to environmental enhancement and sustainable development has also received greater attention, as discussed further in the chapter.

Given South Africa's propensity to bid for and host mega-events, the merits of these events are highly contested. The 2010 FIFA World Cup, the biggest event the country has hosted to date, will be highlighted as an illustrative case. Oxford Business Group (2012) cited figures by Brand South Africa that report that about 10% of foreign visitors to South Africa annually participate in or watch a sporting event. Furthermore, they cite South African Tourism (SAT) figures that in the year preceding the 2010 World Cup, arrivals increased by 15%, while 2012 witnessed another 3.3% increase despite the global slowdown in international travel. Awareness levels of South Africa as a leisure destination also increased by 9%, with the World Cup acknowledged as the first source of awareness by a third of tourists surveyed (National Department of Tourism and SAT survey cited by Oxford Business Group, 2012).

While the World Cup also contributed to general infrastructural investment, there are concerns about the under-utilisation of stadia, some airports and hotels. This has further fuelled the debate regarding short-term gains and opportunity costs, with South Africa deciding not to pursue a 2020 Olympic Games bid, despite it being awarded as the "World's Leading Sports Tourism Destination" at the 2012 World Travel Awards (Oxford Business Group, 2012). Similarly, the South African government did not sign the host city contract for the 2022 Commonwealth Games, which was awarded to the City of Durban (Swart, 2018).

While one cannot directly link the increases in international travel to South Africa to the World Cup, sport tourists have contributed to the upward trajectory in international tourism arrivals to South Africa. With South Africa only receiving about 3.4 million tourists in 1993 (Swart, 2018), more recently, the numbers increased from 14.16 million in 2012 to 16.44 million in 2018 (Lock, 2019). While forecasts predicted continuous increases in tourism arrivals, there is no doubt that Covid-19 will have a devastating impact on the sport tourism industry in South Africa, as explored further in this chapter. Attention will be turned to the challenges of creating a strategic approach to the development of sport tourism in South Africa.

Swart (2018, p. 325) underscored that despite South Africa's success in hosting mega- and major sport events, "a pro-active bidding and hosting strategy is required". As early as 2005, it was recognised that no overarching strategy existed to proactively grow a portfolio of sport events in order to enhance South Africa's competitiveness (SAT, 2005). It is disconcerting to note that the sport tourism strategy drafted by SRSA in 2012 does not seem to have been finalised. The aim of the strategy was to coordinate and integrate efforts to leverage benefits and position South Africa as a sport tourism destination of choice (Swart, 2018).

While this strategy did not come to fruition, it is interesting to note that another initiative, Sports and Events Tourism Exchange (SETE), was launched in

2011 to further strengthen South Africa's status as a leading sport and event tourism destination after the hosting of the 2010 World Cup (Tourism-Insider, 2011). SETE is an annual trade event which encourages collaboration across the sport, events and tourism industries. It is evident that South Africa still experiences limited linkages between the sport and tourism sector and therefore does not capitalise on mutual beneficiation as underscored by Swart and Bob (2008).

Sustainability

The South African sport and development landscape presents many positive angles; nevertheless, there are still challenges and new trends emerging in the context of sustainability that are decisively impacting South African society and environment. *Sustainability* has many interpretations depending on the field where it has been implemented, ranging from the vaguest definition that highlights the idea of maintaining the 'status quo', especially in the field of economics, to one that underlines the importance of achieving well-being of the society without compromising resources for future generations, which is linked to the concept of development and is considered as the most cited definition. It was conceptualised in 1987 by the Brundtland Commission Report, defining sustainability as the "development that meets the needs of the present without compromising the ability of future generations to meet their own needs" (Roostaie, Nawari, and Kibert, 2019, p. 134) and use to be divided between three spheres: environmental, social and economic (Prizzia, 2017) that will serve as the basis to analyse the contemporary challenges and trends in South Africa's sport industry.

Environmental sustainability

The environmental sphere comprises issues such as climate change, renewable energy, soil quality and erosion, water management as well as air and water pollution, as noted by the United Nations (2019). Regarding water management, the case of surfing can be paradigmatic. This sporting activity has received the attention of the local government of Cape Town in order to attract water-sensitive international tourists, due to the water crisis experienced in the Western Cape in general, and in Cape Town in particular (Zietsman, 2018). The goal of attracting water-sensitive tourists assumes that activities pursued in natural environments enhance sustainable attitudes (Hanna et al., 2019). Nonetheless, this assumption may be unfounded as surfers are highly mobile, leading to a higher carbon footprint than other tourists (Butt, 2015).

Although, these sport participants, and the industry around it, have created innovative ideas, like the Shark Spotters, to preserve marine wild-life in Cape Town (Martin-Gonzalez, Luque-Gil and Swart, 2019). Additionally, the water crisis pushed creativity, giving rise to innovative tools and measures to save water within sports clubs and sport events, reducing the water needs in different ways. For example, the Cape Town Cycle Tour (2018) adopted certain measures, like the use of bottled water from other parts of the country or the reduction of water points along the race circuit. Also, the Two Oceans Marathon took analogous procedures to reduce water usage during the event (Sport24, 2018). Similarly, the beginning of certain leagues like rugby or soccer was postponed in order to preserve dam levels (Blaustein, 2018).

In another vein, Cape Town is embracing the emerging trend of electric engines for sustainable mobility, recently bidding for hosting the Formula E event (Kew, 2020). A bid for Formula E also addresses positioning South Africa as a competitive and sustainable tourism destination.

Social sustainability

Broadly, *social sustainable development* refers to the capacity of systems to achieve social equity, enhancing the quality of life within communities and access to basic goods like healthy food or water and services like transport or recreation (Mckenzie, 2004). It is possible to distinguish between several social issues including gender equity, ageing, poverty, youth, indigenous people, social inclusion and disability (United Nations, 2019), all of which are also addressed in governmental policy as highlighted previously.

Obesity among youth is one of the emerging problems in South Africa, which is closely related to the lack of access to healthy food and active sporting habits (Nordling, 2016). The lack of convenient sport facilities in poor areas, derived from South Africa's apartheid past, has been already pointed out (Claophas, 2018). Additionally, the pressure experienced by young people to become elite rugby players has resulted in an increasing number of doping issues (Henson, 2020).

On the other hand, gender equity is another challenge in terms of women participation as discussed previously. However, it is further discussed in this section given its link to the social sphere of sustainable development. As an example, in the Eastern Cape province, there is a group of women who promote healthy sporting habits amongst them, participating in swimming and triathlons (McCainsh, 2019). In the same vein, South African women are also improving in elite sports, from rugby player Babalwa Latsha, who recently signed up for the Spanish club SD Eibar Femenino (Sibembe, 2020), to football player Refiloe Jane, who became part of the Italian AC Milan in 2019 (Vardien, 2019), to gold medallist swimmer Tatjana Schoenmaker (Houlie, 2020). All are emerging South African young women athletes who can encourage women's' sport participation in South Africa.

Another emerging trend in South Africa is the use of indigenous sports as a driver for sports participation and inclusion with the promotion and addition of traditional Zulu Games in the school curriculum (Roux, Burnett and Hollander, 2008).

Economic sustainability

The economy has been a key aspect of sustainability given that it is the main tool to manage the scarce resources of the world and has received more attention than the previous spheres. Two main goals regarding economic sustainability are pointed out by the Sustainable Development Goals Fund (SDGF, 2015): decent work and economic growth, without damaging the environment. Access to financial services is also important to achieve these two main objectives to balance the share of resources between the disadvantaged and advantaged. Several initiatives to transform the industry from a sport-business perspective are also emerging. Two illustrative examples are highlighted. Based in Johannesburg, the company Zenzele Fitness Group, owned by Katlehong Township entrepreneur Tumi Phake, manages 15 gyms (including commercial, corporate, government and universities) successfully (Ndalana, 2016). On the other hand, black women entrepreneurs are also represented. For example, Nomvuyo Treffers created swimming caps specially designed for voluminous black hair in order to solve the problem of black women who don't want to damage hair with sea or swimming pool water (Head, 2018). She started the business as she could not find swimming caps that could fit her daughter's hair.

Covid-19

Finally, we would like to highlight the new scenario that has arisen over the globe with the Covid-19 pandemic. In the context of sports, it has meant the cancellation and the rescheduling of all sport events worldwide, including the Olympic Games (IOC, 2020). In South Africa, it seems important to mention the impact of it on events, within the context of sport tourism, and sport practice generally. First, it forced a change in protocols before the peak of the crisis (Richardson, 2020a) and, eventually, the cancellation of sport events like the Cape Epic (Cape Epic Organisation, 2020) and the Two Oceans Marathon (Richardson, 2020b), which will generate negative social and economic results. However, it is providing certain benefits for the environment and a change in the paradigm about the future of mobility worldwide since most countries have restricted flights and movements as a result of closing borders.

This new scenario represents a unique opportunity for the South African sport (tourism) industry to increase active sport participation amongst South Africans, especially those that are still marginalised. Additionally, participation could be boosted by improving and investing in sport facilities in poorer areas and taking measures to increase attendance, including providing South Africans with coupons as some regional governments in Italy are planning to do, providing certain groups with 500€ to spend in tourism (Wilson, 2020) to support the local sport tourism industry in rural and underdeveloped areas in South Africa.

Conclusion

While South Africa has made great gains in transforming the development of sport in post-apartheid society, it is evident that the legacy of apartheid remains a central feature. While the South African government has developed policies and implemented strategies to address the inequities of the past and has attempted to address this from both mass participation and elite performance perspectives, the development of sport is still plagued with transformation issues across race and gender. More holistic measures to address transformation have been introduced with greater success in some sports than in others.

Since South Africa's successful hosting of the 1995 Rugby World Cup, it has also recognised the benefits of using sport to create a competitive tourism industry; however the linkages between sport and tourism can be further strengthened. Furthermore, like other nations, South Africa continues to grapple with contemporary challenges and trends in developing a sustainable sport (and sport tourism) industry. It has resulted in some successes in relation to how sport stakeholders are adapting to climate change and has also spurred innovation in the surf (tourism) industry as well as entrepreneurship in the sport and fitness industry that contribute to addressing some of the transformation issues outlined.

Finally, while initial observations have been presented as to how the global coronavirus pandemic is affecting major sport events in South Africa as well as the practice of sport, it remains to be seen how the development of sport in South Africa will be transformed moving forward.

References

Apartheid, (n.d.). In *Britannica*. [online]. Available at https://www.britannica.com/topic/apartheid [Accessed 15 May 2020].

Black, D. and Nauright, J. (1998). *Rugby and the South African nation*. Manchester: Manchester University Press.

Blaustein, L. (2018). *Cape Town sports are hit hard by its water crisis*. [online]. greenbiz.com. Available at: https://www.greenbiz.com/article/cape-town-sports-are-hit-hard-its-water-crisis [Accessed 26 Mar. 2020].

Butt, T. (2015). Surf travel: The elephant in the room. In: G. Borne and J. Ponting, eds., *Sustainable stoke: Transitions to sustainability in the surfing world*, 1st ed. Plymouth: University of Plymouth Press, pp. 200–213.

Cape Epic Organisation, (2020). *Official statement 2020 Absa Cape Epic cancellation*. [online]. Cape Epic. Available at: https://www.cape-epic.com/riders/the-2020-race/official-statement-2020-absa-cape-epic-cancellation [Accessed 26 Mar. 2020].

Cape Town Cycle Tour, (2018). *Cape Town Cycle Tour takes unprecedented steps during water crisis*. [online]. Cape Town Cycle Tour. Available at: https://www.capetowncycletour.com/blog/in-reaction-to-the-water-crisis-cape-town-cycle-tour-takes-unprecedented-step/ [Accessed 11 Apr. 2020].

Claophas, F. (2018). *South Africa must look to history to level the playing field for school kids*. [online]. Theconversation.com. Available at: https://theconversation.com/south-africa-must-look-to-history-to-level-the-playing-field-for-school-kids-95551%0D [Accessed 26 Mar. 2020].

Clark, N.L. and Worger, W.H. (2011). *South Africa: The rise and fall of Apartheid*. Abingdon, Oxon: Routledge.

Clarke, M. and Bassett, C. (2016). The struggle of transformation in South Africa: Unrealised dreams, persistent hopes. *Journal of Contemporary African Studies*, 34(2), pp. 183–189.

CNN, (2018). *South Africa names first black rugby captain in 127-year Test history*. [online]. Available at: https://edition.cnn.com/2018/05/28/sport/siya-kolisi-first-black-test-captain-south-africa/index.html [Accessed 22 Apr. 2020].

Hanna, P., Wijesinghe, S., Paliatsos, I., Walker, C., Adams, M. and Kimbu, A. (2019). Active engagement with nature: Outdoor adventure tourism, sustainability and wellbeing. *Journal of Sustainable Tourism*, 27(9), pp. 1355–1373.

Head, T. (2018). *Afro-friendly swim caps are now a thing, thanks to this SA entrepreneur.* [online]. TheSouthAfrican.com. Available at: https://www.thesouthafrican.com/lifestyle/swim-caps-for-natural-hair-sa-entrepreneur-swimma-caps/ [Accessed 26 Mar. 2020].

Henson, M. (2020). *Steroids at 16: South Africa's schoolboy rugby scene faces a widespread doping problem.* [online]. BBC Sport. Available at: https://www.bbc.com/sport/rugby-union/50785122 [Accessed 26 Mar. 2020].

Houlie, M. (2020). Tatjana Schoenmaker bio. [online]. SwimSwam,com. Available at: https://swimswam.com/bio/tatjana-schoenmaker/ [Accessed 13 Apr. 2020].

Ibrahim, Y. (1991). Olympics; Olympics Committee ends its ban on participation by South Africa. *New York Times*, [online]. p.1. Available at: https://www.nytimes.com/1991/07/10/sports/olympics-olympics-committee-ends-its-ban-on-participation-by-south-africa.html [Accessed 22 Apr. 2020].

Investec, (n.d.). *Investec hockey. Supporting women's hockey in South Africa.* [online]. Available at: https://www.investec.com/en_za/sponsorships/hockey-sa.html [Accessed 22 Apr. 2020].

IOC, (2020). *Joint statement from the International Olympic Committee and the Tokyo 2020 Organising Committee.* [online]. Available at: https://www.olympic.org/news/joint-statement-from-the-international-olympic-committee-and-the-tokyo-2020-organising-committee [Accessed 22 Apr. 2020].

Kew, M. (2020). *Cape Town declares intention to host South Africa Formula E race.* [online]. autosport.com. Available at: https://www.autosport.com/fe/news/148536/cape-town-declares-intention-to-host-formula-e-race [Accessed 22 Apr. 2020].

Kidd, B. (1998). The campaign against sport in South Africa. *International Journal*, 43(4), pp. 643–666.

Langkilde, D. (2016). *Quantifying sports tourism.* [online]. Available at: https://www.tourismtattler.com/articles/events/quantifying-sports-tourism/62728 [Accessed 22 Apr. 2020].

Lock, S. (2019). *Number of tourists in South Africa from 2012 to 2023.* [online]. Statista. Available at: https://www.statista.com/statistics/300683/number-of-tourists-in-south-africa/ [Accessed 22 Apr. 2020].

Maralack, D. (2014). Sport policy in South Africa. In: M. Keim and C. de Coning, eds., *Sport and development policy in Africa – Results of a collaborative study of selected country cases* Stellenbosch: Africa Sun Media, pp. 119–138.

Maralack, D., Keim M. and de Coning, C. (2013). South Africa. In: K. Hallman and K. Petry, eds., *Comparative sport development: Systems, participation and public policy.* New York: Springer, pp. 253–268.

Martin-Gonzalez, R., Luque-Gil, A.M. and Swart, K. (2019). Surf tourism knowledge system: A conceptual approach. In: K. Tajeddini, V. Ratten, and T. Merkle, eds., *Tourism, hospitality and digital transformation: Strategic management aspects.* Abingdon: Routledge, pp. 175–220.

zzMckenzie, S. (2004). *Social sustainability: Towards some definitions.* [pdf]. Working Paper Series No 27. Hawke Research Institute University of South Australia. Available at: https://naturalcapital.us/images/Social%20Sustainability%20-%20Towards%20Some%20Definitions_20100120_024059.pdf [Accessed 22 Apr. 2020].

Murray, B. and Merrett, C. (2004). *Caught behind: Race and politics in Springbok cricket.* Johannesburg and Scottville: Wits University and University of KwaZulu-Natal.

Nauright, J. (1997). *Sport, culture, and identities in South African sport.* London: Leicester University Press.

Nauright, J. (2010). *Long run to freedom: Sport, culture and identities in South Africa*. Morgantown: Fitness Information Technology.

Ndalana, L. (2016). *Meet the man who wants to disrupt SA's fitness industry*. [online]. fin24. com. Available at: https://www.fin24.com/Entrepreneurs/My-Business/meet-the-man-who-wants-to-disrupt-sas-fitness-industry-20161212%0D [Accessed 26 Mar. 2020].

Nongogo, P. (2011). *The Olympic Movement and South Africa - The effect of the sport boycott and social change in South Africa: A historical perspective, 1955–2005*. PhD. University of Pretoria.

Nordling, L. (2016). *Rising to the nutrition challenge: South Africa's new obesity research centre*. [online]. The Guardian. Available at: https://www.theguardian.com/global-development-professionals-network/2016/feb/24/south-africa-obesity-nutrition-health-issues [Accessed 22 Mar. 2020].

Oxford Business Group, (2012). *Debating sport tourism benefits. South Africa*. [online]. Available at: https://oxfordbusinessgroup.com/news/south-africa-debating-sports-tourism-benefits [Accessed 22 Apr. 2020].

Prizzia, R. (2017). Sustainable development in an international perspective. In: K.V. Thai, D. Rahm, and J. D. Coggburn, eds., *Handbook of globalization and the environment*, 2nd ed. Boca Raton: Routledge, pp. 19–42.

Richardson, J. (2020a). *Cape Town Cycle Tour 2020: Coronavirus protocols introduced*. [online]. TheSouthAfrican.com. Available at: https://www.thesouthafrican.com/sport/cape-town-cycle-tour-2020-coronavirus-protocols-introduced/ [Accessed 26 Mar. 2020].

Richardson, J. (2020b). *Two Oceans Marathon cancelled due to Covid-19 outbreak*. [online]. TheSouthAfrican.com. Available at: https://www.thesouthafrican.com/sport/two-oceans-marathon-cancelled-due-to-covid-19-outbreak/ [Accessed 26 Mar. 2020].

Roostaie, S., Nawari, N. and Kibert, C.J. (2019). Sustainability and resilience: A review of definitions, relationships, and their integration into a combined building assessment framework. *Building and Environment*, 154, pp. 132–144.

Roux, C., Burnett, C. and Hollander, W.J. (2008). Curriculum enrichment through indigenous Zulu games. *South African Journal for Research in Sport, Physical Education and Recreation*, 30(1), pp. 89–103.

SAT, (2005). *Overview of the South African sports industry competitiveness*. [pdf] Johannesburg: South African Tourism. Available at: https://live.southafrica.net/media/26768/overview-of-south-african-sports-industry-competitiveness-2005-2010-06-23.pdf [Accessed 22 Apr. 2020].

SASCOC, (2013). South African Sports Confederation and Olympic Committee. [online]. Available at: https://www.teamsa.co.za/ [Accessed 22 Apr. 2020].

SDGF, (2015). *Goal 8 Decent work and economic growth*. [online]. Sdgfund.org. Available at: https://www.sdgfund.org/goal-8-decent-work-and-economic-growth [Accessed 11 Apr. 2020].

Sibembe, Y. (2020). *SA rugby prop goes pro -in Spain- and makes history*. [online]. Daily Maverick. Available at: https://www.dailymaverick.co.za/article/2020-02-26-babalwa-latsha-sa-rugby-prop-goes-pro-in-spain-and-makes-history/ [Accessed 22 Apr. 2020].

South African Government, (n.d.). *Sport and recreation white paper*. [online]. Available at: https://www.gov.za/documents/sport-and-recreation-white-paper [Accessed 22 Apr. 2020].

Sport24, (2018). *Two Oceans Marathon tackles Cape water crisis*. [online]. sport24.com. Available at: https://www.sport24.co.za/OtherSport/Athletics/South-Africa/two-oceans-marathon-tackles-cape-water-crisis-20180206 [Accessed 22 Apr. 2020].

SRSA, (2009). *A case for sport and recreation: The social and economic value of sport*. Pretoria: Government Printer.

SRSA, (2012). *National sport tourism strategy*. Pretoria: Government Printer.

SRSA, (2013). *The white paper on sport and recreation for the Republic of South Africa*. Pretoria: Government Printer.

SRSA, (2019). *EPG: Sport federation transformation status report overview 2018/2019*. [pdf] Pretoria: Government Printer. Available at: https://www.srsa.gov.za/sites/default/files/EPG%20Summary%20Transformation%20Audit%20Report%202018_2019_LR.pdf [Accessed 22 Apr. 2020].

SRSA, (2020). *The national sport and recreation amendment bill, 2020*. [pdf] Pretoria: Government Printer. Available at: https://www.srsa.gov.za/sites/default/files/SRSA%20Amendment%20Bill%20202%20-%20Notice%20-%20Memorandum%20-%20Bill.pdf [Accessed 22 Apr. 2020].

Swart, K. (2018). The South African sport industry. In: J. Jianhui, R.H. Huang and J. Nauright, eds., *Sport business in leading economies*. Bingley: Emerald Group Publishing, pp. 277–339.

Swart, K. and Bob, U. (2008). The eluding link: Toward developing a national sport tourism strategy in South Africa beyond 2010. *Politikon*, 34(3), pp. 373–391.

Tourism-Insider, (2011). Sport tourism, a new spin on an old theme. Tourism-Insider Online Magazine, 9 May. Available at: http://tourism-insider.com/en/2011/05/english-sport-tourism-a-new-spin-on-an-old-theme/ [Accessed 23 Apr. 2020].

United Nations, (2019). *Social development for sustainable development*. [online]. UN.org. Available at: https://www.un.org/development/desa/dspd/2030agenda-sdgs.html [Accessed 16 Mar. 2020].

UNWTO, (n.d.). *Sports tourism*. [online]. Available at: https://www.unwto.org/sport-tourism [Accessed 22 Apr. 2020].

Van der Merwe, J. (2007). Political analysis of South Africa's hosting of the Rugby and Cricket World Cups: Lessons for the 2010 football World Cup and beyond? *Politikon*, 34(1), pp. 67–81.

Vardien, T. (2019). *Banyana star Refiloe Jane signs for Italian giants AC Milan*. [online]. Sport 24. Available at: https://m.sport24.co.za/Soccer/BafanaBafana/banyana-star-refiloe-jane-signs-for-italian-giants-ac-milan-20190906 [Accessed 22 Apr. 2020].

Wilson, A. (2020). *Sicily to subsidise post-Covid holidays as Italy ponders reopening to tourists*. [online]. The Guardian. https://www.theguardian.com/travel/2020/may/05/sicily-to-subsidise-post-covid-holidays-as-italy-considers-reopening-to-tourists [Accessed 15 May. 2020].

Wren, C.S. (1991). Olympics; An era begins: South Africa to go to Olympics. *New York Times*. [online]. p. 19. Available at: https://www.nytimes.com/1991/11/07/sports/olympics-an-era-ends-another-begins-south-africa-to-go-to-olympics.html [Accessed 22 Apr. 2020].

Xasa, T. (2018). *Speech on women and sport dialogue*. [online]. 24 August, Gauteng. Available at: https://www.srsa.gov.za/speech-women-and-sport-dialogue-ms-tokozile-xasa-mp-minister-sport-and-recreation-sa [Accessed 22 Apr. 2020].

Zietsman, G. (2018). *#ItsAllStillHere: Cape Town dropping into surf tourism + best waves in SA*. [online]. Traveller24. Available at: https://m.traveller24.com/FindYourEscape/CapeTown/itsallstillhere-cape-town-dropping-into-surf-tourism-best-waves-in-sa-20180911 [Accessed 22 Apr. 2020].

Chapter 12

Sport and development in South Korea

A critical analysis of media discourses on the unified Korean women's ice hockey team in the PyeongChang 2018 Olympic Games

Yeomi Choi

Introduction

Since the establishment of the North and South Korean administrations in 1948, the two sides have steadily engaged in various inter-Korean sport exchanges with each other. Given their special political relationship, in many cases, such attempts have been planned and conducted to develop positive mutual relations through sport rather than for the development of Korean sport itself. In particular, sport mega-events such as the Olympic Games have been consciously employed in that they not only contribute to the enhancement of peaceful bilateral ties but also serve to display them and each side's national prestige on the global stage with the help of the media.[1]

Thirty years after the 1988 Seoul Olympics, the 2018 Olympics was held in PyeongChang, South Korea. To host the event, the Korean government emphasised the Olympic ideal of 'peace' throughout the bidding process and finally won the right to host the Games on its third attempt. The host's sport-for-peace initiative to promote and sustain peace on the Korean Peninsula and in Northeast Asia gained momentum with North Korea's participation. In particular, a unified North-South Korean team was formed for the first time in Olympic history. Yet, in contrast with the wishes of the South Korean government and the International Olympic Committee (IOC), which were both looking forward to fostering an atmosphere of peace and development in and through the Olympics, the South Korean public did not fully support North Korea's participation in the PyeongChang Games and especially the decision to form a unified team. Why and how did the state-led attempt to use the Olympics as an opportunity to promote peace, which may sound innocuous and righteous, stir up controversy in Korean society? This chapter approaches these questions by examining how the PyeongChang Olympics and the unified team were discussed and narrativised in the media.

While the meaning of development through hosting the Olympics is often interpreted within the context of economic growth and infrastructure (Darnell, 2012a), this particular Korean context sheds light on the aspects of post-war reconciliation and détente in and through the Olympics. To be clear, the focus of this chapter is not on interrogating whether the hosting of the Olympic Games in PyeongChang effectively contributed to the promotion and advent of peace on the Korean Peninsula and providing an explicit answer to that question. Instead, through a critical reading of media texts on the controversy over the unified team at the PyeongChang Games, it seeks to understand how Korea's sport-for-peace initiative and related major notions and issues are discursively constructed through media coverage today, which could yield important and meaningful implications leading to the achievement of development and peace through the Olympics within the region and beyond.

To do this, 47 articles that narrated the unified Korean team from 13 South Korean daily newspapers (published between 11 January 2018 and 25 February 2018) were collected and analysed using content analysis. The following section focuses on North Korea's participation, providing a historical contextualisation of the PyeongChang Games and sketches out the landscape of the controversy surrounding the unified team in South Korea.

PyeongChang 2018, two Koreas and the joint Korean team

South Korea's liberal administration, in power since 2017, which favoured engagement with North Korea, endeavoured to make the Northern neighbour come to the Winter Games. South Korea's President Moon Jae-in envisioned the event as building momentum for the resumption of dialogue for a better relationship with the North and eventually for a peace settlement on the Korean Peninsula. In addition to the inter-Korean political issue, to the host, North Korea's participation was also a necessary condition that had to be achieved for the event to go ahead as planned as the international situation was against the South's hosting aspirations, regarding North Korea as a threat to global peace and security.

On 3 September 2017, just a few months before the event, North Korea claimed that it had successfully tested an intercontinental ballistic missile (ICBM), which was its sixth and "most powerful nuclear test" (Orjoux and George, 2018). The international community voiced concerns over the North's provocations and the United Nation's sanctions on the state followed. US President Donald Trump warned and mocked North Korea's leader Kim Jong-un saying that "Rocket Man is on a suicide mission for himself" during his speech at the United Nations General Assembly (UNGA). He also added, "If it is forced to defend ourselves or our allies, we will have no choice but to totally destroy North Korea" (cited in Borger, 2017, 8). A few days later, Kim Jong-un responded to Trump, calling him a "dotard" and "mentally deranged" (cited in Samuelson, 2017, 3).

The insult exchange between the two world leaders was never helpful to the Olympic host. It instead sparked some countries' anxieties over security on the Korean Peninsula. France publicly stated that it might boycott the Olympics if safety was not guaranteed. Germany and Austria agreed saying that they were also considering not attending the Olympics. Reporting that PyeongChang is situated just 80 km (50 miles) from the Demilitarized Zone (DMZ) that separates South Korea from North Korea, and the two states are still technically at war, foreign media also seemed to incite such fears (McCurry, 2017). To reassure other countries and encourage them to come to South Korea, the Korean officials made efforts to provide an optimistic view arguing that the PyeongChang Games, which particularly sought the value of peacebuilding, would be the safest in Olympic history.

This point was accentuated again during the 72nd session of the UNGA held on 13 November 2017. In support of the Olympic Truce resolution for the Pyeong-Chang Games, Kim Yuna, South Korean Olympic gold medalist figure skater and a goodwill ambassador for the PyeongChang Games, in her short speech, stressed several times the significance of the peace and solidarity that the PyeongChang Games would build and sustain. Kim said, "PyeongChang represents perhaps the most sincere effort to cross frozen borders between North and South Korea and foster a peaceful environment" (cited in Kim and Jung, 2017, p. A5). Nevertheless, concerns over a possible military provocation by North Korea were not entirely resolved, and many still remembered North Korea's terror attacks during the Seoul Olympics in 1988.

However, Kim Jong-un's New Year's Day address, which was made only a month before the Olympics, suddenly broke the ice. In the address, he declared his willingness to send a team to the PyeongChang Games. Moon Jae-in welcomed Kim's suggestion and ordered the officials to swiftly draw up measures to restore inter-Korean dialogue and realise North Korea's participation in the games (KBS, 2018). The government's eagerness to construct the PyeongChang Olympics as a peace festival became visible. The US also assisted in decreasing tensions in PyeongChang by agreeing to suspend joint South Korea-US military drills during the Games, which had been requested by Moon Jae-in.

On 9 January 2018, at the inter-Korean talks held at the Peace House of Panmunjom, both sides consented to the North's participation in the PyeongChang Olympics. A week later, follow-up talks were held at the same place, and a joint statement containing 11 agreements was announced after the meeting. The deal included a joint march with the use of the Korean Peninsula flag at the opening ceremony, the formation of a unified women's ice hockey team, the dispatch of North Korean cheering squad and art troupe and joint ski training at the Masikryong Ski Resort located in North Korea. Following this, after a consultation at the IOC headquarters in Lausanne, Switzerland, with the North and South Korean Olympic Committees and the PyeongChang Organising Committee, Thomas Bach, the IOC President, officially announced on 20 January 2018 that the Democratic People's Republic of Korea (DPRK) would participate at the PyeongChang Games. By the agreement, 22 North Korean athletes in three sports and five disciplines were accredited to take part in the games.

This announcement was quickly and widely disseminated in South Korean society through the news media. Contrary to expectations from the government and the IOC that the reconciliation mood at the Olympics would contribute to the peace and harmony on the Korean Peninsula and in Northeast Asia, many media outlets responded to the decision in a pessimistic tone. In addition, the South Korean public did not seem to welcome North Korea's engagement in the event.

Negative public opinion about the Olympics was especially amplified over the formation of the unified team in women's ice hockey. The public ire towards the government became sharper when South Korea's Prime Minister Lee Nak-yon defended the decision with the reasoning that the women's ice hockey team was out of medal contention. A few days later, he apologised for his remarks, but the controversy over the team continued. The presidential Blue House website was flooded with petitions against forming a unified team with the North. One particular petition was made to the National Human Rights Commission of South Korea against Do Jong-hwan, South Korean Minister of Culture, Sports and Tourism, arguing that such a move violated the human rights of South Korean athletes, specifically the right to pursue happiness and freedom of occupation. Some pointed out that it was a sexist decision, implying that women's sport and its athleticism are not crucial and thus the last-minute insertion of new players is not a big deal (Jeong, 2018).

The fact that there was no prior consultation between the team and the government further angered the public. Sarah Murray, the head coach of South Korea women's national ice hockey team, said she was "shocked" to hear the joint team proposal only 20 days before the Olympics. She added in the interview that:

> I think there is damage to our players [...] It's hard because the [South Korean] players have earned their spots and they think they deserve to go to the Olympics. Then you have people being added later. It definitely affects our players.
>
> (Cited in Fifield, 2018, 7)

The administration attempted to placate the squad as well as the broader public. The day after Murray's interview was released, Moon Jae-in visited the Jincheon National Training Centre where South Korean Olympic athletes were training. During the visit, Moon met with the ice hockey players and explained the meaning of a unified team and a joint parade saying that "It can be the beginning of developing relationship between South and North Korea with a bigger significance than just the North participating in the Olympics" (cited in the *Dong-A Ilbo*, 2018). Moon also stressed that the plan would be a good opportunity for the Korean ice hockey teams to attract more public attention.

Despite the government's explanation that the North's participation is both for *sport for development* (i.e., for the purpose of peace) and *sport development* (i.e., for Korean hockey itself), negative public opinion that a unified team would rob South Korean players of a rare chance to play in the Olympics was not dampened. The well-known conservative newspaper, *Chosun Ilbo*, cited conservative parties' remarks that the PyeongChang Games was becoming "Pyongyang Olympics", deeming the North's agreement to form a unified team a disguised peace gesture. The suspension of the South Korea-US joint military drills and the imprinting of the image of North Korea's pursuit of peace to people around the world were mentioned explicitly as the North's underlying motive behind its participation (C.H. Lee, 2018, 1). Although various media outlets acknowledged that the "Pyongyang Olympics" analogy was immoderate and absurd, the controversy over the PyeongChang Olympics continued.

Amid such a domestic clamour, the Olympics began on 9 February 2018, and the unified team had matches against Switzerland, Sweden and Japan, in turn. Switzerland and Japan initially complained that forming a joint team was unfair and against the rules, but they eventually accepted the decision. To assist reaching this agreement, Thomas Bach, the IOC president, and René Fasel, the president of the International Ice Hockey Federation (IIHF), sent their full support. Furthermore, they approved the inclusion of more players for the joint team, and as a result, the team's quota was increased to 35 by adding 12 North Koreans to the existing 23-member South Korean team. Yet, the number of players allowed to compete in each game was 22, just like any other participating country, and at least three North Korean players had to play each game.

As the Olympics progressed, public antipathy towards the unified team and the event seemed to gradually ease, and the media began to dramatise the squad after watching its historic debut. The coach and South Korean players who had either voiced dissatisfaction with the government's decision or declined any comment on the new members also seemed to embrace and support the North Korean players finally. According to a poll conducted in February 2018, 56.8% of South Koreans thought the unified team was a "good decision" while 38.7% thought it was a "wrong decision" (Kang and Jeong, 2018). The approval rating for Mr. Moon, which had hit a record low since taking office, was also revived.

Nevertheless, given that even the government-friendly liberal media critiqued the Moon administration in their early narratives, it is argued that this high-profile incident and the social dispute involved function as an important and interesting cultural context to suggest what has to be considered in the process of devising and implementing a concrete peace agenda in and through the Olympics. In the section that follows, key media discourses surrounding the joint team are addressed and discussed, including themes of de/politicisation of sport and Korean nationalism.

Media construction of the unified team

De/politicisation of sport

Relying on an ideological frame of liberalism, mainstream news media stressed that one of the key rhetorical claims undergirding the negative public opinions about a single team was the government's violation of fairness of sport. In the media coverage, the young generation was especially cited as the main actors who strongly expressed such antipathy. The results of a poll were often used as the rationale of such a view's legitimacy: When asked if forming a unified team was unfair, 74% of the respondents said "yes", and among them, those in their 20s and 30s answered so at a higher rate than other generations (Cho, 2018). The fact that the decline in presidential approval rating was noticeable among the under-40 age group was also highlighted (S.J. Lee, 2018). One reporter in the *Kukmin Ilbo* pointed out that this difference in approval rating among younger people was unusual:

> Young people in their 20s and 30s are the age group that showed the highest approval rating in various surveys since the inauguration of the Moon Jae-in administration. They were called the president's strong base of support. On the issue of inter-Korean exchanges at the PyeongChang Olympics, which President Moon is actively pushing for, the unwavering supporters are raising their dissenting voices against it. This situation shows that the younger generation's important 'value' is different from the past.
>
> (Tae, 2018, 6)

Another reporter stated that young people turned their backs on "the violent and old sensibility of the name 'nation-state,' which easily ignores individuals invoking a medal haul" (B.C. Lee, 2018, p. A26). According to their analysis, today's young people in South Korea are driven to give up getting a job and marriage due to intensified competition amid the unreasonable economic and social systems. Thus, they have a keen sensitivity to social issues and problems of inequality. In this sense, they were understood as a group prone to sympathise with the Korean athletes, with the belief that the players' opportunity to go to the Olympics, which had been gained by years of hard work, was stolen by the nation.

In contrast, the North Korean players were highlighted as free riders to the Olympics, thanks to the tickets earned by South Korean players. Moon Jae-in's remarks which had been a core part of his inauguration speech were also attacked: "There is even criticism that Mr. Moon broke his promise he made in his inaugural address that 'the opportunity will be equal, the process will be fair, and the outcome will be just'" (Lee, Sohn and Park, 2018, p. A1). As such, various media outlets conveyed disapproval that the government unfairly built a unified team under the pretext of restoring inter-Korean relations, turning a blind eye to Korean athletes who had been trying for years to go to the Olympics.

Furthermore, the issue of fairness was intermingled with the rhetoric of de/politicising sport or the Olympics. The media regarded the unified team as improvised for a political purpose, and thus politics was accused of polluting the purity of sport, causing unfairness in and through the Olympics. For example, a journalist in the *Dong-A Ilbo* stated that:

The life of sport lies in keeping the rules, and in purity. Another thing is to rule out ideological or political intervention. [...] The existence of past cases does not justify the same logic. The PyeongChang Olympics is an opportunity to complete the [South Korea's] world sport grand slam and the winter dream that has been waiting for more than a decade, and to establish sport justice right.

(T.Y. Lee, 2018, p. A37)

Here, the real value and spirit of the sport were identified as having to be irrelevant to politics, considering the hasty push for a unified team could undermine sport justice. The accusation was also directed at the IOC, devaluing it as a highly political group. One reporter noted that the IOC, which strictly bans athletes from politics in principle, used nationalism and international conflict as its driving force for a hit of the Olympics, and the decision regarding the joint team also demonstrated that the IOC placed its political goals above the spirit of sport (K.W. Lee, 2018). In a similar manner, some argued that the reason why the IOC president was paying particular attention to the PyeongChang Olympics was to establish the foundation for his re-election by successfully hosting the Games (T.H. Kim, 2018a).

Many scholars have argued that there is a close tie between sport and politics, and in particular, that the Olympics and politics have been inextricably linked since the foundation of the Games (Cha, 2009; Lee, 2016; Sage, 2010). Nevertheless, a sport purist's view that politics should be kept out of sport was accentuated in the South Korean media which reflects today's Korean society, where social inequality has deepened. It further implies that unless the governmental engagement in *sport for development and peace* (SDP) is expanded to a social development strategy considering how to address and resist structural inequality in Korea, the imperative of the development policy of establishing peace on the Korean Peninsula may not be supported by the local community.

The development logic featuring fairness is seemingly related to the connectivity of sport and politics only, but it is inevitably combined with a nationalist discourse in that the young generation is predominantly identified with the South Korean team and its members, not the North's squad. This is the point where the concepts of 'we' and 'they' are generated, which are discussed next.

Korean nationalism in divided Korea: defining 'we' and 'they'

When the controversy over the unified team flared up, the Moon administration emphasised that 'our' players would not suffer much damage to defend the decision to include North Korean players (T.G. Park, 2018). The news media also reported in a worried tone that pushing for a unified team would be an unfair act that would penalise 'our' team. It is thus fair to ask and ponder: Who are 'we'? How are 'we' defined in the media? And who are not 'we'? In some progressive media, 'we' were often deliberately used to refer to both North and South Koreans (i.e., 'we are one'), but in many other examples, the term 'we' was identified with South Korean nationals only. In contrast, North Koreans were depicted as those increasingly moving away from the 'we' category:

> There are many reasons for their strong disapproval of the unified team. However, most of all, the fact that public sentiment toward North Korea has deteriorated as the two Koreas have been in conflict over the past decade cannot be left out. The worsened public perception toward North Korea is also confirmed through figures. According to the 2016 Unification Consciousness Survey by the Institute for Peace and Unification Studies at Seoul National University, the number of South Koreans who view North Korea as a 'cooperative object' was reduced from 56.6% in 2007 to 43.7% in 2016, while that of those who view the North as a 'hostile object' increased from 6.6% to 14.8%. The controversy cannot be free from criticism that the government pushed for itself without careful consideration of such changes in public perception.
>
> (B.S. Park, 2018, p. A26)

The majority of scholarship over inter-Korean relations suggests that South Koreans have mixed and ambivalent emotions towards North Korea and its people: North Koreans are neighbours sharing the same blood as South Koreans, but at the same time, they are enemies of South Koreans (Jeong, 2017; Joo, 2012; Lee, 2014; Shin, 2006). As a poll cited in the newspapers revealed, however, South Koreans' sentiment towards North Korea has worsened in recent years. Certainly, to South Koreans today, North Korea is mostly seen as an unpredictable autocratic state that threatens the security of South Korea and the international community with nuclear tests and missiles, and thus, its citizens, too, are considered either enemies or at least dissimilar entities rather than compatriots (Jeong, 2017; Shin, 2006).

The media reports on the controversy over the hockey team were mostly based on this public perception. Quoting remarks by Sohn Ki-woong, former head of the Korea Institute for National Unification, that "after 70 years of division, the meaning of 'we are one' was lost", the *Segye Ilbo* emphasised that a growing number of people, especially the younger people, disagree with the idea that the two Koreas should be reunified no matter what the cost (T.H. Park, 2018, p. A31). As such, despite the assumption of shared blood, culture and history among Koreans, the media tend to illuminate North Koreans as those who do not necessarily have to be woven into the same group as South Koreans. Such a perspective appeared to resonate the view that North and South Korea represented 'two nations-two states', not 'one nation-two states' (Jeong, 2017).

Instead, it was noted that contemporary South Korea was reimagined by embracing new nationals. As one media outlet named the hockey team as "bibimbap", a Korean rice dish mixing various ingredients, the joint women's ice hockey team for the PyeongChang Games featured unprecedented diversity indeed (K.H. Lee, 2018, p. A30). In addition to the 12 players from North Korea, four players of Korean descent from the US and Canada joined the team, and a white Canadian was recruited as the head coach. The three players from North America, including Randi Griffin, Danelle Im and Caroline Park, were naturalised in South Korea, and Marissa Brandt (who had been adopted to the US) recovered her South Korean nationality so that they were able to compete in the Olympics as members of Team Korea.

In addition to the Korean passports they obtained, they joined the national team in 2017 and trained together with the original members for years. As a result, the four immigrants were portrayed as 'our' players who were baffled and disappointed by the news of the sudden decision for a joint Olympic team (H.C. Park, 2018). Moreover, many newspapers noted that the players' parents are 'overseas Koreans' who were born to Korean parents in the Korean Peninsula but live abroad. For example, the *Dong-A Ilbo* stressed that "Their backgrounds are different, but they all share the same Korean blood" (Han, 2018, p. A30).

In such a media rhetoric, a qualification to be Korean seems to depend on whether they are persons of Korean heritage. A biracial player, such as Randi Griffin, who was born to a white American father and a Korean mother, was not an exception to such embracement by being presented as ethnically and racially Korean.[2] While the ethnic affinity to North Koreans tended to be increasingly weakened, the notion of a blood connection among Koreans was rather markedly applied to include overseas Koreans (in North America) as South Korean nationals. As Kang (2007) argues, belonging to the political community of the Republic of Korea or not has become very meaningful in defining Koreans' identity. Whereas the notion of shared blood and culture has been a potent measure of defining Koreans in the past, he reminds us that political membership plays a more crucial role in distinguishing 'us' from 'others' in contemporary South Korea. Such a transformation mirrors South Korea's desire to improve its national power and global prestige, contributing to the shaping ideas of global 'Koreanness' (Joo, 2012).

Furthermore, it is worth noting that Sarah Murray was often interactively situated in and with the media's construction of the unified team and thus 'Korean/ness'. By and large, in the representation of the squad, the media tended to draw attention to Murray's leadership and authority. Reporting the public's antipathy towards the formation of a unified team, several media frequently cited Murray's initial response to the news, which displayed discontent and embarrassment, and her remarks that, "I would not comply with the [government's] order to field North Korean athletes" (T.H. Kim, 2018b, p. 17).

As such, Murray was depicted as a guardian, protecting 'our' players as underdogs from a possible exercise of governmental power. Certainly, against the move, she said, "It would definitely affect *our* players" as cited above [emphasis added]. On the other hand, Murray was given the status of a saviour who successfully integrated the North and South Korean players as one team. One reporter in the

Hankook Ilbo stated that the head coach made "small reunification" in the ice link by contributing to the reconciliation of the players of two Koreas who were forced to gather as part of the regime's peace policy (J.S. Kim, 2018, p. 3).

Even though Murray does not share the ethnic affinity with South Koreans, unlike the athletes mentioned above, she was regarded as South Koreans' 'neighbour' or 'companion' properly interacting with them, and accordingly, her foreignness merged with her whiteness, and North American citizenship was not interrogated or problematised. In this way, the category of 'we' was strategically manufactured in the media, which acted as soil for creating understandings of the single team.

Conclusion

In this chapter, the South Korean media narratives surrounding the controversy over the combined inter-Korean team for the 2018 PyeongChang Olympics have been examined. In contrast to the former sport exchanges in and through sport mega-events with the North, which were largely welcomed and supported by the majority of the South Korean nationals (i.e., the 2002 Busan Asian Games), the recent sport cooperation provoked a public backlash, and the South Korean government was perplexed by the unexpected response.

In South Korea, the conflicting perceptions of North Korea have been the primary criterion for separating political conservatives and liberals, causing ideological strife among them (Lee, 2016). In general, the liberal public and media tend to recognise North Korea as a partner and prefer the engagement policy towards the North. In contrast, the conservative side tends to regard the North as an enemy and support its hard-line policy towards Pyongyang. In some ways, the 2018 Olympics, which was held under the current liberal administration, was not an exception to such dichotomous frames (i.e., 'PyeongChang Olympics' vs. 'Pyongyang Olympics'). Nevertheless, not only the conservative but also the liberal media expressed concerns and criticisms over the state-led peace initiative, specifically, the formation of a unified team.

One distinctive media narrative surrounding the incident was related to a logic of sport purism: 'Keep politics out of sport'. Through the discourse, it was stressed that even if the unified team is for 'the great cause' of realising peace on the Korean Peninsula, it should not be achieved at the expense of athletes and sport spirit. Young people in their 20s and 30s were revealed as the main voices resistant to various issues of social inequality in a highly competitive Korean society. On the one hand, through such coverage, how meanings of sport and inter-Korean sport exchanges are constructed in today's public discourse in South Korea can be understood.

On the other hand, the discourse suggests the need to rethink the meaning, method and directionality of the sport-focused development project between the two Koreas, demonstrating that it is becoming more critical to attend to domestic social change and seek public consent when it comes to envisaging state-led development and peace initiatives through sport mega-events such as the Olympics.

The conceptualisation of 'Korean/ness' was also conspicuous in the reading of the media narratives. The Korean ethnic identity was ambivalently employed to set the scope of South Koreans. As the ethnic affinity between North and South Koreans became increasingly weakened, North Koreans tended to be excluded from the 'imagined community' of South Korea (Anderson, 1983). In contrast, through the very ideas of blood and ethnicity, naturalised players seemed to be welcomed as members of South Korea.

The envisioned Korea here was not a unified Korea but a global South Korea, a political entity, caring about promoting its economic liberalisation and global prestige. The naturalised Koreans were embraced because they were considered beneficial to be global Korea, while North Koreans were not. In a similar vein, interestingly, without sharing blood, history and culture with South Koreans, Murray was positioned as a representative of South Korea.

According to Kobierecki (2018), 'the sports cooperation between North and South Korea from the very beginning was, in a way, a reflection of political relations' (p. 146). Indeed, as the PyeongChang Olympics also partly substantiated, inter-Korean sports diplomacy was depressed in the times of political impasse, while it thrived when the political tensions and confrontations were alleviated. This Winter Games and especially the unified team, despite their historical significance and the expectations of the international community, may also have little to do with continuous sport exchanges and development and forming a climate of conciliation on the Korean Peninsula and beyond. Two months after the Olympics, the historic North-South Summit was held, and the improved atmosphere led to the meeting between Donald Trump and Kim Jong-un. However, at the time of writing, North Korea is again arousing international concerns, resuming military provocation.

Even though it could be agreed that development and peace initiatives and policies connected to the Olympics are limited in their ability to bring about a complete thaw in relations between the two Koreas, this chapter has shown the close relationship between sport mega-events, development and the media.

Sport mega-events have the potential to reach more people through media coverage, and accordingly, the development agenda of the events can get more public attention (Darnell, 2012b). Therefore, how the media reproduce and interpret sport mega-events, and the development and peace content ascribed to it, is significant for the effective contributions of sport to the broader social good. Although few South Korean media captured the North Korean human rights issues along with their reports on the PyeongChang Olympics and the unified team, in this sense, the dire humanitarian situation in the North also needs to get attention and be discussed in connection with the mega-events held on the Korean Peninsula.

Notes

1 For a discussion of the history of inter-Korean sport exchanges focusing on large-scale and mega-events of sport, see Bridges (2015), Cha (2009), Chung (2002), Kobierecki (2018), Lee (2017), Manzenreiter (2009), Merkel (2008) and Min and Choi (2019).
2 The naturalised female players were ambivalently constructed in the media, depending on whom they were situated with. The media tended to describe the four women as 'strangers' when they were displayed in relation to indigenous South Korean players (the 'we'), while the four were regarded as more qualified Koreans when non-ethnic Koreans (i.e., white immigrants) were their counterparts (Choi, 2020).

References

Anderson, B. (1983). *Imagined communities: Reflections on the origin and spread of nationalism.* London: Verso.

Borger, J. (2017). Donald Trump threatens to 'totally destroy' North Korea in UN speech. *The Guardian.* [online]. Available at: https://www.theguardian.com/us-news/2017/sep/19/donald-trump-threatens-totally-destroy-north-korea-un-speech [Accessed 26 Jan. 2020].

Bridges, B. (2015). Flags, formulas and frustrations: North-South Korean Olympic 'cooperation'. *Asia Pacific Journal of Sport and Social Science,* 4(3), pp. 211–222.

Cha, V. (2009). *Beyond the final score: The politics of sport in Asia.* New York: Columbia University Press.

Cho, H.J. (2018). A society where hard work can't guarantee results … There should be a test. *The Hankyoreh.* [online]. Available at: http://www.hani.co.kr/arti/society/society_general/830816.html [Accessed 24 Jan. 2020].

Choi, Y.M. (2020). Stranger fetishism: Race, gender, and nationalism in the construction of naturalised Koreans for the 2018 Olympic Games, paper presented at the Asia Research Institute's workshop (New Racism and Migration: Beyond Colour and the West), National University of Singapore, Singapore, 16–17 January.

Chung, C.M. (2002). The history of exchanging North-South Korean sports and developmental scheme. *Korean Journal of History for Physical Education, Sport and Dance,* 10, pp. 51–76.

Darnell, S. (2012a). Olympism in Action, Olympic hosting and the politics of 'sport for development and peace': Investigating the development discourses of Rio 2016. *Sport in Society,* 15(6), pp. 869–887.

Darnell, S. (2012b). *Sport for development and peace: A critical sociology.* London: Bloomsbury Academic.

Dong-A Ilbo (2018). Convincing the public on N. Korea's participation in Olympics. *The Dong-A Ilbo.* [online]. Available at: http://www.donga.com/en/article/all/20180118/1194853/1/Convincing-the-public-on-N-Korea-s-participation-in-Olympics [Accessed 25 Jan. 2020].

Fifield, A. (2018). Koreas plan Olympic first with joint women's hockey team. But many in the South are not happy. *Columbia Daily Tribune.* [online]. Available at: https://www.columbiatribune.com/zz/shareable/20180117/koreas-plan-olympic-first-with-joint-womens-hockey-team-but-many-in-south-are-not-happy [Accessed 26 Jan. 2020].

Han, K.S. (2018). Dong-a square/Han Kyu-sub: Brandt, I support your 'woo-saeng-soon'. *The Dong-A Ilbo.* [online]. A30. Available at: http://www.donga.com/news/Top/article/all/20180203/88490863/1?comm [Accessed 25 Jan. 2020].

Jeong, H.W. (2017). National identity change in South Korea: An empirical study on the rise of two nations-two states identities. *Korea University Peace & Democracy Institute*, 25(2), pp. 43–86.

Jeong, Y.C. (2018). Sarah Murray says 'I can't control the formation of a unified Korean team, but I will control the strategy. *The Dong-A Ilbo*. [online]. p. A26. Available at: http://www.donga.com/news/article/all/20180123/88312505/1 [Accessed 25 Jan. 2020].

Joo, R.M. (2012). *Transnational sport: Gender, media, and global Korea*. Durham: Duke University Press.

Kang, W.T. (2007). The national identity and ethnic identity of South Koreans: Korean nationalism. In: W. Kang, ed., *The national identity of Koreans and Korean politics*. Seoul: East Asia Institute, pp. 15–38.

Kang, B.H. and Jeong, H.B. (2018). 'Single team, good work' 56.8%... the increase in approval since the opening of the Olympic Games. *Kyunghyang Shinmun*. [online]. p. A3. Available at: https://news.khan.co.kr/kh_news/khan_art_view.html?art_id=201802141659001&code=910100 [Accessed 27 Jan. 2020].

KBS, (2018). S. Korea welcomes Kim Jong-un's new year's speech, proposes dialogue. *KBS*. [online]. Available at: http://world.kbs.co.kr/service/news_view.htm?lang=e&Seq_Code=132822 [Accessed 26 Jan. 2020].

Kim, J.S. (2018). What's wrong with losing all the games? ... Murry who made 'small reunification' in the ice link. *Hankook Ilbo*. [online]. p. 3. Available at: https://www.hankookilbo.com/News/Read/201802201846774305 [Accessed 27 Jan. 2020].

Kim, T.H. (2018a). Why is Bach obsessed with the unified team? *Kukmin Ilbo*. [online]. p. 14. Available at: http://news.kmib.co.kr/article/view.asp?arcid=0923894792 [Accessed 26 Jan. 2020].

Kim, T.H. (2018b). Murray says, 'Even if the government orders me to field North Korean players, I will not follow'. *Kukmin Ilbo*. [online]. p. 17. Available at: http://news.kmib.co.kr/article/view.asp?arcid=0923888998 [Accessed 26 Jan. 2020].

Kim, J.E. and Jung, I.H. (2017). Olympic Truce resolution adopted by UN General Assembly. *The Hankyoreh*. [online]. p. A5. Available at: http://english.hani.co.kr/arti/english_edition/e_international/818978.html [Accessed 27 Jun. 2020].

Kobierecki, M. (2018). Inter-Korean sports diplomacy as a tool of political rapprochement. *Humanities and Social Sciences*, 25(4), pp. 139–153.

Lee, B.C. (2018). 2030 and the unified team. *Kyunghyang Shinmun*. [online]. p. A26. Available at: http://news.khan.co.kr/kh_news/khan_art_view.html?art_id=201802022102015 [Accessed 27 Jan. 2020].

Lee, C.H. (2018). Hong Joon-pyo says '[They are] preparing for the Pyongyang Olympics, not the PyeongChang Olympics'. *The Chosun Ilbo*. [online]. Available at: https://news.chosun.com/site/data/html_dir/2018/01/18/2018011801523.html [Accessed 27 Jan. 2020].

Lee, J.W. (2016). A game for the global north: The 2018 Winter Olympic Games in PyeongChang and South Korean cultural politics. *The International Journal of the History of Sport*, 33(12), pp. 1411–1426.

Lee, J.W. (2017). Do the scale and scope of the event matter? The Asian Games and the relations between North and South Korea. *Sport in Society*, 20(3), pp. 369–383.

Lee, K.H. (2018). A very special unified team. *Kyunghyang Shinmun*. [online]. p. A30. Available at: http://news.khan.co.kr/kh_news/khan_art_view.html?artid=201802041641001&utm_source=livere&utm_medium=social_share [Accessed 27 Jan. 2020].

Lee, K.W. (2018). IOC's paradox ... requiring a unified inter-Korean team but prohibiting the use of 'Taiwan'. *Kukmin Ilbo*. [online]. p. 16. Available at: http://m.kmib.co.kr/view.asp?arcid=0012105363 [Accessed 28 Jan. 2020].

Lee, N.Y. (2014). What determines Korean perception and attitude on national unification? Searching for the new analytical model. *Korea University Peace & Democracy Institute*, 22(1), pp. 167–206.

Lee, S.J. (2018). Gallop: 'President Moon's approval rating dropped by 6 per cent to 67 per cent' ... Impacted by the unified ice hockey team. *The Hankyoreh*. [online]. Available at: http://www.hani.co.kr/arti/politics/politics_general/828531.html [Accessed 27 Jan. 2020].

Lee, T.Y. (2018). North Korea's participation in the Winter Olympics is good, but do not lose the purity of sport. *The Dong-A Ilbo*. [online]. p. A37. Available at: http://www.donga.com/news/article/all/20180118/88220021/1 [Accessed 25 Jan. 2020].

Lee, H.M., Sohn, J.H. and Park, G.I. (2018). Young people opposing the unified Korean team want 'fair rules' regardless of whether they are right or wrong. *Kukmin Ilbo*. [online]. p. A1. Available at: http://news.kmib.co.kr/article/view.asp?arcid=0923886370 [Accessed 26 Jan. 2020].

Manzenreiter, W. (2009). Football diplomacy, post-colonialism and Japan's quest for normal state status. In: S. Jackson and S. Haigh, eds., *Sport and foreign policy in a globalising world*, London: Routledge, pp. 66–80.

McCurry, J. (2017). South Korea Winter Olympics: doubts raised over American athletes taking part. *The Guardian*. [online]. Available at: https://www.theguardian.com/world/2017/dec/07/south-korea-winter-olympics-doubts-over-american-athletes-taking-part [Accessed 27 Jan. 2020].

Merkel, U. (2008). The politics of sport diplomacy and reunification in divided Korea. *International Review for the Sociology of Sport*, 43(3), pp. 289–311.

Min, D. and Choi, Y. (2019). Sport cooperation in divided Korea: An overstated role of sport diplomacy in South Korea. *Sport in Society*, 22(8), pp. 1382–1395.

Orjoux, A. and George, S. (2018). Kim Jong Un offers rare olive branch to South Korea. [online]. CNN. Available at: https://edition.cnn.com/2017/12/31/asia/kim-jong-un-new-year-address-nuclear/index.html [Accessed 27 Jan. 2020].

Park, B.S. (2018). After the unified Olympic team. *The Hankyoreh*. [online]. p. A26. Available at: http://www.hani.co.kr/arti/opinion/column/828710.html [Accessed 27 Jan. 2020].

Park, H.C. (2018). A little special national team ... Four women ice hockey players' 'Olympic Story'. *The Hankyoreh*. [online]. Available at: http://www.hani.co.kr/arti/sports/sports_general/830698.html [Accessed 25 Jan. 2020].

Park, T.G. (2018). Do Jong-hwan says 'At least 5 North Korean players in the unified team were requested by the IOC'. *The Dong-A Ilbo*. [online]. Available at: http://www.donga.com/news/East/MainNews/article/all/20180202/88478919/2?comm= [Accessed 25 Jan. 2020].

Park, T.H. (2018). 2030's regret for PyeongChang. *Segye Ilbo*. [online]. p. A31. Available at: https://www.segye.com/newsView/20180131006565 [Accessed 27 Jan. 2020].

Sage, G. (2010). *Globalising sport: How organisations, corporations, media, and politics are changing sports*. Boulder: Paradigm.

Samuelson, K. (2017). Here are all the times Kim Jong Un and Donald Trump insulted each other. *Time*. [online]. Available at: https://time.com/4953283/kim-jong-un-donald-trump-insults/ [Accessed 26 Jan. 2020].

Shin, G.W. (2006). *Ethnic nationalism in Korea: Genealogy, politics and legacy*. Stanford: Stanford University Press.

Tae, W.J. (2018). 2040 turning away from the unfair single team ... President Moon's approval rating is 67 per cent. *Kukmin Ilbo*. [online]. Available at: http://news.kmib.co.kr/article/view.asp?arcid=0012063349 [Accessed 27 Jan. 2020].

Chapter 13

Sport and development in Turkey

Community sport participation, leisure spaces and social inclusion

*Selçuk Açıkgöz, Gökben Demirbaş
and Reinhard Haudenhuyse*

Introduction

The Republic of Turkey, with a population of approximately 83 million (TUIK, 2020a), is one of the largest countries amongst the Southeast-Mediterranean countries, located between Europe and the Middle East. As of 2019, the gross domestic product (GDP) of Turkey is 754.8 million US dollars, and the country has become one of the fastest developing countries in the world, particularly with the actions taken in the early 2000s (OECD, 2018). In the last decade, however, developmental investments have declined due to an economic recession, lack of investors and, most recently, the Covid-19 pandemic. The country also experienced social turmoil and several related problems in the last decade. The most notable ones were an increasing youth unemployment rate (24.6% as of May 2020), a 2016 failed coup attempt and the dismissal of hundreds of academics over a peace petition that condemned the conflicts in Southeast Turkey. Apart from the negative economic impact, these problems also are said to have had an impact on the democratisation processes.

Despite these recent social issues and economic setbacks, Turkey continues to prioritise developmental actions. In this regard, sport has received an increasing amount of attention. The Ministry of Youth and Sport (MYS) has commenced various sport-based developments such as athlete development systems, community sport initiatives, sport for development programmes, investments in sport mega-events and sport infrastructure (e.g., football stadiums, multi-purpose sport gyms, athletic fields and recreational areas). Aiming to contribute to youth development, MYS has invested in Youth Centres. Such centres often not only include different aspects of athlete development but also include leisure opportunities and the organisation of social, cultural and religious activities for youth.

Despite the high investment in sport for development initiatives, the extent to which youth centres in Turkey produce sport and social developmental outcomes is unknown. Therefore, this chapter presents findings of a qualitative research study conducted at three youth centres, as a part of the sport for development policies in Turkey. The study utilised Lefebvre's (1991) spatial trialectic concept (i.e., perceived, conceived and lived spaces) to interrogate the rationale behind the construction and execution of youth centres as leisure and sport space. The chapter proceeds with an outline of sport and development in Turkey, where different sport and development programmes initiated in Turkey are presented. Subsequently, we give information on youth centres and their current status and importance for the achievement of government objectives. The chapter also provides more insight on space and leisure and, in particular, why it is important to support leisure and community sport from the perspective of sport for development.

Policy areas of sport and development in Turkey

Sport development and sport for development have increasingly been used by the Turkish government's policies in the 21st century (Açıkgöz, Haudenhuyse and Aşçı, 2019; Tinaz, Turco and Salisbury, 2014). Sports have been used widely in political and social spheres as well as within athlete development. Sport development initiatives have accelerated with the launching of Turkish Olympic Preparation Centres (TOHM) project which prioritises developing sport athletes, signing agreements with public institutions (e.g., universities and the Ministry of Education) to increase participation in sport in school settings and to support the dual career of athlete-students. Besides investing in athlete development, policy authorities in Turkey continue to naturalise foreign-born athletes to increase the number of medals in international competitions (Reiche and Tinaz, 2019). To strengthen sport mega-event experiences as a host, Turkey hosted many international sports competitions at different levels, hoping that this would increase the chances of hosting a Summer Olympic Games, for which Istanbul has applied five times (Leopkey, Salisbury and Tinaz, 2019). Mega-sport events are also being used by Turkey for "nation branding", similar to other developing nations such as South Africa and states within the Arab Peninsula (Knott, Fyall and Jones, 2017; Testa and Amara, 2015). The sport for development concept, on the other hand, is still an emerging concept in Turkey. There are a limited number of sport for development projects organised and financed by MYS. The majority of the projects are short-term, poorly planned and primarily focused on football (cf. Açıkgöz, Haudenhuyse and Hacısoftaoğlu, 2020).

Sport infrastructures, both as economic and social development, are the focus of the MYS's current policy objectives. Like in other emerging nations, the construction industry has a predominant role for Turkey (Gregori and Pietroforte, 2015). Previous research has defined the construction sector as the locomotive of the Turkish economy and demonstrated how the Justice and Development Party (AKP) government, in the last two decades, has worked side-by-side with the private sector (Balaban, 2016; Gürek, 2008). The government facilitates the regulations to allow the private sector to continue to invest in its construction business and, even more, supports the private sector through public subsidies and bidding processes for constructions demanded by the government (i.e., urban transformation) (Balaban, 2016).

In line with the economy-politics of the AKP government, in 2011, the re-established MYS invested in infrastructural development and new sports facilities such as stadiums, sports gyms and youth centres. The initial investments in football stadiums in Turkey also helped merge football with the private sector. The MYS spent 4.4 billion Turkish lira on 32 football stadiums that were built and planned in the last eight years (MYS, 2019). Together with these 32 football stadiums and another 2,000 neighbourhood sport fields, the MYS has also built over 300 youth centres across the country since 2012 (MYS, 2019).

The significant increase of the annual budget of the MYS (from approximately 4.4 billion in 2012 to 17.8 billion Turkish lira in 2020) is an indicator of the increased focus on sport investments in Turkey (Resmi Gazete, 2011, 2019). On the other hand, Erturan-Öğüt (2014, 2020) addressed the questionable contribution of the infrastructural development on social life and instead focused on the development's encouragement of the construction sector through public-private partnerships, financing contracts and public subsidies. In a similar vein, Amara (2012) questioned the legacy issues of sporting infrastructures and how they become ineffective and economically burdensome for countries in the Arab World.

In addition to the high level of sport infrastructure investment and sport development, participation in sport competitions has also increased in Turkey. The total number of people with a license to compete in sport competitions increased from 278,046 in 2002 (Yüce and Sunay, 2013, p. 97) to 4,957,000 in 2018. As of 2018, the number of active participants in sport competition in Turkey is 695,000, with 433,000 male and 262,000 female participants (SHGM, 2018).

These figures, however, do not provide information on how often citizens actively participate in sport in their daily lives. The data show that the youth segment of the population, which could be expected to participate in sport at a higher percentage, lacks participation. For example, in 2015, the ratio of children in the 10–17 year age group participating in sport activities was 4.1% for basketball, 6% for cycling, 13.7% for football, 4.1% for volleyball, 4.8% running, 1.9% for swimming and 3% in other categories (TUIK, 2016). These low figures lead us to question the legacy of the sport (for) development investments in the country.

In the midst of social and economic development, community sports also gained attention from the public authorities. However, there is limited knowledge of how sport facilities are used for social inclusion purposes, which is considered to be one of the objectives of sport for development programmes. In this regard, the following section highlights the importance of youth centres as a social space.

Sport for all: the production of leisure spaces and social in/exclusion

Community sports participation (i.e., *sport for all*) is part of the right to leisure, which is considered a right of all human beings, yet it is not equally accessible to everybody (Henderson, Bialeschki and Shaw, 1989). This issue attracted many sport for development programmes around the world to focus on increasing social inclusion opportunities for diverse groups in sport activities (Haudenhuyse, 2017). Similar to any social practice, leisure is embedded within a multitude of discourses which are all implicated in relation to power (Friedman and Van Ingen, 2011, p. 87). It is, then, meaningful to treat leisure as a social space involving all kinds of social rules, conventions and expectations which may limit or expand opportunities for leisure-related decisions (Wearing, 1998, p. 42) and produce exclusionary or inclusionary and socio-spatial practices.

Public leisure spaces, for instance, are 'ideally' defined as common places where people from diverse backgrounds can share and interact with each other. Yet, such spaces form a homogenous group of participants (e.g., Thompson, Russell and Simmons, 2014). For instance, Yuen and Johnson (2017) discuss how the characteristics of customers in certain places are exclusionary towards some underserved, lower-income communities. Social exclusion, a multidimensional and dynamic process, manifests itself in spaces and determines the access to social resources and services (Akkan, Deniz and Ertan, 2017, pp. 74–75). Consequently, it was crucial to understand the characteristics of space when assessing sport-related development investments.

The study used Lefebvre's theoretical toolbox to understand the production of space and, in particular, to analyse operations, and sport and social outcomes of youth centres, a social space built to promote and support sport (for) development in Turkey. Lefebvre's (1991) production of space framework consists of three forms of social space: (1) spatial practice (perceived space); (2) representations of space (conceived space) and (3) representational space (lived space).

First, spatial practice (perceived space) forms the very basic phase of social space, a material environment where daily routines take place. For instance, physical activities or engaging with certain activities within a space can be defined as a spatial practice from walking through the streets to playing sports (van Ingen, 2004). Second, the representation of space (or conceived space) defines the imagined and constructed space. Here, social space is designed by a certain dominant vision that belongs to, for example, policymakers, city planners and authorities. Conceived spaces directly reflect the space of power holders, and they aim to sustain 'routine subject formation' (van Ingen, 2004, p. 203). Lastly, representational space (or lived space) explains the unfolding of conceived spaces. It defines whether conceived spaces are deconstructed by actual practices in social spaces, in that users reproduce social spaces based on their own needs, interests and worldviews.

In his conceptual framework, Lefebvre (1991) underlines the unequal role and power of mediators in the production of space. The representations of space, conceived with a combining ideology and knowledge, have a substantial role and a specific influence in the production of space: "By production of space, ideology, which is characterised by rhetoric, by meta-language,…by 'culture' and 'values'… achieves consistency" (Lefebvre, 1991, p. 44). The representations of space, according to Lefebvre (1991, p. 50), leave a limited margin for representational space to displace the former and achieve symbolic force; yet, the latter is capable of disrupting the expected forms of social practice in a conceived space. For instance, young people are able to reimagine or reconstruct spaces through their social interactions with peers, such as using spaces for their own priorities instead of what is expected from them (Lashua and Kelly, 2008; Sharpe, Lashua and van Ingen, 2019).

Youth centres in Turkey

Turkey invests in and develops its own version of Western leisure practices in relation to the government's neoliberal and neoconservative agenda (Tinaz, Turco and Salisbury, 2014; Yabanci, 2019). Building and utilising youth centres have become instrumental in achieving various development objectives. The statistics show that the number of youth centres has expanded exponentially from just 16 in 2011 to 300 in 2019. The number of centre members has also skyrocketed from 8,610 in 2011 to 2 million in 2018 (MYS, 2019). Just in 2018 alone, the MYS had 146 youth centre projects that were in different phases of construction with a total project cost of 578 million Turkish lira (approx. 83 million Euro) (MYS, 2019).

While building youth centres involves the aim of contributing to the economic development of the country, the activities in these centres are designed to meet two different development objectives: sport development and youth development through sport and leisure activities. Sport development objectives are pursued through weekly talent searches and sport activities for different age groups where children can regularly attend one of the available sport activities or prepare for local, national and international competitions. Some of these sport activities are basketball, volleyball, judo, taekwondo and 'talent search' trainings, which are organised to select skilled candidates to develop them as competitive athletes. Leisure activities, such as language, music and handcraft courses, are included alongside sport activities.

As the second objective, youth development through sport and leisure focuses on youth development for social, economical and ideological purposes. In addition to the previous activities, the main activities in this area are Quran courses, spiritual education, theatre plays and social trips (MYS, 2020).

Sport and youth development, owing to the high percentage of youth in the population of the country (24.3% of the total population is within the 15–29 age group according to the Ministry of Development, 2018), have historically been interlinked within the policy frameworks of Turkey (Aykın and Bilir, 2013). In the last two decades, the AKP government reinvigorated the existing approach of nation-building through youth and sport development with an enormous increase in sports infrastructure, especially the opening of youth centres throughout the country.

Similar to Turkey, the countries in the Middle East and North Africa (MENA) region also craft sport development policies in a way that strengthens national identity and contributes to their nation-building processes (Amara, 2012). Youth objectives comprise the main priority of MYS, and the activities are planned to construct the "ideal youth citizen". As defined in their purpose, youth centres aim to generate "nationalist", "moral" youth that "glorify its nation, family" with high skills in "social, cultural and sports fields" (MYS, 2019, p. 59). The MYS announced its responsibility of "inseminating consciousness in youth and encouraging them to transcend their private interests and personal liberties for the higher interests of the nation and the country" (MYS, 2019, p. 59). This responsibilisation of youth requires constant engagement with young people. As the numbers indicated above, the MYS invested significantly in youth centres to accomplish this task.

Youth centres are given a key role for sport and youth-related development objectives, as they provide free access, organise after-school programmes, are flexible to encourage participation and provide a range of activities that potentially attract young people to participate. Youth centres are potentially the most suitable space for young people to participate in and for sport authorities to implement sport and leisure activities. For these reasons, this chapter examines the case study of a middle-sized city in Turkey to explore how sport development and youth development through leisure and sport are realised in multiple youth centres.

Analysis of three youth centres in Edirne, Turkey

The remainder of this chapter focuses on an analysis of three youth centres located in different districts of Edirne. Edirne is a middle-sized city located in the north-west area of Turkey in a region called Trakya. It has a total population of 413,903 (TUIK, 2020b). Interviews, observations and a focus group were used to collect data from young people and centre personnel. In total, 12 participants were interviewed, and a focus group was held (comprised of five young people). The semi-structured interviews were conducted with local officials of the youth centres, who were directors, youth leaders, sport education experts, sports trainers and young participants. The focus group participants were selected from young people who regularly attend basketball courses in the youth centres. The 21 hours of observation at the youth centres and in the neighbourhoods around the centres also provided some insightful data.

The emerging research questions were mainly guided by the theoretical framework and topics that were deemed important by participants. Thematic analysis was used, where themes were identified inductively during data collection and analysis. Then, statements were sorted into identified themes, and certain regularities were highlighted. The following analysis reflects both similarities and contradictions that were revealed from the views of the participants (Sparkes and Smith, 2014).

Sport for development outcomes and organisational challenges

Increasing socialisation and opportunities of youth

Youth centres that are built all around the country, particularly in rural areas, offer a promising option for meeting sport for development objectives since they assist young people to improve their sport and social skills. One of the officials stressed the importance of the centres in this regard:

> One of the reasons youth centres are built in the country is this: Although I am an individual who wanted to have a hobby but could not get one and, in this matter, you cannot find the materials, cannot find a teacher, cannot draw very good. Ask many people they will say they were good in drawing, for example, but they never had any lecturer [who supported them] in their lives, they cannot find that opportunity. Here, there is an incredible chance to provide that opportunity. Once you step into this centre, everything is free, from your water to tea...
>
> (P1, youth centre official)

Experiencing new opportunities and being able to get support for skill development can flourish new aspirations and opportunities for young people and contain the possibility to generate long-term impacts for young people (e.g., Massey and Whitley, 2016). Providing various activities free of charge is much needed for underserved communities. While youth centres provide different activities for young people who may not have similar opportunities, the local officials generally frontline the individual stories to emphasise the impact of the centres. Although individual stories are important and show the care given by service providers at the centre, they are not representative of the general outcomes obtained from young participants. Our findings, on the other hand, suggest that several factors (e.g., location of centres, organisational incapacity, not targeting certain excluded groups) limit the potential of achieving specific social outcomes.

Distant space: a barrier to participation

Young people considered the location of youth centres as the main barrier to participating in activities. The proximity of services to lower-income communities is an essential facilitator for the participation of individuals who face exclusion and poverty (Collins, 2014). While local officials acknowledge that youth centres are built far away from lower-income communities, they approach the problem as the perception of individuals rather than reality:

> If it [the youth centre] would be in the [district] centre, of course, it would be better but [it is] too congested... Mostly, it is bad for our brothers in the disadvantaged area... sometimes they even need 1 lira, as an allowance. For the child to take a bus and come, and it is not possible to take such responsibility [for a child]. Also, they [local people] are a society who get bored for half an hour ride to here.
>
> (P2, youth centre official)

What local officials overlook is the time-dependent life of young people. The principal attendants of youth centres are students. Mostly, high-school and university students race against time after school and strive to organise different responsibilities (Thompson, Russell and Simmons, 2014). Considering this factor, young people face difficulties to attend the activities in their limited time. Young participants also mention what drives their preferences to come to a youth centre:

KEREM: I mean, young people can come however they want to but there are some problems such as transportation.

INTERVIEWER: Is transportation a severe problem for participation?

YASIN: It is for some people coming from certain places. For example, it is a problem for me. I live on the other side of the town.

I: Would you still participate if the activities were not free of charge?

YASIN: If I had to pay a fee, I wouldn't come here, [I would go to] somewhere close, I would go to [course] that is next to my home.

MERT: I wouldn't come here either [if it was not free].

The reasons for young people's participation in the youth centre activities are mainly pragmatic, and it offers something young people give importance to, despite the distance of the centres. The view of young people also shows that the location of the centres was not prioritised for the benefit of the disadvantaged, lower-income communities during the planning process. In the next section, we present findings to understand whether this lack of consideration is related to the incapacity of organisations.

Organisational incapacity

Despite multi-purpose spaces and multifaceted objectives, youth centres seem to struggle to fulfil these expectations, as they have, quantitatively, very few personnel. All the interviewed personnel underlined that the lack of personnel affects the quality of services:

> In the 3 year-period [since the youth centre was built], we have one bureau personnel, one sports education expert, one youth leader and one security personnel. We have only one in each of these. If you ask me if the duties finish on time, we do our best. Does it challenge us to organise new projects? It challenges us a lot...
>
> (P1, youth centre official)

The statements of local officials also demonstrate that the facilities were opened with as few personnel as possible, and they usually lacked the experts who had a speciality in different disciplines to consult young people for their age-related concerns and problems. As a result of the incapacity, the existing personnel often directed their priorities to the one-off, short-termed projects rather than conducting long-term, sustainable programmes (e.g., Açıkgöz, Haudenhuyse and Hacısoftaoğlu, 2020).

Invisible underserved youth

Although youth centres exhibit a general interest towards the "socially excluded" (out-of-school young people who graduated from university and high school or dropped out of the education system), their efforts are most likely an 'invitation' rather than developing concrete and well-rounded strategies to enable these groups' engagement in the centres. For instance, the Roma youth, who form a considerable number of youth in the city, are not present among the young attendants. The lack of support from parents is given as the reason of the Roma youth's non-participation:

> They don't go to school either. We went to their school once; there was almost no students.
>
> (P7, youth centre official)

> It is hard to find a solution [to their participation] because they are not supported by their parents, and they struggle to support their children because families are uneducated.
>
> (P5, youth centre official)

As a solution, the centre staff developed a project named "If you don't come, we come to you" to pay regular visits to the schools close to Roma neighbourhoods. The discourse of the youth centre is problematic since the title of the project disconnects the lack of attendance of Roma youth from their status of social exclusion, disregards it as a structural problem and, instead, reduces it to Roma youths' agency. In other words, the centre takes the nonattendance of Roma youth at face value and stigmatises them as "uncooperative". However, the findings also showed that it was the multi-layered barriers (i.e., poverty, racism and school dropout) that Roma youth face in participating in urban life.

The incapacity of youth centres in terms of human resources adds another barrier for local staff to give priority to young people who cannot benefit from the activities of the centres. Although some local personnel make an effort to reach more young people from different backgrounds, their attempts appear as tokenistic, one-off events without offering tangible benefits:

> We couldn't make the continuity persistent. We need a lot more argument [resources] to provide that persistency. Like transportation, tangible possibilities, from time to time, we tried to do this. We spoke to young people who have bad habits, but it is very hard for us to direct to a psychologist or a rehabilitation centre, but we do it to the best of our abilities.
>
> (P1, youth centre official)

The failure of staff to find resources that go beyond sport and leisure activities demonstrates that the goals of the sport for youth development programme have yet to be achieved. In relation to current literature, sport policies do seem inconsiderate in terms of sport for development in that social inclusion strategies are not secured for the participation of young people from different backgrounds in youth centres. Youth centres, as they are today, are examples of the spaces that belong to power, which maintain the inequalities and conceal its existence (van Ingen, 2003).

Youth centres as *lived spaces*: sport vs. expected ideological outcomes

The findings indicate that most young people come to the centres to take part in sport activities or to use sport gyms. Sport, specifically football in this case, seems to be used by local officials as an 'entry activity' to attract youth to the centres:

> Mostly they come for sports activities. One sport activity, and besides that we definitely try to direct them to fine arts, in whatever incomers have talent, likeness.
>
> (P5, youth centre official)

This is reminiscent of Coalter's (2007) emphasis on how sport is used as a 'hook' to invite and inform young people for other social and cultural activities. The aim of creating a spillover effect, however, seems to fall through since the interviewed high-school students, who take part in the basketball activities, state that they only use centres for sports and social activities. They come to "learn basketball", "socialise with friends", "spend free time wisely" and "relax after school". Such discrepancy between the intended and experienced outcomes directs our focus onto youth centres as representative of the relation between the conceived and lived spaces. The interior design of the youth centres represents the investment of the AKP governments on constructed space with symbolic meaning. The symbols, pictures, quotes hanging on the wall exhibit priorities of the youth centres and make references to nationalistic and religious values. Sport activities and ideological expectations coexist in the space.

Other countries in the region (e.g., Qatar, Tunisia, Algeria and Morocco) also nest their nationalist, ideological priorities with sport development policies. They support decolonised sports, practice sport activities according to Sharia or use sport to strengthen the nation-building process (Amara, 2012). The aim in the analysed centres is to stimulate popular conceptions of history and nostalgic glorification of national culture. Although symbols and codes are used to organise meanings and interpretations into a single, unified sense, as Gottdiener (2001) highlights, conveying the intended meaning varies from one social group to another. Young attendants and their families are not interested in the cultural activities that the centres offer to the youth:

One of the centre staff showed me the centre. At the main area, there used to be a 'HAS room', a room that represents Ottoman-style of conversation environment and designed with ethno-political symbols and materials. However, later on, this room was replaced with a judo gym and the has room was moved to the back of the centre. The has room has not been used for its purpose yet and currently functions as storage where they keep gifts for another project.

(19 February 2020, Youth Centre II)

As briefed in the field note, the diversion from the initial purpose generates a new purpose for the space based on the preferences of its users (Lefebvre, 1991). The local officials also highlight the nonattendance of young people to the religion-based 'value lectures' and ideologically oriented activities. Despite attempts to use the conceived space based on nationalist, religious and spiritual values education, young people have different, mostly sport-related, expectations from youth centres. When asked about the activities they would like to see in the centres, different expectations unfold:

I'd like it if they would have ballet courses. I went there for three years and left it after the trainer left the town and there isn't any ballet trainer in the town.

(P9, Funda, 15-years-old)

I wasn't interested in other activities they mentioned; dart and wrestling. I'd wished they had golf, bowling.

(P10, Yasemin, 15-years-old)

As the excerpts suggest, young people expect different sport activities in youth centres. Whether this resides as a form of resistance towards the youth centre or not, young people passively experience the space and attend only the activities they selected beforehand. The local officials, on the other hand, continue to 'fill the space' with users and overcome this non-verbalised resistance. Having assemblies and attracting people are also addressed by the officials. The comments of a local authority refer to the importance of including everyone at the centre:

This is a state investment, and there is a government who administers the state as always but be sure that this is not a party building, we classify nobody here based on their political views, [however] the state has a stand, an attitude as well…. people who do not violate this stand, and what I mean by that is [conducting] terror activities, are welcome. The door is open for every kind of young person, for every kind of thought.

(P1, youth centre official)

In the above quotation, the official responds to local people's views of the centre as a highly political space, the space of the ruling party and their unwillingness to participate in the activities of the youth centre. The resistance of the local people who were identified as 'prejudiced', forced local officials to reappropriate the space as 'diverse', 'apolitical' and 'tolerant', which is crucial for the maintenance of the centre.

The dominant discourse is that youth centres aim to be open for everyone because only then, the diversity of thoughts can be challenged, and people can be 'ideally' unified. Lefebvre (1991) explicates this as disconnecting the productive labour and the product (e.g., youth centres) which indicates that there is a need to obscure the elements that belong to the producer (the MYS) to secure the participation of young people in the youth centres. Local officials adapt their discourse to the reactions by foregrounding the centres' *public space* identity welcoming every citizen. In this way, they attempt to take the attention away from the ideological components underpinning the design of the youth centre activities. Provision of musical and sport activities are utilised in maintaining the socially inclusive and 'neutral' appearance of the centres and prevent the possible resistance of local people.

Conclusion

This chapter has analysed the sport (for) development policies and programs in Turkey with a special focus on their social results. Lefebvre's (1991) spatial trialectic concept was used to understand the social and ideological outcomes of sport (for) development investments with regard to utilisation of space. The strategies of the MYS involved continuous preparations and applications to host sport mega-events like the Olympic Games, increasing its athlete development capacity as well as increasing community sports participation. Investing in sport infrastructure is seen as the most important step to meet the summarised strategies. Increasing sport participation is an aim shared by both sport development (i.e., the legacy of mega-events, athlete development and promoting physical activity) and sport for development policies.

Youth centres are constructed by the MYS in Turkey to provide social, educational and sport activities for young people. An interrogation of the operations of youth centres and their impact on the development of young people was conducted. Youth centres were built at unprecedented speed to complete 'infrastructural development', and it is promising that young people in Turkey have a space to be themselves and develop their skills. However, in the analysed centres, this is rather a meagre development, as these urban spaces face the risk of unsustainability due to their distance from disadvantaged communities, lack of personnel and inconclusive vision to implement long-term community transformation programs for young people. Such inadequacies reduce youth centres to mere physical spaces (i.e., sport gym, football field and library) for young people who have the ability to attend, a common problem amongst the MENA and Arab countries that disproportionately invest in sport infrastructures.

The findings also suggested that although the nationalist, religion-induced activities, symbols, rituals are dominant and apparent throughout youth centres, the ideological objectives are not strictly practised, mainly due to the lack of personnel and the local characteristics of the region. Hence, the personnel use sport opportunities to attract young people to the centres due to the higher demand for sport activities in comparison to other leisure courses. Different priorities of local people disrupt the conceived outcomes and lead to significant changes in the space and discourses at the centres.

Suggestions for policymakers and practitioners

Considering the findings that exhibited the difficulty young people have to participate, particularly from underserved communities, we can see there is a need to develop alternative policies to increase community participation in sport and leisure activities. The current problems of transportation and lack of personnel highlight the lack of emphasis given to the socio-spatial aspects of the centres in the planning procedure, and these problems show how youth centres can be far from maximising their potential to provide services for diverse communities. To avoid ineffectiveness at sport fields and youth centres, the countries who invest in sports infrastructure should coordinate infrastructural and social development before the construction of sport and leisure fields are completed. By planning the possible programmes of sport and leisure fields, sport authorities can realise the possible needs of local people and the proximity of centres to low-income communities. This would help authorities to ensure that the centres are needed and built at the best possible location where diverse communities have easy access.

Despite organisational incapacity, youth centres are all-in-one spaces, conducting programmes on various subjects and aiming to simultaneously achieve different (social, sportive, ideological) outcomes. We suggest youth and sport institutions redefine the goals of their youth centres in cooperation with local authorities who are aware of the needs of young people. Local authorities should trust young people's agency and consult them in terms of which activities and skills should be developed. Also, to use their organisational capacity more wisely and offer more than a physical space, youth and sport institutions need to be specialised and, thus, focus on certain objectives that the organisational staff are capable of contributing to in order to make an impact in their respective communities.

In the selected centres, it is observed that the polarised political climate of Turkey challenges local sport authorities to invite and engage more directly with local beneficiaries as some young people show resistance to the use of youth centres due to some of the activities (e.g., religion-themed activities). Local staff can engage better with local people to explain themselves regarding the purpose of the facilities and be more transparent about the activities that are not mandatory and, instead, subject to voluntary involvement. This would also require youth centres to claim and advocate diversity not only in their discourse but also in their practices to be more socially inclusive through rigorous policies. A youth-friendly space that emphasises concepts such as peace, cultural diversity and tolerance may also welcome more young people and help to overcome prejudices.

References

Açıkgöz, S., Haudenhuyse, R. and Aşçı, H. (2019). Social inclusion for whom and towards what end? A critical discourse analysis of youth and sport policies in Turkey. *Journal of Youth Studies*, 22(3), pp. 330–345. doi: 10.1080/13676261.2018.1506571.

Açıkgöz, S., Haudenhuyse, R. and Hacısoftaoğlu İ. (2020). 'There is nothing else to do!': The impact of football-based sport for development programs in under-resourced areas. *Sport in Society*, 1–18.

Akkan, B., Deniz, M.B. and Ertan, M. (2017). The Romanization of poverty: Spatial stigmatization of Roma neighborhoods in Turkey. *Romani Studies 5*, 27(1), pp. 73–93.

Amara, M. (2012). *Sport, politics and society in the Arab world*. Basingstoke: Palgrave Macmillan.

Aykın, A.G. and Bilir, F.P. (2013). *Hükümet Programları ve Spor Politikaları*. [Government programs and sport policies]. *Ç.Ü. Sosyal Bilimler Enstitüsü Dergisi*, 22(2), pp. 239–254.

Balaban, O. (2016). İnşaat sektörü neyin lokomotifi [What the construction sector islocomotive of]. In: T. Bora, ed., *İnşaat Ya Resulullah*. İstanbul: Birikim Kitapları, pp. 17–32.

Coalter, F. (2007). *A wider social role for sport: Who's keeping the score?* London: Routledge.

Collins, M. (2014) *Sport and social exclusion*. London: Routledge.

Erturan-Öğüt, E.E. (2014). Türkiye'de Spor Yönetiminin Neoliberal Dönüşümü [Neoliberal transformation of sport management in Turkey]. *Amme İdaresi Dergisi*, 47(4), pp. 31–58.

Erturan-Ogut, E.E. (2020). Neoliberalizing football and fandom: The authoritarian e-ticketing system in Turkish stadiums. *International Journal of Sport Policy and Politics*, 12(1), pp. 91–110.

Friedman, M.T. and van Ingen, C. (2011). Bodies in space: Spatializing physical cultural studies. *Sociology of Sport Journal*, 28(1), pp. 85–105.

Gottdiener, M. (2001). *The theming of America: American dreams, media fantasies, and themed environments*, 2nd edn. Oxford: Westview Press.

Gregori, T. and Pietroforte, R. (2015). An input-output analysis of the construction sector inemerging markets. *Construction Management and Economics*, 33(2), pp. 134–145.

Gürek, H. (2008). *AKP'nin Müteahhitleri* [The contractors of AKP]. İstanbul: Güncel Yayıncılık.

Haudenhuyse, R. (2017). Introduction to the issue "sport for social inclusion: Questioning policy, practice and research". *Social Inclusion*, 5(2), pp. 85–90.

Henderson, K., Bialeschki, M.D. and Shaw, S.M. (1989). *A leisure of one's own: A feminist perspective on women's leisure*. Oxford: Venture Publishing.

Knott, B., Fyall, A. and Jones, I. (2017). Sport mega-events and nation branding. Sport mega events and nation branding: Unique characteristics of the 2010 FIFA World Cup, South Africa. *Journal of Contemporary Hospitality Management*, 29(3), pp. 900–923.

Lashua, B.D. and Kelly, J. (2008). Rhythms in the concrete: Re-imagining relationships between space, race, and mediated urban youth cultures. *Leisure/Loisir*, 32(2), pp. 461–487.

Lefebvre, H. (1991). *The production of space*. Oxford: Blackwell Publishing.

Leopkey, B., Salisbury, P. and Tinaz, C. (2019). Examining legacies of unsuccessful OlympicBids: Evidence from a cross-case analysis. *Journal of Global Sport Management*. [online]. Available at: doi: 10.1080/24704067.2019.1604072.

Massey, W. and Whitley, M. (2016). The role of sport for youth amidst trauma and chaos. *Qualitative Research in Sport, Exercise and Health*, 8(5), pp. 1–18.

Ministry of Development, (2018). The 11th Development Plan (2019–2023), child and youth specialisation commission, youth working team report [11. Kalkınma Planı (2019–2023) Çocuk ve Gençlik Özel İhtisas Komisyonu Gençlik Çalışma Grubu Raporu]. [online]. Available at: http://www.sbb.gov.tr/wp-content/uploads/2020/04/Cocuk_ve_GenclikOzelIhtisasKomisyonuGenclikCalismaGrubuRaporu.pdf [Accessed 27 Jul. 2020].

MYS (Ministry of Youth and Sport), (2019). Annual activity report 2018 [2018 YıllıkFaaliyet Raporu]. [online]. Available at: https://www.gsb.gov.tr/Sayfalar/3253/3143/dosyalar.aspx [Accessed 04 Apr. 2020].

MYS (Ministry of Youth and Sport), (2020). Youth centres academy [Gençlik Merkezleri Akademisi]. [online]. Available at: https://ghgm.gsb.gov.tr/Sayfalar/3277/3187/genclik-merkezleri-dairesi.aspx [Accessed 23 Jul. 2020].

OECD [Organization for Economic Cooperation and Development]. (2018). Economic Surveys of Turkey overview. [online]. Available at: http://www.oecd.org/economy/surveys/Turkey-2018-OECD-economic-survey-overview.pdf [Accessed 23 Jul. 2020].

Reiche, D. and Tinaz, C. (2019). Policies for naturalisation of foreign-born athletes: Qatar and Turkey in comparison. *International Journal of Sport Policy and Politics*, 11(1), pp. 153–171.

Resmi Gazete [Official Gazette], (2011). 2012 Merkezi Hükümet Bütçe Kanunu [2012 Central Administration Budget Act]. [online]. Available at: https://www.resmigazete.gov.tr/eskiler/2011/12/20111229M1-1.htm [Accessed 23 Jul. 2020].

Resmi Gazete [Official Gazette], (2019). 2020 Merkezi Hükümet Bütçe Kanunu [2020 Central Administration Budget Act]. [online]. Available at: https://www.resmigazete.gov.tr/eskiler/2019/12/20191231M1-1.htm [Accesed 23 Jul. 2020].

Sharpe, E.K., Lashua, B. and van Ingen, C. (2019). A good place for what? Placing "value" in youth centers. *Leisure Sciences*. [online]. Available at: https://doi.org/10.1080/01490400.2019.1604277 [Accessed 20 Feb. 2020].

SHGM [General Directorate for Sport Services], (2018). *Statistics of the number of licensed and active athletes in Turkey*. Ankara: Ministry of Youth and Sport [Gençlik ve Spor Bakanlığı]. [Online]. Available at: https://shgm.gsb.gov.tr/Sayfalar/175/105/istatistikler.aspx [Accessed 14 Jul. 2020].

Sparkes, A.C. and Smith, B. (2014). *Qualitative research methods in sport, exercise and health: From process to product*. London: Routledge.

Testa, A. and Amara, M. (Eds.). (2015). *Sport in Islam and in Muslim communities*. Oxon: Routledge.

Thompson, R., Russell, L. and Simmons, R. (2014). Space, place and social exclusion: Anethnographic study of young people outside education and employment. *Journal of Youth Studies*, 17(1), pp. 63–78.

Tinaz, C., Turco, D.M. and Salisbury, P. (2014). Sport policy in Turkey. *International Journal of Sport Policy and Politics*, 6(3), pp. 533–545.

TUIK (Turkish Statistical Institute), (2016). The rate of children participating in sport activities [Sportif faaliyetlere katılım sağlayan çocukların oranı]. [online]. Available at: https://biruni.tuik.gov.tr/medas/?kn=201&locale=tr [Accessed 23 Jul. 2020].

TUIK (Turkish Statistical Institute), (2020a). Address-based population registration system. [Adrese Dayalı Nüfus Kayıt Sistemi Sonuçları]. [online]. Available at: http://www.tuik.gov.tr/PreHaberBultenleri.do?id=33705 [Accessed 23 Jul. 2020].

TUIK (Turkish Statistical Institute), (2020b). Address based population registration re-sults for Edirne [Adrese Dayalı Nüfus Kayıt Sistemi]. [online]. Available at: https://biruni.tuik.gov.tr/medas/?kn=95&locale=tr [Accessed 25 Mar. 2020].

van Ingen, C. (2003). Geographies of gender, sexuality and race: Reframing the focus on spacein sport sociology. *International Review for the Sociology of Sport*, 38(2), pp. 201–216.

van Ingen, C. (2004). Therapeutic landscapes and the regulated body in the Toronto FrontRunners. *Sociology of Sport Journal*, 21(3), pp. 253–269.

Wearing, B. (1998). *Leisure and feminist theory*. London: Sage Publication.

Yabanci, B. (2019). Work for the Nation, Obey the State, Praise the Ummah: Turkey's Government-oriented Youth Organizations in Cultivating a New Nation. *Ethnopolitics*, [online]. Available at: https://doi.org/10.1080/17449057.2019.1676536 [Accessed 03 Mar. 2020].

Yuen, F. and Johnson, A.J. (2017). Leisure spaces, community, and third places. *Leisure Sciences*, 39(3), pp. 295–303.

Yüce, A. and Sunay, H. (2013). Türk Sporuna İlişkin Nicel Gelişimin Dönemsel Olarak İncelenmesi ve Bazı Ülkelerle Karşılaştırılması. [Periodical research of quantitative im-provement of Turkish sport and comparison with some countries]. *Ankara Üniversitesi Spor Bilimleri Fakültesi Dergisi*, 11(2), pp. 95–103.

Chapter 14

Conclusion

Lessons learned from the emerging nations

Brendon Knott and Cem Tinaz

This book sets out to provide answers to the question: "How is sport contributing to development (in terms of social, economic, cultural, political, technological or environmental advancement) in emerging nations?" From the themes that have run through the cases in this book, it is clear that although there are many similarities among emerging nations in terms of their socio-economic developmental status and challenges that they face, they also each face their own unique circumstances, priorities, policies and development agendas. Sport and development in these emerging nations must be understood within the context of each nation's social and economic sphere as well as its historic and political legacy.

This book aimed to highlight the subtle nuances and unique variations in the sport and development discourse among the different global regions and emerging nations by gaining perspectives, examples and research findings from authors with academic standing in this field within each of these nations. The editors made no attempt to define, delimit or set the agenda for the content of each chapter, leaving the authors a great deal of freedom to focus on priorities, cases and assessments that they felt would contribute most to the global understanding of sport and development. Authors were encouraged to write for the global audience, highlighting unique issues, challenges, examples and research data that would be relevant for international academics, students and practitioners linked to the sport industry who would benefit from these global perspectives.

This chapter reviews the cases in this book to consider key themes that emerged across the chapters, indicating how this book has achieved its primary objective and proposing future directions for the study of this topic. The chapter begins by reviewing the contribution of sport to development across the emerging nations. It then proposes a set of potential solutions to counter some of the most pressing obstacles mentioned in the cases in achieving these aims. The chapter concludes on a more personal reflection by the editors and the identification of future academic directions in this field of study.

The contribution of sport to development in emerging nations

In Chapter 1, several definitions of sport and development were discussed. The chapter explained the challenges in defining this term, with its broad, encompassing and overlapping reach. The six distinctions made in Astle, Leberman and Watson's (2018) model highlighted the desire to clarify and separate the broader understanding of this term. However, rather than supporting these distinctions, the chapters of this book have once again shown that sport and development is multi-faceted and overlapping. In attempting to provide an overview of key elements of sport and development in emerging nations, this book has not been able to separate the understanding of this term into components. Even the broader distinctions between development of sport and development through sport (Houlihan and White, 2002), while distinct in theory and definition, are difficult to separate within the practical context of the discourses presented in this book.

While the generic aims and expectations of sport and development appear to be widely accepted among the emerging nations, particularly embraced within public policy, this book affirms Houlihan's (2005, p. 163) assertion that, "governments more frequently view sport as a panacea for a diversity of social and economic concerns". While the cases in this book have revealed evidence to support this assertion and expectation of governments in many diverse ways, it has also indicated that the achievement of these aims through sport is not a guarantee by any means. Similarly, Chapter 8 referred to the "lasting power of the Great Sport Myth" (Coakley, 2015). This is anchored on the beliefs that sport holds an inherent purity and goodness that can be transferred by a sort of osmosis process to those who practice or consume sport and that sport practices inevitably lead to individual and community development.

The cases in this book have emphasised that there is clearly no cut-and-paste means of applying sport programmes, policies or sport development agendas that works automatically to achieve developmental aims. Historic, political and socio-economic nuances, as well as implementation, support or partnerships and financial sustainability are all key influencing factors in the successful attainment of these aims. The following sections indicate the key development themes that were highlighted across the cases, providing an overview of the complexities and mitigating factors that have affected the realisation of developmental ambitions through sport for these nations.

Sport and socio-cultural development

Most of the emerging nations indicated their historic and political development over the past century as crucial to understanding the role of sport in development. Whether emerging from a colonial past (as indicated by Indonesia), a repressive regime (as documented by the Czech Republic), isolation or fragmentation (as detailed by South Korea) and racial or societal divisions (as described by South Africa), sport has been embraced for its unifying effect for many historically or currently divided nations.

In the case of South Korea, the political separation from the north has entrenched societal divisions that appear to have heightened over time. Sport participation, especially on global stages, has proved to be one of the sole means of bridging these divisions and normalising relations to some extent. However, as Chapter 12 indicated, although the international media narrative reflected the unification story of the Games, this sentiment was not universally embraced domestically. The chapter suggests the need to rethink the meaning, method and directionality of sport-focused development between the two Koreas. The case demonstrates that it is critical to attend to domestic social change and to seek public consent when it comes to envisaging state-led development and peace initiatives, especially through sport mega-events.

Although the South African example of historic division is rather different and based on racial classification and economic inequality, sport has proved once again to be a unifying catalyst, even if more symbolic in its effect. Chapter 11 described how the 1995 Rugby World Cup stands out as a significant moment in the history of South African sport – symbolic of the transformation that was taking place in the aftermath of apartheid. As a result, government policies and strategies have aimed to address the inequities of the past and attempted to address this from both mass participation and elite performance perspectives (including the subsequent hosting of the 2010 FIFA World Cup). Despite these historic moments of social cohesion through sport, the development of sport in the nation is still plagued with transformation issues across race and gender – a challenge that remains across all sectors of the nation's business and society.

Beyond bridging social and political divisions, sport has also fostered the development of national identities as described in the cases of the Czech Republic and Indonesia. These nations emerged from decades of oppressive regimes and serve as examples of the development of national pride and identity through global sporting achievement and the connection between sport and cultural identity formation. Chapter 4 details the political and historical rise of sport through Czech history. The stages of its historical progress are heavily interwoven with political and nationalist goals, chiefly using sport in the fight for national independence and self-determination. However, the Czech Republic case also highlights the negative side to this politicisation of sport as it described how a totalitarian political regime aimed to spread its values and ideology through sporting practices, albeit with questionable success.

Sport-related programmes have been utilised by public, private and non-profit organisations to address a wide variety of the socio-cultural challenges faced by emerging nations. The aim to address social issues prevalent in these nations through sport is a constant refrain across the chapters. Primary issues targeted include education, livelihoods, gender and peace. The examples given by Mexico and Turkey indicate a focus on children and youth development. The case of Turkey adds the element of cultural and religious integration of these sport and leisure activities. Chapter 8 identified a gap in literature and advocates for the need to identify what sport-based interventions work better to address vulnerable groups, not only children and youth, but also deprived populations in rural settings, indigenous peoples, those with a mental or physical disability, and even seniors.

The case of Turkey indicated that its government's neoliberal and neoconservative agenda has led to a large-scale investment in sport infrastructure development. While the case mentions the investments at the elite and professional sport levels, it focused on government investment in community leisure spaces, and specifically, youth development centres. This case raises several serious obstacles to developing effective sport development facilities. Chapter 13 argued that urban sport development spaces face the risk of unsustainability due to their distance from disadvantaged communities, lack of personnel and inconclusive vision to implement long-term community transformation programmes. This is viewed as a common problem amongst the MENA and Arab countries, which disproportionately invest in sport infrastructure. The solution suggested is to match the aims of the development with the needs of the local population and ensure close proximity to low-income communities.

Sport mega-events as political "soft power"

The political use of sport as "soft power" to promote national and political prestige is already established in the literature, particularly through the hosting of mega-events (see Grix, Brannagan and Lee, 2019). Among emerging nations, the political ambitions of utilising sport mega-event hosting and elite sport achievement on the global stage, is more apparent, as indicated by Heslop et al. (2013), who asserted:

> Many emerging nations have risked a great deal in betting that hosting of a mega-event can be a fast-track to world recognition and reputation enhancement, and there is considerable evidence that this bet has payoffs in positive impacts on country images and reputations as producers of products and as tourism destinations.
>
> (p. 13)

Table 14.1 below lists the sport mega-events mentioned in this book. This is a clear indication of the increasing hosting ambitions of emerging nations, especially in the 21st century.

Both the cases of South Africa and Poland support the assertion of Heslop et al. (2013). South Africa's hosting of the 2010 FIFA World Cup left a legacy of global branding gains for the nation, providing a boost to its emerging status and aiding the development of its sport tourism industry. For Poland, achievements in elite sport and the hosting of mega-events have been perceived as a medium to showcase the country's 'new face' internationally as it emerged from its communist legacy. This goal was clearly visible when Poland co-hosted the European football championships, UEFA EURO 2012. The tournament is believed to have strengthened the Polish image among visitors and football fans and enhanced its international competitiveness. However, it also argued that the hosting of the mega-event was not part of the original long-term policy and planning for sport

Table 14.1 Emerging nations hosting sport mega-events

Country	Sport mega-events hosted (as mentioned in this book)
Brazil	2007 Pan-American Games
	2014 FIFA World Cup
	2016 Olympic Games
China	2008 Olympic Games
India	2008 Commonwealth Youth Games
	2010 Commonwealth Games
	2011 Cricket World Cup
	2011 Formula One Grand Prix
Indonesia	2018 Asian Games
Poland	2012 UEFA EURO
Qatar	2022 FIFA World Cup
South Africa	1995 Rugby World Cup
	2003 Cricket World Cup
	2010 FIFA World Cup
South Korea	1988 Olympic Games
	2002 Asian Games
	2002 FIFA World Cup
	2018 Winter Olympic Games

and development. Although, once awarded the hosting rights, the event became a central point for many development projects, primarily relating to infrastructure development, and many sport development programmes were designed to accompany the tournament.

While the cases in this book have highlighted positive impacts from hosting mega-events, they have also revealed the complexities and challenges that have mediated the legacies of these events to varying degrees and drawn attention to a more critical assessment of the hosting of sport mega-events by emerging nations. For example, the case of South Korea indicated that through the 2018 Olympic Games, the host nation aimed to portray one aspect of its identity, that of the 'global' South Korea, highlighting its economic liberalisation and global prestige. The chapter emphasised the role of the media in reproducing and interpreting the discourses surrounding sport mega-events.

This was also mentioned in Chapter 10, which described an international communication strategy employed by Qatar to emphasise the host nation of the 2022 FIFA World Cup's endeavour in contributing to international aid, conflict resolution, and peace-building in order to counter serious negative publicity surrounding the event. Although Qatar's preparations for hosting the 2022 FIFA World Cup have been mired in global scepticism and controversy, it is also heartening to read the positive examples of initiatives that have used the mega-event as a platform to leverage local sport development initiatives.

The case of Brazil highlighted the intentional political strategy behind its government bidding for and hosting serial sport mega-events for both political and economic benefits. The chapter revealed that while this may have been beneficial to a few sport sectors, it negatively disadvantaged certain population groups. This chapter clearly highlighted a more critical assessment of sport mega-event hosting, proposing a need for future studies to consider the paradoxes of development within underdevelopment, investments in world-class sport facilities that cause exclusion and the redirection of investment from other means of development. Added to this is the fact that sport mega-events in emerging nations have become associated with several human rights issues. This chapter makes a strong case for a more critical assessment of sport mega-event hosting in emerging nations as part of a future research agenda.

Sport and economic development

Grix, Brannagan and Lee (2019) indicated that an outcome of the 20th century has been the decentring of wealth and power from the major developed states to the fast-developing nations in Africa, Asia, the Middle East and South America. Rapidly growing economies is a hallmark of most emerging nations. Increased globalisation has offered new opportunities for sport leagues, teams, events, and manufacturers in emerging economies as they have modelled or been influenced by the many commercial sport successes of the established economies in North America and Europe.

The impact of private investment in sport by corporates (and in some cases, individuals), alongside increased commercialisation and professionalisation of the sporting sector, is predominant in the cases of China and India. An example of this growing investment is Chinese private companies that are now investing in global football, international sport marketing companies and international football stadium construction projects. The Chinese case contends that this increased investment in and through sport, both within China and globally, is an indicator of the social and economic development of the nation.

Similarly, the rapid commercialisation of Indian sport through professional league systems highlights the growing economic power of the sub-continent. The success of the Indian leagues reveals the importance for sport governing bodies in emerging nations to develop multiple revenue streams, for example, through events, sponsorship, broadcasting rights and increased attendance and/ or participation. In the case of India, private investment in sport by individuals and celebrities has also contributed to its sport and development.

Although not to the same scale as China and India, the case of Hungary and the CEE region also indicates how the recent development of sport and leisure reflects the significant expansion of the service sector in the region. As emerging-market economies continue to grow, demand for leisure sport products and services is likely to increase significantly. Chapter 5 indicated the value chain from investment in leisure sport development at both the micro- and macro-levels: Improvements in human capital, health conditions, quality of life, social capital and cohesion, productivity and GDP are value-creating factors that contribute to regional and global competitiveness.

Potential solutions for sport and development in emerging nations

While the hindrances, obstacles and challenges faced by emerging nations in sport and development are often unique and context-specific, this section notes some areas of commonality and draws together potential solutions for the future of sport and development in these nations, based on the cases in this book.

Sport policy consistency, governance and accountability

Differing public policies for the development of sport are evident throughout the chapters. While this book does not attempt to suggest a best-case model for development, several chapters indicate challenges with regard to public policy development and implementation. Many emerging nations have suffered from frequent changes in political leadership that can result in shifting policies and priorities, which can deeply affect the development of sport. As Chapter 7 indicated, sport development in Indonesia in the reformation era stagnated due to frequent leadership transitions (namely five different presidents between 1998 and 2020) and the resulting political turbulence. While Indonesia highlighted the severity and impact of political instability for sport and development, several other nations also mentioned the hindering effect of changing government policies and aims. This is especially significant for nations where sport investment and development are highly government-led and controlled.

Similarly, the case of Turkey reveals that sport for development has increasingly been used within the Turkish government's policies in the 21st century. Sport has been used widely in the achievement of political aims. This has led to increased public and academic contention, especially given the backdrop of the failed coup attempt of 2016 and the dismissal of hundreds of academics over a peace petition that condemned the conflicts in Southeast Turkey. Chapters 2 and 8 advocate the need for good governance and accountability within the public sectors when it comes to sport policy development and implementation, especially given the highly bureaucratic environments in which they operate. They bemoan the lack of critical assessment of policies and programmes and advocate for increased systematic and rigorous evaluations.

A potential solution to countering problems of corruption within public sport associations is offered in Chapter 9. Poland's Ministry of Sport and Tourism adopted a Code of Good Governance for Polish sport associations, where compliance with the Code is a precondition for receiving additional public funding. Although the authors admit that it is too early to assess the effectiveness of this measure, it is certainly an encouraging step towards improved governance and accountability.

Public, private and third-sector partnership

The cases in this book argued the need for public, private and third-sector collaborations for the achievement of sport and development aims. The Chinese case exemplifies the clash between traditional government influence and the emerging commercial and market elements in professional sport and sport consumption among many emerging nations. Chapter 3 advocates a new model of governance for sport in that nation, and one that could serve as a prototype for other emerging nations that currently face high levels of government control in sport. Chiefly, this would revolve around an intensified marketisation of sport and greater autonomy for sport organisations, permitting the market to play the predominant role in determining resource allocation. However, as Chapter 5 cautions, government leaders should also understand that the market cannot solve everything on its own.

Support and partnership across sectors are, therefore, vital. A key to future sport development programme success may lie in the revelations from the Mexican case. Chapter 8 indicated that most of the NGO's operating in Mexico that they surveyed had been delivering programmes in partnership with business corporations (national and transnational), the Mexican government, international funding agencies and national universities.

The role of the third sector emerged as a significant actor within sport and development through a number of chapters. These organisations have seemingly been able to innovate and adapt better to external forces to keep their work sustainable over time. In some cases, the work of not-for-profit, NGO and community-based organisations is contrasted to government policy initiatives, with Chapter 8 labelling this as 'developmental interventionism'. In the case of Brazil and Mexico, the organisations described were able to target disadvantaged populations more effectively. Furthermore, Chapter 2 promotes the idea of third-sector sport organisations adopting a social entrepreneur approach to achieve social change through the adoption of business-like practices that allow them to fill the gap between the social demands and existing public policies.

Innovation for sustainability

Chapter 11 used the following definition of sustainable development, namely: "development that meets the needs of the present without compromising the ability of future generations to meet their own needs" (Roostaie, Nawari and Kibert, 2019, p. 134). Very little has been mentioned across the cases of the responses of the sport industries in emerging economies to the global environmental sustainability issues of climate change, renewable energy, soil quality and erosion, water management as well as air and water pollution. The South African case draws attention to this as a major threat to the sport industry, detailing a recent water crisis that drastically impacted the local sport industry, but which also proved to be a catalyst for innovation and education around this theme. The adoption and promotion of energy-efficient sport and event practices is also mentioned as an area for future innovation.

Social inclusion and transformation

Many emerging nations face the challenge of addressing obstacles or negative attitudes towards sport participation. Chapter 5 revealed an increase in leisure sport spending coupled with a decrease (or stagnation) in the frequency of recreational sport participation across Hungary and the CEE region. This was deemed to be a reflection of people in higher income brackets, city dwellers and people with higher levels of educational attainment, being more likely to participate in sport than people in other sectors of society. This is a challenge faced across the emerging nations. Not everyone has the aptitude or the money for sport participation. Since there has been a significant rise in expenditures on leisure sport in developed nations, we can assume that similar increases can be expected in emerging nations in future. Besides promoting leisure sport participation, the South African case also proposes the promotion of indigenous sports as a driver for sport participation and inclusion.

Related to sport participation and inclusion is the aspect of "transformation". Improved racial and gender representation in sport is mentioned as a key imperative for South African sport development and looms large as a potential obstacle to social sustainability across emerging nations in general. While representation has become a global issue in sport, it is perhaps the emerging nations that are at the forefront of this as they grapple more intently with their political and historical legacies, economic growth challenges and societal disparities. Chapter 11 provides encouraging examples of potential solutions in this regard, describing a group of Black African women who are promoting healthy sporting habits in underprivileged and rural areas of the country as well as female elite athletes who are becoming role models for female participation and achievement in sport in the nation.

Concluding reflections

This book has provided diverse insights into the development, challenges and future opportunities that exist within a range of emerging nations. While not proposing that these nations be considered as a singular entity, this final chapter has highlighted the similarities across the cases from these nations and drawn attention to the most pertinent examples. In this way, the book has achieved its objective of answering the question: "How is sport contributing to development in emerging nations?"

While the areas of socio-cultural, economic and political development are well represented, the areas of technological advancement and environmental sustainability are under-represented. The editors therefore draw attention to these topics as core areas for future discourse and study. Several chapter authors have also advocated for future studies in emerging nations to take a more critical perspective in the assessment of sport programmes, policies and interventions and especially in the hosting of sport mega-events. The authors have called for more evidence-based assessments of sport and development through systematic and rigorous evaluations.

The chapters of this book have accelerated the analysis of sport and development within these emerging nations and have added to the limited English language literature available on this topic, in the case of many of these nations. The nuanced, critical and reflective analysis represented in this book is a testament to the growing academia in sport development in these nations. The global co-operation across these emerging nations that has resulted in the realisation of this book is commendable. It will surely strengthen and extend the academic networks through these regions.

The co-editors trust that the book has authentically represented their passion for the field of sport and that the book itself has conveyed the energy, ambition and potential they perceive in the sport industries in the emerging nations.

References

Astle, A., Leberman, S. and Watson, G. (2018). *Sport development in action: Plan, programme and practice*. London and New York: Routledge.

Coakley, J. (2015). Assessing the sociology of sport: On cultural sensibilities and the great sport myth. *International Review for the Sociology of Sport*, 50(4–5), pp. 402–406.

Grix, J., Brannagan, P.M. and Lee, D. (2019). *Entering the global arena: Emerging states, soft power strategies and sports mega-events*. Singapore: Palgrave Macmillan.

Heslop, L.A., Nadeau, J., O'Reilly, N. and Armenakyan, A. (2013). Mega-event and country co-branding: Image shifts, transfers and reputational impacts. *Corporate Reputation Review*, 16(1), pp. 7–33.

Houlihan, B. (2005). Public sector sport policy: Developing a framework for analysis. *International Review for the Sociology of Sport*, 40(2), pp. 163–185.

Houlihan, B. and White, A. (2002). *The politics of sport development*. London: Routledge.

Roostaie, S., Nawari, N. and Kibert, C.J. (2019). Sustainability and resilience: A review of definitions, relationships, and their integration into a combined building assessment framework. *Building and Environment*, 154, pp. 132–144.

Index

Note: **Bold** page numbers refer to tables; *italic* page numbers refer to figures and page numbers followed by "n" denote endnotes.